Access Behind the Veil

The Coming Glory

Second Edition

Dr. Michael Petro

Access Behind the Veil: The Coming Glory

March 2021

Second Edition

ISBN 978-1-954919-20-4 HARDCOVER
ISBN 978-1-954919-19-8 PAPERBACK
ISBN 978-1-954919-18-1 EBOOK

Published and Distributed by:
The Voice of Healing Publishing
Website: voh.church

This book is dedicated to the hungry and thirsty souls seeking truth, who have sat under misconstrued teachings of the Word of Yahweh. This book is dedicated to those who have eyes to see and ears to hear the revelation of the Torah – the living Word of God, Yehoshua Himself. This book is dedicated to the final move of God during which the great harvest will have access through the veil into the Holy of Holies and experience the glory of the Almighty God.

Table of Contents

Preface

This book is based on many of the revelatory teachings given to me straight from God. After several years of hearing and preaching sermons relaying that God's grace covers all sin and that one day a group of believers would be caught up into heaven to avoid the mass destruction of the world, I was taken through the veil, and He began to reveal to me the hidden secrets of the kingdom as taught by the Early Church. All of my Christian doctrine leading up to that point went out the window. Since this awakening, I have never been the same. This complete alteration, and the existence of this book, all started with an impregnation of new DNA.

Growing up, I could see that my father had many attributes of my grandfather. The similarities came by natural means, through genetics. I could see so much of my grandfather in my dad, who, by the way, was a great father. In the same way, I could see a lot of the traits of my mom's dad in my aunts and uncles. One day, my oldest sister said, "Michael, I see so much of Dad in you." As I thought about it, I began to see it as well, and I knew that it was also the nature of my grandfather. It was evident that my grandfather's DNA was in me too.

God shows us something tremendously important about genetics and DNA. Yeshua states that the seed is the Word (Luke 8:11) and in His Word contains the mysteries of the kingdom (Matthew 13). The *seed* also means the *sperm* or the DNA. I know that the seed of my Grandpa, YHVH, has the power to create universes. I see my mind constantly being impregnated with the seed of creation.

Many times Grandpa has taken me into His glory, where I have seen many wonderful and exciting things. I have seen Him heal deaf ears and blind eyes and even raise the dead. I have come to a point where I truly know that through Him, *all* things are possible, for He is limitless in His ability. But His greatest work is us – the creation of His children.

The entire universe is only an afterthought. His true heart is to have us come into our destiny of restoring the Earth.

One morning He showed me His love – His agape love. I couldn't contain it. I wasn't ready for it. I found myself with Grandpa's thoughts. It was overwhelming, like pouring the ocean into a teaspoon, and I was wrecked with His love for months. The first thing He showed me was how much He hated to see us in these bodies. It was like His children had cancer and He would do anything to heal us of it. He desires to see us back in the perfected body He created for us, which is the glorified body Adam had before he fell.

He wants full access to just overwhelm us with His amazing love. One day we will be able to handle it, even though we aren't yet able. Nothing will stand in the presence of His love and glory. I'm swept up in that love even now as I write this Preface while flying from the United States to Belgium. I just feel that love wave crashing over me, as well as the difficulty to contain my feelings especially surrounded by people who have never experienced such great love. But it doesn't matter because my love for my Father is greater than life itself. I don't see any purpose in life other than to tell everyone about His great love. Everything becomes reduced to this type of relationship – a love sickness for Him. Nothing in this life compares to Him. In His love for us, He created the Earth as a great classroom, in order to open the eyes of his children…But do we have eyes to see?

I understand why Yeshua says, "You will forsake all." It is not only because He requires it; it is because we become so consumed to know Him more that we will simply drop everything else to follow Him. I cannot imagine ever being separated from this great love – from this wonderful Savior who came and gave His life for a world and people who do not even recognize Him. But I know that His agape love will be like an atomic explosion when fully released in the glory. It will catch the whole world on fire for Him, and the world will burn with love for the greatest Lover of all. He deserves to reap the love He has sown into us.

Saints have asked me why I want to know so much about the Father. Simply put, I'm in love. I feel Him and see Him in every letter and every word, and it amazes me how He does and is everything. It intrigues me to see how Yeshua was always present in the Scripture, yet many of us do not see Him because we have thrown away the beauty of His manifestation as the Word. I know my relationship with Him has changed immensely because I endured persecutions and trials. Even during the times of testing, I only wanted Him. He has made my hunger insatiable for Him, and I am so addicted to His presence that I feel as if I can never get enough. There are examples of those who understood and had that great love – Enoch, Elijah, and others – who were just one day consumed by that love. He had to take them because they were just too heartbroken to not be in His presence. A fire burns inside me to make all see His agape love so they can experience it too. Just as God took me behind the veil and completely changed my relationship with Him, my desire is for all to have access behind the veil and obtain a deeper understanding of our awesome Creator and His divine love, plan and purpose for us as His children.

- Dr. Michael Petro

Introduction

The declaration that the Church has left its first love (Revelation 2:4) should be a sounding alarm that it has left the foundational, hidden teachings of Yeshua – the teachings of the Early Church. The Early Church teachings are based on the parabolic and prophetic understanding of the Torah, and much of this understanding is lost today. So much of God's Word and doctrine is lost in translation that without returning to the Hebrew roots, it is difficult to recover the original meaning of Scripture. Even the name *Jesus*, derived from the Greek name *Iesous* ("hail Zeus"), is a serious divergence from His name in the original Hebrew language: *Yehoshua* ("Yahweh is salvation"), or *Yeshua* ("salvation").

The Torah is a book of secrets and mysteries that are hidden in parables. God speaks in parables and dark sayings (Psalms 78:2), and Yehoshua taught the masses in parables (Matthew 13:11-17, Mark 4:11-12). The hidden teachings of the kingdom take us beyond the veil and into the Holy of Holies, considered by the Early Church to be the garden of Eden, which was the original dwelling place of the first high priest, Adam. Today's Church has strayed from Early Church teachings that the temple is a pattern of all of creation, wherein the three sections of the temple – the Outer Court, Holy Place, and Holy of Holies – depict different levels of understanding of God's Word, His prophetic Scriptures. Until we begin to see His Word from the spiritual and prophetic, instead of from the natural and literal, we have not yet gone through the veil into the Holy of Holies.

It is in the Holy of Holies that the glory of God resides, and it is only accessed through revelation – an *apocalypse*, or a *removal of the veil.* In Mark 4:11, Yeshua told His disciples, "**To you it has been given to know the mystery of the kingdom of God; but to those who are outside, all things come in parables**." He was speaking about being outside of the veil leading into the Holy of Holies.

The symbolism found throughout Scripture is described in 1 Corinthians 2:7 as "the hidden wisdom." When we recognize the hidden meanings within the Word of Yahweh, we begin to experience ascension and illumination. The Early Church taught that this ascension occurred when one learned the secrets of the kingdom. The cry for us to return to our first love is a cry to return to righteousness – the right understanding of Torah, which encompasses learning the hidden mysteries and a transformation of life.

The purpose of this book is to remove the veils that have been covering many eyes and to reveal the hidden secrets and mysteries of the kingdom contained within the Word of God. Just as God speaks in parables and mysteries, the Torah is also parabolic. It contains the pattern of creation and the steps to restore what Adam lost in the garden. Throughout Scripture and Early Church teachings, God continually points to the restoration of creation and the reestablishment of truth.

This book is a journey behind the veil through revelation and an intimate relationship with Yeshua, ultimately providing fuller understanding of the coming glory of God – the same glory in which Adam lived before the fall. Likewise, it is intended to awaken those who are slumbering and blinded by lack of (or wrong) understanding of the Torah. The desire is to remove the veil and show that sin is missing the mark of Torah, that God's grace is specifically given to those who act on faith (the *correct* understanding of His Word), and that the entire redemption process is a marriage covenant bringing us back into the garden of Genesis – back into the glory of God. Most importantly, this book aims to reveal God's divine plan of reestablishing His kingdom on Earth *through* His people. We are the temple of God, the garden, the Holy of Holies, the Tree of Life, and the Torah. It is through a people – the Christ generation, the love slaves (Obadiah 1:21) – that God will reestablish His kingdom in this final move.

Throughout Scripture, Yeshua rebukes those who do not have eyes to see or ears to hear. Those who neither see nor hear the deeper revelation of the kingdom have yet to pass beyond the veil. God's ultimate and divine plan is about restoration and includes access to the deeper teachings within the Holy of Holies. Yeshua did not come to judge the world; He came to bring redemption (John 12:47). His desire is to bring His children back into Eden and back into His glory through His divine plan if we can see it. By returning to the foundational teachings of the Early Church and reading the Scriptures from a Hebraic mindset, we begin to pass through the veil. Let us begin our journey and clothe ourselves that we might not be found naked. May our desire be to fall so in love with this great King of Righteousness and allow Him to fully consume every part of our lives with His love. Only then can we say we have the mind of Christ. Let us now proceed toward the veil. . .

Chapter One

A Glimpse at the Early Church

Can any who spend several years in those seats of learning be excused if they do not read the Fathers, the most authentic commentators on Scripture, as being both nearest the fountain, eminently endued with the Spirit by whom all Scripture was given. It will be easily perceived, I speak chiefly of those who wrote before the Council of Nicea.

John Wesley
Address to the Clergy

In order to properly set the foundation of God's divine Word and His divine plan, it is imperative to recognize that the instruction from Yehoshua to His disciples were the teachings of the Early Church.

Early Church Fathers

The Early Church Fathers, often referred to as the Ante-Nicene Fathers, are the core foundation of the teachings of Christ. The Early Church Fathers can be categorized into three major generations:

First Generation:

Peter, John, Paul, Luke, Timothy

Second Generation:

Clement, Ignatius, Aristides, Polycarp, Papias

Third Generation:

Justin, Melito, Athenagoras, Theophilus, Irenaeus

The first generation was taught directly by Yeshua Himself or close disciples thereof. One of Paul's closest ministry assistants was Timothy, to whom he writes:

> **And the things that you have heard from me among many witnesses, commit these to *faithful men* who will be able to *teach others* also (2 Timothy 2:2).**

Timothy was instructed to pass on the teachings to the *faithful men* who would then be able to teach others. These faithful men are the following generations of catechumen. The second generation consists of Fathers who learned from the first generation. Even Paul, in his letter to the Philippian Church, mentions his fellow worker Clement:

> **And I urge you also, true companion, help these women who labored with me in the gospel, with *Clement* also, and the rest of my *fellow workers*, whose names are in the Book of Life (Philippians 4:3).**

The term *fellow worker* is the word *sunergos,* used in the New Covenant meaning *co-worker, fellow laborer,* especially in Christian work. Clement, who became the pastor of the church in Rome, received instruction from Peter. Polycarp was the pastor of the church in Smyrna, who was the protégé of, and ordained by, the Apostle John. Ignatius was the pastor of the church in Antioch until 110 A.D. and likely knew the last of the direct apostles of Yeshua. The next generation included Justin Martyr, a famous teacher in Rome (around 150 A.D.), and Irenaeus, a pastor of the church in Lyons (around 180 A.D.), both of whom knew Polycarp, John's pupil.

The Early Church Fathers span a range of a several hundred years, as depicted in Figure 1.

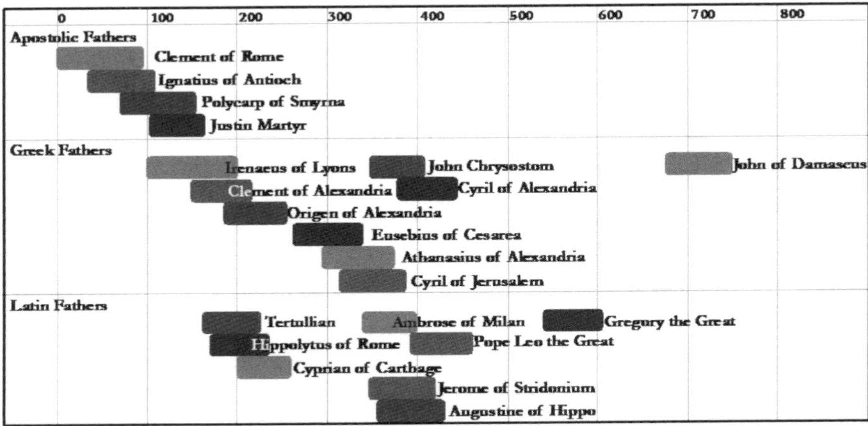

Figure 1: Early Church Fathers

The Early Church Fathers made up the original Orthodox Church. The term *orthodoxy* is defined by the Vatican Council as such:

> Orthodoxy (*orthodoxeia*) signifies right belief or purity of faith. Right belief is not merely subjective, as resting on personal knowledge and convictions, but is in accordance with the teaching and direction of an absolute extrinsic authority. This authority is the Church founded by Christ, and guided by the Holy Ghost. As *divine revelation* forms the deposit of faith entrusted to the Church for man's salvation, it also, with the *truths* clearly deduced from it, forms the object and content of orthodoxy (Callan, 2015).

The truths of the Orthodox teachings were the secret teachings and divine revelation of the Word of God. The right teaching is within the discipline of the secret.

Discipline of the Secret & Mysteries

Mysteries

All throughout Early Church teachings one finds ubiquitous mention of *mysteries*. The word *mystery* comes from the word *mustees*, meaning "one initiated into a revealed secret;" and the related word *mueoo,* meaning "to conceal." The Fausset's Bible Dictionary defines *mystery* as "a spiritual truth heretofore hidden, incapable of discovery by mere reason, but now revealed . . . to the initiated few." Those who did not believe the mysteries were considered the uninitiated. As initiation infers a select few, the word *mystery* inherently correlates with a remnant.

The concept of theological *mysteries* is treated with the utmost seriousness. In its Dogmatic Decrees, the Vatican Council states: "If anyone says that in Divine Revelation there are contained no *mysteries* properly so called that through reason rightly developed all the dogmas of faith can be understood and demonstrated from natural principles; let him be *anathema* (cursed, condemned)." Those who did not believe that the teachings of God contained *mysteries* were condemned and cursed.

Not only did the Early Church teach mysteries, but they also considered these secret teachings most sacred and holy. They were not meant for just anybody to learn; for the mature, the deeper teachings are the meat of the Word, not the milk for babes (1 Corinthians 3:1-2). In fact, many of these teachings were not even documented in writing. Clement of Alexandria writes in his work, *The Stromata*, that Yeshua taught "knowledge of the past, present and future," and that He only revealed the mysteries concealed in the Scripture through oral communication to his closest disciples.

Origen of Alexandria, in his work *Contra Celsus*, describes that many prophets knew greater things than could be found in Scripture, but that these things were not documented in writing. In the Early Church, the function of the prophet was to dig out greater spiritual truths through revelation. Origen writes that even the Apostle Paul heard "unspeakable words, which is not lawful for a man to utter," and that "John, in teaching us the difference between what ought to be committed to writing and what not, declares that he heard seven thunders instructing him on certain matters, and forbidding him to commit their words to writing." Further, Yeshua conversed with His disciples in private especially concerning the Gospel of God, but His teachings were not preserved because the evangelists felt they could not adequately convey the teachings to the multitude through writing or speech. As a result, many teachings were not recorded in writing but instead were only given to select individuals, or a remnant. The Early Church clearly taught that the remnant consisted of those who had learned the secrets and mysteries from their teachers. Early Church Father Mathetes wrote:

> **For who that is rightly taught and begotten by the loving Word, would not seek to learn accurately the things which have been clearly shown by the Word to His Disciples, to whom the Word being manifested has revealed them, speaking plainly (to them), not understood indeed by the unbelieving, but conversing with the disciples, who, being esteemed faithful by Him, acquired a knowledge of the mysteries of the Father? (Mathetes, a disciple of Paul the Apostle, 130 A.D.).**

The Qumran texts (Dead Sea Scrolls), which contain Jewish documents dating from the third century B.C.E. to 68 C.E., are full of references to visions and mysteries. Barker notes some examples:

> **Thou hast made me . . . a discerning interpreter of wonderful *mysteries* (1QH X, formerly II).**
>
> **Thou hast given me knowledge through thy marvelous *mysteries* (1QH XII, formerly IV).**
>
> **In thy marvelous *mysteries* . . . thou hast granted me knowledge (1QH XV, formerly VII).**
>
> **He has opened your ears to the *mystery* of existence (4Q416).**
>
> **Meditate on the *mystery* of existence (4Q417).**

Catechumen

The Early Church method of instruction was much different than that of today's Church. While most of the modern church believes that the sinner's prayer will lead to eternal life, the Early Church understood that a true confession of Christ was shown through one's spiritual works, which was accomplished through a process of revelation first transforming the inner man:

> **Let us then not only call Him Lord, for that will not save us. For He saith, "Not everyone that saith to Me, 'Lord, Lord,' shall be saved, but he that worketh righteousness." Therefore brethren, let us confess Him by our works, by loving one another, by not committing adultery, or speaking evil of one another, or cherishing envy; but being continent, compassionate, and good. We ought also to sympathize with one another, and not be avaricious (Clement, *2nd Epistle of St. Clement*).**

Early Church instruction was done through *catechesis*, or *catechism*, which means "the act of teaching," and "the knowledge imparted by teaching." *Catechesis* and *catechism* come from the Greek word *katecheo*, which is made up of the words *kata* (*down*) and *echos* (*noise, sound*) and means *to sound down into the ears, indoctrinate ("catechize"), instruct, teach.*

The root word *katecheo* is found in Galatians 6:6, 1 Corinthians 14:19, Luke 1:4, and Acts 18:25:

> **Let him who is *taught* [*ho katechoumenos, is qui catechizatur*] the word share in all good things with him who *teaches* (Galatians 6:6).**

> **I would rather speak five words with my understanding, that I may *teach* [*katecheso*] others also, than ten thousand words in a tongue (1 Corinthians 14:19).**

> **...that you may know the certainty of those things in which you were *instructed* [*katechethes, in quibus eruditus es*] (Luke 1:4).**

> **This man [Apollos] had been instructed [*katechemenos, edoctus*] in the way of the Lord; and being fervent in spirit, he spoke and taught accurately the things of the Lord, though he knew only the baptism of John (Acts 18:25).**

The word *katechesis* means *instruction by word of mouth, especially questioning and answering*, and is commonly used to describe the preparation for initiation into Christianity. In fact, *katechesis* technically means "oral religious instruction," although it is applied to both the act of instructing and the subject of instructing. The French word *catéchisme* even still applies to the small printed book in which questions and answers are contained.

Catechism – oral instruction by questions and answers – was practiced even among the Hebrews in the Old Testament (Exodus 12:26, Deuteronomy 6:7, 20). Three forms of catechizing existed:

- **Domestic**: conducted by the head of the family for children and servants

- **Scholastic**: conducted by teachers in schools

- **Ecclesiastical**: conducted by priests and Levites in the Temple and synagogues

Regular instruction of children began when they were twelve years old, the age at which Yeshua began sitting among the doctors in the temple and astonishing them with His wisdom:

> **And when he was twelve years old, they went up to Jerusalem after the custom of the feast. . . . And it came to pass, that after three days they found him in the temple, sitting in the midst of the doctors, both hearing them, and asking them questions. And all that heard him were astonished at his understanding and answers (Luke 2:42, 46-47).**

The Early Church taught in two distinct categories: (1) preliminary instruction to new converts, and (2) the Holy mysteries to the initiated (few, mature). *Catechumen* was the name given to one who was not yet initiated into the sacred mysteries and still going through preparatory courses for the initiation. Catechumens were divided into two groups: ***inquirers*** (*audientes, akromeni*) and ***proper catechumen.*** Each stage had a three-fold preparation: catechetical, ascetical, and liturgical.

If a pagan desired to become a Christian, he was given elementary instruction in the fundamental doctrines and practices of the Church, and he was considered to be only in the stage of inquiry. Allowed to be present at the first part of Mass, he was dismissed immediately after the sermon before the second part, which was for the initiated. After the inquirer's instructors (the catechists) were satisfied that the inquirer was likely to persevere, he was promoted to a *catechumen proper*. At this point, the catechumen could be *initiated*, which came *before* instruction of the deeper teachings.

The Holy mysteries and teachings of the initiated were treated with the utmost seriousness. In fact, the *discipline of the secret* is a theological term used to describe the custom of the Early Church that entailed keeping the knowledge of the more intimate mysteries from the heathen or those still undergoing instruction in the Faith. Once catechumens were taught the holy mysteries, they were instructed to guard their teachings from those who were not yet taught the mysteries:

> When, therefore, the Lecture is delivered, if a Catechumen asks you what the teachers have said, tell nothing to him that is without. For we deliver to you a mystery, and a hope of the life to come. *Guard the mystery* for Him who gives the reward. Let none ever say to you, "What harm to you, if I also know it?" So too the sick ask for wine; but if it be given at a wrong time it causes delirium, and two evils arise; the sick man dies, and the physician is blamed. Thus is it also with the Catechumen, if he hear anything from the believer: both the Catechumen becomes delirious (for he understands not what he has heard, and finds fault with the thing, and scoffs at what is said), and the believer is condemned as a traitor. But you are now standing on the border: take heed, pray, to tell nothing out; not that the things spoken are not worthy to be told, but because his ear is unworthy to receive. You were once yourself a Catechumen, and I described not what lay before you. When by experience you have learned how high are the matters of

> our teaching, then you will know that the Catechumens are not worthy to hear them (Cyril, *Procatechesis*).

The Council of Laodicea forbade the speaking of Holy aspects taught in the Church, as it was "not lawful to reveal everything to those who are yet uninitiated." The discipline of the secret was kept with utmost confidentiality for the initiated.

Baptism, Enlightenment & Resurrection

While the catechumen was entitled to be called a Christian, he was not entitled to be called one of the "faithful." After some years in the catechumen stage, he was promoted to the rank of *competentes* – those ready for *baptism*, which entailed learning the deeper teachings. The Greeks called the catechumens who were ready to learn the deeper mysteries and go through baptism *photizomenoi*, entailing that they were being *enlightened* in the mysteries of the faith. In fact, baptism is referenced as "light," and being baptized entailed becoming *enlightened* or *illuminated*, which is depicted in Hebrews 6 and Hebrews 10:

> **For it is impossible for those who were once *enlightened*, and have tasted the heavenly gift, and have become partakers of the Holy Spirit, and have tasted the good word of God and the powers of the age to come, if they fall away, to renew them again to repentance, since they crucify again for themselves the Son of God, and put Him to an open shame (Hebrews 6:4-6).**

> **But recall the former days in which, after you were *illuminated*, you endured a great struggle with sufferings (Hebrews 10:32).**

Baptism is also associated with the concept of *ascension*, or *resurrection*. To the Early Church, resurrection entailed being raised up and transformed into an angel figure, or a son of God. One who was raised up (or resurrected) was considered an Anointed One – an angel raised up into the presence of God. The word *Messiah* is the Hebrew word *mashiyach*, which is the Greek word *christos*, and means *anointed, smeared (one who is smeared with oil as a sign of authority)*. Resurrection is equated to becoming an anointed one – an angel, or son of God:

> **But those who are counted worthy to attain that age, and the resurrection from the dead, neither marry nor are given in marriage; nor can they die anymore, for they are *equal to the angels* and are *sons of God*, being *sons of the resurrection* (Luke 20:35-36, emphasis added).**
>
> **Now if we died with Christ, we believe that we shall also live with Him (Romans 6:8).**

Those who were *baptized* – learning the deeper secret teachings of God – were associated with the mystical experience of *heavenly ascent*. Resurrection was therefore connected to the baptism of the mysteries. In fact, the Early Church taught about *two* resurrections, with the first resurrection being the aforementioned baptism of learning the sacred mysteries, and the second resurrection being the return to the glorified state that Adam had in the garden of Eden before he fell. Hermas, a second century apostle, wrote about this as follows:

> **"They were obliged," he answered, "to ascend through water in order that they might be made alive; for, unless they laid aside the deadness of their life, they could not in any other way enter into the kingdom of God"… "For," he continued, "before a man bears the name of the Son of God he is dead; but when he receives the seal he lays aside his deadness, and obtains life. The seal, then, is the water: they descend into the water dead, and they arise alive" (Hermas, *The Shephard*).**

The Early Church knew that Yeshua gave secret teachings to an inner group of disciples. The first teaching was to a group of just three: James, John, and Peter. Eusebius writes, "James the Righteous, John and Peter were entrusted by the Lord after his resurrection with the higher knowledge. They imparted it to the other apostles and the other apostles to the seventy, one of whom was Barnabas." Here again, resurrection is associated with obtaining the higher, secret knowledge. Barker points out that "after his resurrection" refers to after Yeshua's own experience of birth as Son of God, and His baptismal anointing with the Spirit.

During His ministry, Yeshua taught the secret teachings to His disciples, who asked Him why He taught the masses in parables.

> **And He said to them, "To you it has been given to know the *mystery of the kingdom of God*; but to those who are *outside*, all things come in *parables*" (Mark 4:11).**

The secret teachings were not taught to those on the *outside* or those who were not part of the initiated group of catechumens (who therefore did not receive baptism). This word *outside* speaks of a people who are outside the door, meaning they have not entered into the house of Yah. It even illustrates being outside the veil of the Holy of Holies, wherein lie the deeper mysteries of God. When Yeshua says He stands at the door and knocks (Revelation 3:20), He seeks to initiate the immature into maturity by teaching them the secrets of the kingdom. The inner group of disciples to whom the secrets were taught would experience resurrection from the dead nature and carnal way of thinking to a new life in the Spirit of God. The Early Church understood that the mystery of the kingdom was only for the initiated:

> **And if you come to the books written after the time of Jesus, you will find that those multitudes of believers who hear the parables are, as it were, "without," and worthy only of exoteric doctrines, while the disciples**

learn in private the explanation of the parables. For, privately, to His own disciples did Jesus open up all things, esteeming above the multitudes those who desired to know his wisdom (Origen, *Against Celsus*, 184-253 A.D.).

Resurrection of Water and Spirit

Yeshua spoke about resurrection to Nicodemus, saying,

> **". . . Most assuredly, I say to you, unless one is *born again*, he cannot see the kingdom of God. . . . Most assuredly, I say to you, unless one is *born of water and the Spirit*, he cannot enter the kingdom of God" (John 3:3, 5).**

The word *again* in John 3:3 is the Greek word *anothen*, meaning *from above, from a higher place, from the first, from the beginning.* One must be born from above – a higher place, the beginning – in order to see the kingdom. This *higher place* depicts the heavenly realm, and even more so, the *place of the beginning*, the **garden of Eden**, the place of learning. This higher place requires ascension, or enlightenment.

In John 3:5, the water is the teaching of the secrets and mysteries. The Greek word for *water* is the word *hudor* or *hudatos*, which comes from the base word *huetos*, meaning *rain*. The Song of Moses (Deuteronomy 32) begins as follows:

> **Let my *teaching* drop as the *rain*, My speech distill as the dew, as raindrops on the tender herb, and as showers on the grass (Deuteronomy 32:2).**

God's teaching is as the rain. The word *teaching* is the Hebrew word *leqach*, meaning both the instruction received by a student and the instruction that is taught from an instructor, which describes *catechism*. Essentially, this teaching is the discipline of the secret. Further, the word *leqach* comes from the word *laqach*, meaning *to take, carry away* (or even *rapture*). This carrying away depicts the ascension and enlightenment that comes from learning the deeper and secret teachings. The instruction of the secrets, which causes one to *ascend*, is as *rain* (or *water*).

The kingdom of God is for those who have been resurrected through water – the secret teachings – and the Spirit. As with water, to be born of the Spirit is associated with learning the secret teachings of God and the corresponding transformation and ascension into a higher, or angelic state (Matthew 22:30). Yeshua even refers to John the Baptist as His angel, or messenger (Matthew 11:10). Much of the work done by angels in the Earth is through mature believers who understand the covenant and divine plan of Yeshua.

The word *spirit* is the Greek word *pneuma*, meaning *a spirit higher than man but lower than God, i.e., an angel*, and *the spiritual nature of Christ, higher than the highest angels and equal to God, the divine nature of Christ.* The Early Church taught that resurrection (learning the secret teachings) caused one to become an *angel.* Thus, being born again of the Spirit implies the *transformation* into an angelic state, which is achieved by learning the secret teachings of God. On the Mount of Transfiguration, the inner circle of disciples, Peter, James, and John, witnessed Yeshua's transfiguration into a higher, angelic (non-human) state:

> **...and He was *transfigured* before them. His face shone like the sun, and His clothes became as white as the light (Matthew 17:2).**

While Peter, James, and John themselves did not become transfigured as Yeshua did, they still partook of the heavenly ascension through *observation* of His ascension. There existed two degrees of involvement of the heavenly realm, which might be considered as two stages of initiation. One was the observation of the heavenly realm, such as the experience of Daniel, who watched the Man ascend to the heavenly throne (Daniel 7:13-14). The other was the actual participation in the heavenly realm, such as the experience of Enoch being taken up before the throne (1 Enoch 14) and even being transformed into an angel (2 Enoch, 3 Enoch), and that of John, who was in the heavenly Holy of Holies (Revelation). The three disciples on the Mount of Transfiguration can be placed into the first stage of initiation, where they observed Yeshua's interaction with the heavenly realm. The two types of initiation can even possibly be attributed to the two resurrections taught by the Early Church: the first being the baptism into the secret teachings, and the second being the transformation into the glorified body.

The baptisms of water and of the Spirit extend beyond the physical submersion into water and the invitation of the Holy Spirit to enter one's life, respectively. The definition of baptism must be understood from the Early Church point of view. The baptisms of water and of the Spirit point back to learning the secret teachings of God, the very teachings of the Early Church. Only those who learned the deeper teachings would see the kingdom of God.

The Early Church taught that learning the mysteries of the kingdom would bring resurrection, and that departing from the mysteries was considered *falling away*. We live in the time of the great apostasy that Paul wrote about and even Yeshua warns about the **great falling away** at the end of the age:

> **Let no one deceive you by any means; for that Day will not come unless the *falling away* comes first, and the man of sin is revealed, the son of perdition, who opposes and exalts himself above all that is called God or that is worshiped, so that he sits as God in the temple of God, showing himself that he is God (2 Thessalonians 2:3-4).**

The term *falling away* is the Greek word *apostasia*, which, in addition to *falling away,* also means *defection from truth, apostasy*. The Hebrew equivalent words for *apostasia* include *beliyaal* (*without profit, worthless, destruction*), *maal* (*treachery, transgression*), and *mered* (*rebellion*). The great falling away is the departure from truth – the teachings received in the Early Church. Falling away is equivalent to committing transgression, treachery, and rebellion. The Early Church taught that those who have fallen away are enemies of God:

> **And being raised from the dead and exalted at the Father's right hand, He awaits the time appointed by the Father for the judgment, when all enemies shall be put under Him. Now the enemies are all those who were found in apostasy, angels and archangels and powers and thrones, who despised the truth. And the prophet David himself says thus: The Lord said unto my Lord, Sit on My right hand, until I make thine enemies thy footstool (Irenaeus, *Demonstration of the Apostolic Preaching*).**

Anyone who has fallen away must *turn* back – *repent* – to the discipline of the secret. Only turning back to the teachings of the kingdom mysteries brings salvation. Today, many churches teach that the world has fallen away, but one cannot fall away if one never had truth to begin with. So, if the world cannot fall away, it is only the Church that can (and has) fallen away. Early Church Father Hippolytus rebukes the Church for falling into deception:

> **How have we been beguiled by the deceiver! How have we been joined to him! How have we been caught in his toils! How have we been taken in his abominable net! How have we heard the Scriptures and understood them not! For truly those who are engrossed with the affairs of this life, and with the lust of this world, will be easily brought over to the accuser then, and sealed by him. But many who are hearers of the divine Scriptures, and have them in their hand, and keep them in mind with understanding, will escape his imposture, and will flee from his hands... (Hippolytus, *The Sacred Writings of St. Hippolytus*).**

The Scriptures

Early Church Texts

Numerous sacred texts referenced by the Early Church are not in the current canon of the Bible. The Bible has undergone several iterations of *canonization*. The word *canon* comes from the Greek word *kanon*, which means *reed, measurement*. A canonical book is thus one that measures up to the standard of the Holy Scripture – written by a prophet, apostle, or one closely associated with such an individual.

The formation of the New Testament canon began in the early part of the second century A.D., with the earliest list drawn up in Rome in 140 A.D. By the end of the second century, all but seven books (Hebrews, 2 and 3 John, 2 Peter, Jude, James, and Revelation) were recognized as apostolic, and by the end of the fourth century, all 27 books in today's canon were recognized by Western churches.

While no man or council can pronounce a work to be canonical or scriptural, man can *collect* and preserve the works:

> The New Testament books did not become authoritative for the Church because they were formally included in a canonical list; on the contrary, the Church included them in her canon because she already regarded them as divinely inspired, recognizing their innate worth and generally apostolic authority, direct or indirect. The first ecclesiastical councils to classify the canonical books were both held in North Africa – at Hippo Regius in 393 and at Carthage in 397 – but what these councils did was not to impose something new upon the Christian communities but to codify what was already the general practice of these communities (Bruce, 1981).

While numerous sacred texts are left out of the current canon of the Bible, their importance is evident by their influence on the Early Church and the corresponding references to them in many other biblical books. For example, the books of Enoch considerably influenced early Christianity until the third century C.E. and the Essene community at Qumran in the first centuries B.C.E. and C.E. In fact, the testimonies of Enoch closely parallel John's accounts in the Book of Revelation. The Books of Enoch are referenced in Jude 4, 6, 13, 14-15, as well as 2 Peter 2:4 and 2 Peter 3:13. Other examples include the Book of the Wars of the Lord, referenced in Numbers 21:14-15, and the Book of Jasher (Book of the Righteous) referenced in Joshua 10:13 and 2 Samuel 1:18, just to name a few.

It should further be noted that terms like 'Bible,' 'biblical,' 'non-biblical,' 'canonical,' 'non-canonical,' 'apocryphal,' 'pseudepigraphical,' 'deuteron-canonical,' and 'de-canonization' are all anachronistic terms that did not exist in the formative stages of either Judaism or Christianity. All the non-canonical writings originate from the period of Early Judaism during the Greco-Roman period (300 B.C.E. to 200 C.E.), which was a period decisive for the formation of Judaism and Christianity.

Evidence exists that the Early Church often referenced the *Hebrew Gospel.* The earliest apparent quotation of the *Hebrew Gospel* is in Ignatius' *Letter to the Smyrnaeans*:

> For I know that after His resurrection also He was still possessed of flesh, and I believe that He is so now. When, for instance, He came to those who were with Peter, He said to them, "Lay hold, handle Me, and see that I am not an incorporeal spirit." And immediately they touched Him, and believed, being convinced both by His flesh and spirit (Ignatius, *Letter to the Smyrnaeans*).

This passage is also cited by Early Church Fathers Origen, Eusebius, and Jerome. While Origen and Eusebius do not directly attribute this passage from the *Hebrew Gospel*, Jerome, in the chapter on Ignatius in his work, *Illustrious Men*, notes that the passage is a testimony about the person of Christ "from the gospel that has recently been translated by me." On four occasions, Jerome testifies that he translated "the gospel" from Hebrew into Greek or Latin.

Hebrew Foundations

To grasp the fullness of Scripture, God's Word should really be read and understood from Hebraic roots. Numerous Early Church Fathers confirm that Yeshua spoke in Hebrew. The earliest witness is **Papias**, the Bishop of Hierapolis in Asia Minor during the mid-second century, who writes:

> Matthew put down the words of the Lord in the Hebrew language, and others have translated them, each as best he could (Eusebius, *Ecclesiastical History*).

Irenaeus, the Bishop of Lyon in France, whose works mainly spanned the last quarter of the second century A.D., writes:

> Matthew, indeed, produced his gospel written among the Hebrews in their own dialect (Eusebius, *Ecclesiastical History*).

Origen, during the first quarter of the third century, writes on Matthew:

> Among the four Gospels, which are the only indisputable ones in the Church of God under heaven, I have learned by tradition that the first was written by Matthew, who was once a publican, but afterwards an apostle of Jesus Christ, and it was prepared for the converts from Judaism, and published in the Hebrew language (Eusebius, *Ecclesiastical History*).

The entire New Testament can actually be understood from a Hebraic perspective. The Matthew Document (*Mattityahu Document*), containing Matthew, Mark, Luke, and Acts 1:1-15:35, was written on one scroll in Hebrew and later divided into separate scrolls. Further, much evidence exists that the original text of Revelation, which was written by the Apostle John, if not written in Hebrew, was likely recorded first in Aramaic, which is an ancient dialect of Hebrew.

It is commonly assumed that the New Covenant was written in Greek; however, the majority of the New Covenant was translated from Hebrew.

> Matthew, Mark, and Luke all tell essentially the same story of Yeshua and His life on Earth. But more than that, they all tell it in language that uses nearly identical sentence structure, idiomatic expressions, and other distinguishing linguistic features that are all decidedly Hebrew, not Greek (Klein, 2014).

The contents of the Book of Revelation actually contain more than 68% Hebrew Scripture. The 404 verses of Revelation contain as many as 278 quotes or allusions to the Old Testament, particularly Psalms, Isaiah, Ezekiel, Daniel, and Zechariah. The Old Testament as a whole is 78% of the current Bible text.

> When we add the highly Hebraic portions of the New Testament (Matthew, Mark, Luke, Acts 1:1-15:35,

> approximately 43% of the New Testament) to the Old Testament, the percentage of biblical material originally written in Hebrew rises to 88 percent. Not more than 12 percent of the entire Bible was written in Greek. When we subtract from that 12 percent the 176 quotations from the Old Testament (14 Old Testament quotations in John and 162 from Acts 15:36 to the end of the New Testament), the percentage of the Bible originally composed in Hebrew rises to over 90 percent (Bivin, 1994).

It should be noted that the first 15 chapters of Acts show some of the same textual evidence as the Synoptic Gospels of being originally communicated in Hebrew, as they deal with events in Jerusalem and are recounted in Hebrew context. In Acts 15:36 there is a shift to Greek as Luke begins to describe Paul's missionary journeys.

The text of the Hebrew Bible extends back to the Masoretes, who were a succession of Jewish scholars, notably connected with a school at Tiberias and whose work on the text began around 600 A.D. or earlier. The Masoretes introduced an intricate system of accent and vowel notations since Hebrew itself does not contain any vowels; however, the Masoretes did not originate the Hebrew traditional text. They respected the original text in such a way that they even placed in the margins what they believed to be correct and left the text itself unaltered. The Masoretes worked on the text when the Talmud was written, which had previously been in a relatively fixed condition. The Aramaic versions or paraphrases (Targums), the Syriac Peshitto version, and Latin Vulgate version of the Old Testament, and quotations of the Old Testament in the writings of Early Church Fathers (i.e., Origen's Hexapla) point to the existence of a Hebrew text for several centuries *before* the time of the Masoretes.

It is not difficult to recognize that Yeshua was a Jew. His family adhered to Jewish laws and customs, such as returning to Jerusalem during Passover, as depicted in the Gospel of Luke:

> **His [Yeshua's] parents went to Jerusalem every year at the Feast of the Passover. And when He was twelve years old, they went up to Jerusalem according to the custom of the feast (Luke 2:41-42).**

Even in the Book of Acts, Saul (before he became Paul) on the road to Damascus heard Yeshua speak to him in the Hebrew language:

> **And when we all had fallen to the ground, I heard a voice speaking to me and saying in the *Hebrew* language, 'Saul, Saul, why are you persecuting Me? It is hard for you to kick against the goads' (Acts 26:14).**

Hebrew & Greek Hermeneutics

God's Word is often taken from a literal interpretation and point of view. Scripture can be interpreted in an objective manner (*exegesis*) and in a way that goes beyond the literal (*isogesis*). In Hebrew thought, four levels of interpretation exist simultaneously:

P'shat
Remez
D'rash
Sod

The first level, *P'shat* ("simple"), is the literal interpretation of Scripture. The *P'shat* interpretation is for the common people.

The second level, *Remez* ("hint"), reveals a hinted meaning, usually in the form of a parable. The *Remez* interpretation is for nobles and lawyers.

The third level, *D'rash* ("concept"), is an allegory and investigation. The *D'rash* is a kingly interpretation (because it is for kings to search out the matter).

The fourth level, *Sod* ("hidden, secret"), is the hidden and secret meaning of Scripture. The *Sod* level is the apostolic and prophetic level of understanding.

Taking the first letter of each of the four words spells PRDS – the word *pardes* – meaning *garden, orchard.* Understanding Scripture on all four levels brings one back to paradise, or the *garden of Eden.*

On the other hand, the Greek mindset only has two levels of interpretation – the literal and allegorical – and only one is applied at a given time, never both simultaneously. The ancient Greek philosophers therefore took this approach when translating the Hebrew Scriptures. Because Greek philosophers developed their methods by working on mythological texts, they were thus hindered by the assumption that Hebrew text only reflected 75% creative imagination and 25% truth, leaving much room for the insertion of Greek biases.

Not only does the Greek mindset limit the levels of understanding of Scripture, but because the vast majority of Scripture originates from a Hebraic mindset, having a Greek mindset also limits the full understanding of the many Hebrew idioms and cultural references. As an example, it is difficult for one who isn't knowledgeable about a customary Hebrew marriage to recognize wedding references throughout the Scripture, and that God's divine plan revolves around a wedding from Genesis to the Book of Revelation (see **The Marriage Covenant**).

Ancient Hebrew

Hebrew is the original language God used to communicate to His people. The tablets that Moses obtained on the top of Mount Sinai when he spoke with God face to face were written in ancient Hebrew. Also, Moses wrote the first five books of the Bible in Hebrew. The written Hebrew language has evolved over thousands of years. Modern Hebrew writing differs drastically from ancient Hebrew writing, as ancient Hebrew is purely pictorial. Rabbis teach that each Hebrew letter is alive with a spirit, soul, and body. Early texts such as the *Sefer Yesira* describe that God's creation through speech was a manipulation of the letters of the Hebrew Aleph-Bet. Since letters have spiritual substance, they can be formed, weighed, and shaped by God. Such early texts teach that creation was actually the process of shaping the letters to formulate an earthly manifestation of a heavenly creation that already existed.

In fact, in the process of creation in Genesis, God first *spoke* and then *saw*. He *said*, "Let there be light," then *saw* the light was good (Genesis 1:3-4). This same pattern occurs for the heavens and Earth (Genesis 1:9-10), the vegetation on the Earth (Genesis 1:11-12), the celestial lights (Genesis 1:15-18), the sea creatures and birds (Genesis 1:20-21), the beasts of the Earth (Genesis 1:24-25), and the creation of man (Genesis 1:26-31).

Greek misses the mark in terms of definition and the thought behind the Scripture. An example is the word *roar*, which in Hebrew is the word *shaag*, written in ancient Hebrew, 𐤔𐤀𐤂. The root word is 𐤔𐤂, meaning *to be in error*. The Ancient Hebrew Lexicon Bible describes that the pictograph 𐤔 (*shin*) is a picture of the two front teeth representing the idea of double, the 𐤂 (*gimel*) is a picture of a foot representing the carrying of a burden. Combined these mean "double burden." When a work is found to be in error, the work must be redone. 𐤔𐤂 also means an error that is made out of ignorance or accident.

The root to the word *roar* means *to be in error*, so the Hebrew word for *roar* is connected to one who is in error and must redo the work. When Peter writes, "the devil walks about like a roaring lion" (1 Peter 5:8), he is in fact relaying that the devil comes looking like Yeshua but actually deceives the people through the teachings of false ministers; thus, work must be redone to reverse the false teachings.

One facet of the Hebrew Aleph-Bet is the association of a numerical value to each letter, referred to as *gematria*. God reveals the secrets of His Word not only through the pictorial meanings but also the numerical values associated with each letter and word. This book does not pursue gematria secrets much further but does include a few references to gematria values throughout.

The letters of ancient Hebrew are pictures of objects that hold deeper meanings. The following table of the ancient Hebrew Aleph-Bet depicts each letter's modern and ancient forms, its picture, and meaning(s) (Table 1). Combinations of letters yield words laden with intricate and deeper meanings when one understands the individual meaning of each letter.

Table 1 : The Hebrew Aleph-Bet

Modern	Ancient	Name	Picture	Meaning	Gematria
א		aleph	Head of ox	Strong, power, leader	1
ב		bet	Tent floorplan	Family, house	2
ג		gimel	Foot	Gather, walk, carry	3
ד		dalet	Tent door	Enter, movement, hang	4
ה		hey	Man with arms raised	Look, reveal, breath, sign	5
ו	Y	vav	Tent peg	Add, secure, hook, connect	6
ז		zayin	Mattock	Food, cut, weapon	7
ח		chet	Tent wall	Outside, divide, separation	8
ט	⊗	tet	Basket	Contain, surround	9
י		yud	Hand	Work, throw, worship, teach	10
כ		kaph	Open palm	Open, allow, submit, tame	20
ל		lamed	Shepherd's staff	Teach, yoke, authority	30
מ		mem	Water	Power, chaos, mighty, blood	40
נ		nun	Sprouting seed	Son, heir, continue	50
ס		samech	Thorn	Protect, grab, hate, turn	60
ע		ayin	Eye	Watch, know	70
פ		peh	Open mouth	Blow, scatter, edge	80
צ		tsadey	Man on his side	Wait, chase, snare, hunt	90
ק		kuf	Sun at horizon	Gather, circle, time, condense	100
ר		resh	Head of a man	First, beginning, top, mindset	200
ש		shin	Two front teeth	Sharp, press, eat, anointing	300
ת	†	tav	Cross	Mark, sign, covenant	400

Chapter Two

Hidden Temple Foundations

If the law, according to the apostle, is spiritual, containing the images "of future good things," come then, let us strip off the veil of the letter which is spread over it, and consider its true meaning. The Hebrews were commanded to ornament the Tabernacle as a type of the church, that they might be able, by means of sensible things, to announce beforehand the image of divine things. For the pattern which was shown to Moses (Ex. 25:40) in the mount, to which he was to have regard in fashioning the Tabernacle, was a kind of accurate representation of the heavenly dwelling…

Methodius
Ten Virgins

God established all things before the foundation of the world. What was established was *hidden* and revealed through His Word. All things that are revealed are done so by the proper interpretation and belief of His Word. The entire work and plan of God was already finished from the foundation of the world (Hebrews 4:3); everything that has been unfolding, and will unfold, is only a pattern of the finished counterparts in heaven.

Temple Theology

The tabernacle that God instructed Moses to build was a pattern of creation. All of creation lies within this blueprint, and God's divine redemptive plan is captured within temple theology.

> **For if He were on earth, He would not be a priest, since there are priests who offer the gifts according to the law; who serve the copy and shadow of the heavenly things, as Moses was divinely instructed when he was about to make the tabernacle. For He said, "SEE THAT YOU MAKE ALL THINGS ACCORDING TO THE PATTERN SHOWN YOU ON THE MOUNTAIN" (Hebrews 8:4-5).**

God showed Moses the entire process of creation, and Moses captured this in an earthly pattern: the tabernacle. To understand the secrets and *sod* level of teaching, one must also understand that the temple contained three sections: Outer Court, Holy Place, and Holy of Holies (Figure 2). Each section contained a different level of ministry, and entering into each of these sections required passing through a screen, or veil. These three areas also contained three types of people: Hebrews (Outer Court), Levitical priests (Holy Place), and the high priests (Holy of Holies). These offices were different in function.

Hebrews – Outer Court

The work in the Outer Court was difficult, as it included the inspection and killing of animal sacrifices and removing of waste and ashes. Those in the Outer Court were constantly dirty with blood, ashes and smoke. This portion of the temple illustrates us first coming to Christ with the dirt in our lives, burdens to be rid of, and the filth of sin. But the Outer Court is not part of the actual tabernacle structure, and it is done away with in the Book of Revelation. As we move from the Outer Court into the actual tabernacle, consisting of the Holy Place and Holy of Holies, we begin a cleansing and purifying process.

Levitical Priesthood – Holy Place

Those of the tribe of Levi were allowed to be priests and serve in the Holy Place. The Levitical priests' duties included preparing the temple instruments, preparing the sacrificial lambs, standing guard over the gates, singing and playing instruments, and administering the temple services. As we move closer to the presence of our Creator by entering into the Holy Place, we become cleansed by the work of the blood of the Lamb. The work of the Holy Place is to minister to Yahweh. In the Outer Court, man ministers to man, but in the Holy Place, man ministers to Yahweh. In the Holy Place, we come into a state of preparation where we draw closer to the veil leading into the Holy of Holies, in which the secrets of the kingdom lie.

High Priesthood – Holy of Holies

The Holy of Holies was considered by the Early Church to be Eden, and entrance into this most holy part of the tabernacle was reserved solely for the high priest. To be a high priest, one had to be a descendant of Aaron. A high priest carried a prophetic office, since the prophets in the Old Testament had the ability to pass beyond the veil and learn the hidden things of God. The high priest was in charge of the secrets of the temple ministry; he had access and knowledge of things that the other priests did not. These veiled secrets were reserved for the descendants of Aaron, and a prophetic anointing is required to understand these deeper truths. However, there is a level of priesthood that exists even above the high priesthood: a *royal* high priesthood.

> **But ye are a chosen generation, a *royal priesthood*, an holy nation, a peculiar people; that ye should shew**

> **forth the praises of him who hath called you out of darkness into his marvelous light (KJV, 1 Peter 2:9).**

Peter clearly portrays that we are part of a *royal* priesthood, indicating that we not only have access behind the veil to understand the deeper truths and the glory that was released to our Early Church family, but that we actually become *rulers* over the hidden doctrine. The understanding of this realm of glory can only be revealed through secrets, which are hidden from the wicked but plain to the godly. The Early Church taught that when the high priest entered into the Holy of Holies, he was transformed into an angel and came back out covered in the glory – the same glory that clothed Adam before he fell – and with a message to restore man back to the state before the fall. Essentially, with access back into the glory, we have the ability to restore the original condition of the garden. The blood of Yeshua provided this access for us (see **Royal Priesthood**).

Just as the Holy of Holies is the place where God's deeper secrets are revealed, the Book of Revelation is a book of unveiling secrets. The word *revelation* in Greek is the word *apocalypse*, meaning *to remove the veil* (see **Revelation of Mysteries & The Veil**). Throughout Scripture, the revealed secrets give the Church the ability to pass through the veil, enter the Holy of Holies and bring the glory of God back out to restore what Adam lost in Genesis. As a part of a royal priesthood, we are required to learn and fulfill this final stage of God's perfect plan. The Church is called to understand this realm of deeper teaching to fulfill her role in the restoration of creation.

All of creation, including space and time, fits into these three sections of Moses' temple. The walls of the Outer Court are made from fine linen hangings (Exodus 27:9-19), with the surface area of the hangings of the **Outer Court** measuring **1500** cubits squared. This is symbolic of the 1500 years between Moses receiving the Torah and Yeshua coming to Earth. Since the Outer Court had no covering, it was lit by natural sunlight, which is indicative of natural wisdom and understanding.

The Tabernacle, consisting of the Holy Place and Holy of Holies, has a volume of 3000 cubits cubed (10 x 30 x 10 cubits) (Exodus 26:15-18). The **Holy Place** has a volume of **2000** cubits cubed (10 x 20 x 10 cubits). This is symbolic of the 2000 years between Yeshua's First Coming and the present time, which are the 2000 years of the Church Age. The Holy Place was lit by the light of the menorah which contained anointing oil – a manmade light. The Church Age is the anointing realm whereby the works are still of man.

The **Holy of Holies** has a cube volume of **1000** cubits cubed (10 x 10 x 10 cubits), which is symbolic of the Millennial Kingdom Age. The Holy of Holies, containing the ark of the covenant, was lit by the Shekinah glory of God. The Millennial Kingdom Age is the eternal realm in the glory of God. As the New Jerusalem is also a cube, the Holy of Holies is a representation of the New Jerusalem, and the ark is a representation of the throne of God.

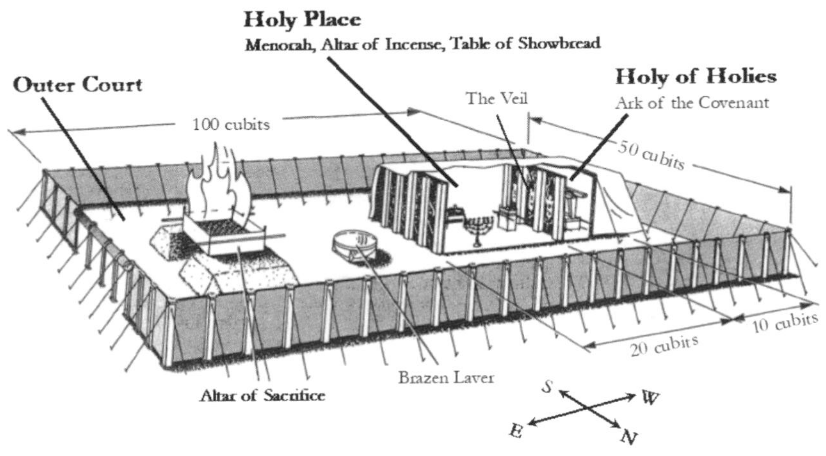

Figure 2: Tabernacle of Moses

Recognizing the partitioning of time into the three sections of the tabernacle is critical to fully comprehending the divine plan of God and the return to Eden. Further revelation of the temple is outlined in Table 2.

Table 2: Mysteries of the Temple

Outer Court	**Holy Place**	**Holy of Holies**
Altar of sacrifice Brazen laver	Menorah Altar of incense Table of showbread	Ark of the Covenant
Hebrews	Levitical Priests	Royal High Priests
Former Rain Feasts *Passover* *Unleavened Bread* *First Fruits*	Pentecost	Latter Rain Feasts *Trumpets* *Atonement* *Tabernacles*
1500 cubits squared	2000 cubits cubed	1000 cubits cubed
Pre-Church Age *1500 years from Moses receiving Torah to Yeshua*	Church Age *2000 years from Yeshua to present*	Kingdom Age *1000 Millennial Reign*
Baptism of Water *Justification*	Baptism of the Holy Spirit *Sanctification*	Baptism of Fire *Glorification*
Carnal Realm *Natural interpretation* *Milk* *Moon glory* *Babies* *30-fold harvest*	Anointing Realm *Hinted meaning* *Bread* *Star glory* *Sons* *60-fold harvest*	Glory Realm *Prophetic meaning* *Meat* *Sun glory* *Fathers* *100-fold harvest*
Cleansing	Teaching, anointing, wisdom	Eternal dwelling in Eden

Secrets

Of the four levels of Hebrew understanding, *sod* is the deepest, whereby the hidden and secret meaning of Scripture is unveiled. God makes it clear that the *sod* level of understanding is revealed to those who fear Him:

> **The *secret* of the LORD is with those who *fear* Him, and He will show them His covenant (Psalm 25:14).**

The word *secret* is the word *sod.* The word *fear* is the Hebrew word *yare*, written in ancient Hebrew, ירא. A related word, *yarah*, also written ירא, means *to throw, pour, shoot arrows, throw water, rain, direct, teach, instruct.* So, the *fear* of God is related to *instruction* from God. The Hebrew letters that form the words *yare* and *yarah* are the *yod* (י, *throw*), *resh* (ר, *mind*), and *aleph* (א, *God*), indicating that both fear of and instruction from God involve giving over one's old mindsets and ways of thinking to Him. *Fear* is associated with *instruction*, and *instruction* is associated with *rain*:

> **Let my *teaching* drop as the *rain*, My speech distill as the dew, as raindrops on the tender herb, and as showers on the grass (Deuteronomy 32:2).**

The word *teaching* is the Hebrew word *leqach*, which is the instruction of *catechism*, the Early Church way of instruction, in which enlightenment occurred when the secret teachings were unveiled to the catechumens **(see Discipline of the Secret & Mysteries).**

The teaching that God speaks about is the revealing of the discipline of the secret. As mentioned, the word *leqach* comes from the word *laqach*, meaning *to take, carry away*. The Early Church considered learning the mysteries of the kingdom to be associated with *ascending*, or *being taken up* – a mental *rapture*. Early Church Father Tertullian describes this ascension:

> **For when a man is rapt in the Spirit, especially when he beholds the glory of God, or when God speaks through him, he necessarily loses his sensation, because he is overshadowed with the power of God... (Tertullian, *Against Marcion*).**

We know that not everyone in the Early Church was given access to the secrets. Similarly, there are only select individuals to whom the kingdom secrets are revealed. Psalms 25:14 tells us that it is those who fear the Lord and are willing to learn from Him who receive the secrets. Further, Amos writes that God reveals His secret to the prophets:

> **Surely the Lord GOD does nothing, unless He reveals His *secret* to His servants the *prophets* (Amos 3:7).**

While the word *secret* may not appear abundantly in English translations of the Bible, the word *sod* appears throughout the Scripture when read in Hebrew. The word *secret* is the word *sod*, meaning *a company of persons in close deliberation, intimacy, consultation, assembly, secret counsel.* The Holy Spirit is the counselor and teacher of secrets.

In ancient Hebrew, *sod* is written 𐤎𐤅𐤃, where the root word *yasad*, 𐤎𐤃, means *level field, level piece of ground for planting crops or setting up tents or structures.* This word *yasad* consists of the letters *samech* (𐤎), a picture of a thorn, and *dalet* (𐤃), a picture of a door. In ancient Hebrew life, entrances into tents commonly entailed hanging curtains from bars; that is, doorways were actually veils, clearly depicted by the letter *dalet.* As thorns pierce and penetrate, the letters 𐤎 and 𐤃 together can be read, "to go through the veil." The word *secret* is associated with *passing beyond the veil* into the Holy of Holies, the place of God's secrets. The very definition of *revelation*, or *apocalypse,* is the removal of the veil (see **Revelation of Mysteries & The Veil**).

A related word to *sod* (סוד) is the word *sadiyn* (סדין), meaning *a sheet, a level garment when laid out, fine linen.* A garment of fine linen is associated with priestly and wedding attires. Fine linen is worn by the high priest and the Bride of Christ and signifies *righteousness.*

> **And the *priest* shall put on his *linen* garment, and his *linen* trousers he shall put on his body, and take up the ashes of the burnt offering which the fire has consumed on the altar, and he shall put them beside the altar (Leviticus 6:10).**
>
> **Then Aaron shall come into the tabernacle of meeting, shall take off the *linen* garments which he put on when he went into the *Holy Place*, and shall leave them there (Leviticus 16:23).**
>
> **Let us be glad and rejoice and give Him glory, for the marriage of the Lamb has come, and His wife has made herself ready. And to her it was granted to be arrayed in *fine linen*, clean and bright, for the *fine linen is the righteous acts of the saints* (Revelation 19:7-8).**

Righteousness is the Greek word *dikaioma*, which comes from the word *dikaios*, meaning *observing divine laws, keeping the commands of God, having right understanding.* In fact, a Hebrew equivalent of the word *dikaioma* is *mitzvah*, which is the word for *commandment* – the same word used for the 613 *mitzvahs* in the Torah. Hence, *sod*, the secrets of the kingdom, is connected with a people who belong to a priestly office and the Bride of Yeshua; they are righteous – they have right understanding of God's Word.

Just as the word *yasad* means a level field, a level foundation is necessary to build a structure or city. The New Jerusalem (the Bride of Christ) is built on a foundation of apostolic teachings:

> **Now the wall of the city [New Jerusalem] had twelve *foundations*, and on them were the names of the twelve *apostles* of the Lamb (Revelation 21:14).**

The foundations of the Church are the secrets and mysteries. The Bride understands the teachings of the apostles. In Ephesians 3, Paul writes that the mysteries of God are given to only two offices: God's holy apostles and prophets. The Bride of Christ cannot be built without first having apostles to bring the revelation of Yeshua. The *secrets* are the *foundations* of *God's kingdom.*

> **For we are God's fellow workers; you are God's *field*, you are God's *building*. According to the grace of God which was given to me, as a wise master builder I have laid the *foundation*, and another builds on it. But let each one take heed how he builds on it (1 Corinthians 3:9-10).**

> **Now, therefore, you are no longer strangers and foreigners, but fellow citizens with the saints and members of the household of God, having been built on the *foundation of the apostles and prophets*, Jesus Christ Himself being the chief *cornerstone* (Ephesians 2:19-20).**

A foundation (*sod*) of the apostles and prophets is required to build the household of God. Yeshua is not only the cornerstone, which is the first stone of a foundation, but He is also the capstone, or the apex of a structure such as a pyramid. The tabernacle of God was patterned after the heavenly temple, whereby the Holy of Holies was considered by the Early Church to be Eden (see **The Garden**). A river flowed *out of* Eden to water the garden and then continued as riverheads (Genesis 2:10), indicating that the elevation increased as one approached and entered Eden.

This picture of increasing elevation from the Outer Court to the Holy of Holies indicates that the heavenly tabernacle was essentially a pyramidal structure. The pyramids in Egypt built by the Nephilim – the fallen ones – were the counterfeit versions of God's tabernacle. With these pyramids, the fallen angels attempted to return to the heavenly realm through resurrection life. A small hole was left at the top of the pyramids as a porthole to the heavens. The Egyptians used the pyramids not to bury the dead, which is a common yet false assumption, but rather to acquire resurrection life. This resurrection was *ascension* into the heavens, or a *catching up*.

Foundations

Any given structure, including the pyramids, requires a solid foundation as well as a cornerstone and capstone. Yeshua is the foundation, cornerstone, and capstone.

> **For no other *foundation* can anyone lay than that which is laid, which is *Jesus Christ* (1 Corinthians 3:11).**
>
> **Therefore thus says the Lord GOD: "Behold, I lay in Zion a *stone* for a *foundation*, a tried stone, a precious *cornerstone*, a sure *foundation*; whoever believes will not act hastily..." (Isaiah 28:16).**
>
> **'Who are you, O great mountain? Before Zerubbabel you shall become a plain! And he shall bring forth the *capstone* with shouts of "Grace, grace to it!"' (Zechariah 4:7).**

The word *stone* in Isaiah 28 is the word *eben*, written in ancient Hebrew, 𐤀𐤁𐤍, whose root word *ben*, 𐤁𐤍, means *tent, build, son.* The addition of the *aleph* (𐤀), a picture of an ox, symbolic of the apostle, further indicates that it is the *apostolic* sons (and houses) that make up the foundations of the kingdom. Just as the earthly temple is a pattern of the heavenly tabernacle, those who God prepared specifically to build the physical sanctuary are patterns of the apostolic teachers who build God's heavenly and glorified Church.

Such individuals include Bezalel and Aholiab. Bezalel, whose name means *under the shadow or protection of God*, and Aholiab, whose name means *father's tent*. They were master builders and given the knowledge to build God's house:

> **And Bezalel and Aholiab, and every gifted artisan in whom the LORD has put wisdom and understanding, to know how to do all manner of *work* for the service of the *sanctuary*, shall do according to all that the LORD has commanded. Then Moses called Bezalel and Aholiab, and every gifted artisan in whose heart the LORD had put wisdom, everyone whose heart was stirred, to come and do the *work* (Exodus 36:1-2).**

The word *work* is the Hebrew word *malakah*, whose root word is *malak*, meaning *angel, or messenger*. The Early Church Fathers taught that those who have ascended through learning the secrets of the kingdom were transformed into the glory of God and became like the angels. So, the *work for the sanctuary* is equivalent to *revealing the mysteries of the kingdom*, leading one into the glory of God in the Holy of Holies. As master builders of the physical temple, Bezalel and Aholiab were only a pattern of catechists unveiling the secret teachings of the kingdom, the building stones of God's government.

The works of God's children will ultimately be revealed by their foundations, or secrets, which will be tested by fire.

> **Now if anyone builds on this *foundation* with *gold, silver, precious stones*, wood, hay, straw, each one's *work* will become clear; for the Day will declare it, because**

> **it will be *revealed by fire*; and the fire will test each one's work, of what sort it is (1 Corinthians 3:12-13).**
>
> **If anyone's *work* which he has built on it endures, he will receive a reward. If anyone's work is burned, he will suffer loss; but he himself will be saved, yet so as through *fire*. Do you not know that *you are the temple of God* and that the Spirit of God dwells in you? If anyone defiles the *temple* of God, God will *destroy* him. For the *temple* of God is holy, which *temple you are* (1 Corinthians 3:14-17).**

The walls of New Jerusalem have precious stones. They are the twelve gems on the ephod, which is the garment of the high priest, symbolic of the Word of God. A city is a community with government and order. A government has laws because without law there is anarchy. The role of government is to keep everything in order, as a kingdom divided cannot stand. The Torah, which is government, is God's order.

> **For who has stood in the *counsel* of the LORD, and has perceived and heard His word? Who has marked His word and heard it? (Jeremiah 23:18).**

The word for *counsel* is the word *sod*, which also means *a group of elders of the tribe who sit in counsel as the foundation of a tribe*. The counsel of the Lord is His secrets. The 24 elders who sit around the throne of God have crowns of gold on their heads (Revelation 4:4). As gold is indicative of wisdom, the elders have the divine knowledge and reveal the secrets of God. Seventy elders were set up by Moses (Exodus 24:9, Numbers 11:16, 25). The number 70 is the gematria value for *sod*, and so those with the secrets sit on the throne with God. Those who hear the secrets partake in a face-to-face experience with God. Paul speaks about this face-to-face encounter:

> **For now we see in a mirror, dimly, but then *face to face.* Now I *know* in part, but then I shall know just as I also am *known* (1 Corinthians 13:12).**

The word *face* is the Greek word *prosopon*, whose equivalent Hebrew counterparts include both *paniym*, meaning *face*, and *peh*, meaning *mouth*. So, the face-to-face encounter is a *mouth-to-mouth encounter*, or a *kiss* or *breath* of God. The breath, or the *ruach* of God, is the very breath that He breathed into Adam in Genesis. The word *know* is the word *ginosko*, whose equivalent Hebrew words include *yada* ([illegible]), which means *to learn, to have intercourse with another person*, and *laqach* ([illegible]), which means *to take, capture, snatch, marry, tongs (used to take things)*. Thus, having a true face-to-face encounter with God – an intimate relationship – is for Him to breathe, or impart His *character* into us, just as He did with Adam. The true face-to-face encounter also entails being *caught up*, or *ascending*, which occurs through *revelation*. This *catching up* also brings a *resurrection*. This is what the Egyptians were unable to achieve with their pyramids, which were counterfeit tabernacles.

Revelation of Mysteries & The Veil

The hidden *mysteries* of God are found throughout Scripture, and were established before the foundations of the world as taught by the Early Church. It takes *revelation* of the mysteries to understand them.

> **. . . how that by *revelation* He made known to me the *mystery* (as I have briefly written already, by which, when you read, you may understand my knowledge in the *mystery* of Christ), which in other ages was not made known to the sons of men, as it has now been revealed by the Spirit to His holy apostles and prophets (Ephesians 3:3-5).**

To me, who am less than the least of all the saints, this grace was given, that I should preach among the Gentiles the unsearchable riches of Christ, and to make all see what is the fellowship of the *mystery*, which from the *beginning of the ages has been hidden* in God who created all things through Jesus Christ (Ephesians 3:8-9).

Now to Him who is able to establish you according to my gospel and the preaching of Jesus Christ, according to the *revelation* of the *mystery* kept *secret* since the world began (Romans 16:25).

. . . the *mystery* which has been hidden from ages and from generations, but now has been *revealed* to His saints. To them God willed to make known what are the riches of the glory of this *mystery* among the Gentiles: which is Christ in you, the hope of glory (Colossians 1:26-27).

The word *mystery*, which appears 27 times in the Bible, is the word *musterion*, which means *hidden thing; secret; the secret counsels which govern God in dealing with the righteous, which are hidden from the ungodly and wicked but plain to the godly.* The mysteries make up the secret counsels that govern God. The secret counsels are the foundation of God's government, which are His kingdom. Even the word *musterion* is the equivalent Hebrew word *sod*, or *secret*. His kingdom is built on mysteries for the righteous – those with right understanding.

The word *revelation* is the Greek word *apokalupsis*, which consists of the words *apo* (*off, away*), and *kalypto* (*cover, hide, veil*). The definition of the word *revelation* or *apokalupsis* is "to remove the veil." The **unveiling of the secret counsels of God** was kept hidden since the beginning of creation. *Apokalupsis* is directly tied to the English word *apocalypse*, which from the proper definition does not point to any sort of world ending phenomenon, but rather a revealing, or revelation. Therefore, the Book of Revelation is the **book of unveiling**.

The Veil

The veil that separated the Holy Place from the Holy of Holies is a representation of the threshold between the earthly and heavenly realms. The Early Church Fathers understood the mystery of the veil as being the entrance back into the garden and the glory of God. Barker describes, "[t]hose who were able to pass through the veil passed beyond the limits of the material world." Only the high priest was allowed to enter the Holy of Holies to atone for the people's sin, which indicates that passing through the veil is a *high priestly tradition*. The Early Church understood that Yeshua stood in the high priestly role.

> Ignatius of Antioch, early in the second century C.E., wrote: 'Our own high priest . . . has been entrusted with the holy of holies and to him alone are the secret things of God committed' (Phil. 9). Clement of Alexandria, writing at the end of the second century C.E., also used significant imagery: 'those who have the truth enter in through the tradition of the Lord by drawing aside the curtain' (Barker, 2000).

Further, it was understood that a transfiguration occurred when one passed beyond the veil. This is indicated in 1 Enoch:

> **None of the angels could enter by reason of the magnificence and the Glory and *no flesh* could behold him (1 Enoch 14:21).**

The transformation was from a human state to an angelic state. Even some hymns discovered at Qumran confirmed that the *priests* in the temple were the *counterparts of the angels*, and the high priest was the image of the Lord on Earth.

The veil was composed of blue, red, and purple thread, as well as white linen. The colored fabric symbolized the weaving of the four earthly elements from which creation was made: blue (air), red (fire), purple, made from seashells (water), and the linen, made of a plant, symbolizing the Earth.

> Josephus, who wrote at the end of the first century C.E., knew the significance of the colours, and he also revealed that the cherubim embroidered on the veil were 'a panorama of the heavens' (War 5.212-13). Philo, his older contemporary, knew a similar tradition about the colours and fibres; the veil which screened God's presence represented matter. 'It is right, he said, that the divine temple of the creator of all things should be woven of such and so many things as the world itself was made of, the world being the universal temple which existed before the holy temple was constructed' (Barker, 2000).

Passing through the veil is equivalent to surpassing the flesh. Paul writes in Hebrews that the veil is His flesh:

> **Therefore, brethren, having boldness to enter the Holiest by the blood of Jesus, by a new and living way which He consecrated for us, through the *veil*, that is, His *flesh*, and having a High Priest over the house of God, let us draw near with a true heart in full assurance of faith, having our hearts sprinkled from an evil conscience and our bodies washed with pure water (Hebrews 10:19-22).**

The word *veil* in Hebrews 10:20 is the Greek word *katapetasma*. One of the Hebrew equivalent words is *masak*, which means *covering, booth, screen*. In ancient Hebrew, *masak* is written , where *samech* (, *thorn*) represents protection, *kaph* (, *palm of the hand*) represents covering ("protective covering"), and *mem* (, *water*) represents power. The veil is meant to be a protective covering of God's power.

Another equivalent Hebrew word is *parokhet*, meaning *curtain, veil*. In ancient Hebrew, *parokhet* is written ; the word means *breaking*, and means *whip: as dividing and breaking open the flesh*. The *veil* is Yeshua's flesh. His physical beating tore the flesh off and exposed the meat of His Body. The word *gospel* means a *feast of meat*, and Paul describes the Word as *meat*:

> **I have fed you with milk, and not with *meat*: for hitherto ye were not able to bear it, neither yet now are ye able (KJV, 1 Corinthians 3:2).**
>
> **For when for the time ye ought to be teachers, ye have need that one teach you again which be the first principles of the oracles of God; and are become such as have need of milk, and not of strong *meat* (KJV, Hebrews 5:12).**

The word *meat* is the Greek word *trophe*, whose Hebrew equivalent includes the word *tereph*, meaning *something torn, such as meat or flesh*. Yeshua's flesh being torn is a picture of the veil being removed from the threshold between the Holy Place and the Holy of Holies, the latter of which contains the manifested glory of God. Yeshua taught that the people must eat His Body and drink His blood (John 6:54-56). To *eat His flesh* is to *go through the veil* by ascension into the Holy of Holies, which is achieved through learning the secrets of the kingdom. The veil is the portal between the earthly and heavenly dimensions; the revelation of Yeshua and God's divine plan is the threshold through which one receives resurrection life.

The Holy of Holies is likened to the **womb**. Cosmas Indicopleustes, an Egyptian Christian who wrote much on the symbolism contained in the temple, wrote of Moses, saying that the Lord hid him in a cloud on Sinai, took Moses out of all earthly things "and begot him anew like a child in the womb."

> **Then having taken him up into the mountain to remain for forty days without food, he hid him in a cloud and in a manner abstracted him from all earthly things . . . giving him birth anew as if he were a child in the womb. But at the end of the forty days he gave him a new form and a new soul, and revealed to him all that he had done in the making of the world in six days, and showing him in other six days by means of visions the making of the world, performing in his presence the work of each day . . . (Cosmas, *Christian Topography*).**

One must become pregnant with the Word – the revelation – in order to enter the glory in the Holy of Holies. When the high priest went through the veil, he was considered to be "born again," as resurrection was connected to learning the deeper teachings of God. As Moses ascended Mt. Sinai, he stepped into his high priestly office.

Seeing the Light

Revelation is directly connected to *vision*. The Hebrew word *chazon* appears over 30 times in the Old Testament writings, and is translated as *revelation* or *vision*. This word *chazon* comes from the root word *chaz*, meaning *to see, perceive; to see beyond what is seen in the physical, present as a light piercing through darkness*; also *vision: a perception beyond the normal experiences*. Receiving revelation is thus connected to being *enlightened*, which describes the baptism of catechumens. The root word *chaz* (*vision*) written in ancient Hebrew is ; the letters *zayin* (, *weapon, plow*) and *chet* (𐤇, *wall, separation*) together can be interpreted as "breaking down a wall," or even "removing a barrier," which parallels the concept of "removing the veil."

The ability to see is *as a light piercing through darkness*. Revelation is thereby directly associated with light. In the Gospel of Luke when Simeon holds the infant Yeshua in the temple, he declares:

> **For my eyes have seen Your salvation which You have prepared before the face of all peoples, a *light* to bring *revelation* to the Gentiles, and the glory of Your people Israel (Luke 2:30-32).**

The word *revelation* is the same word *apokalupsis*. Yeshua, the light of Day One of creation, removed the veil from the Gentiles in order that they might see the divine plan of God. Revelation comes from hearing and rightly understanding the Word of God. Because righteousness is right understanding, revelation, or a removal of the veil, is required to obtain it. Righteousness necessitates a destruction of the carnal interpretation of His Word.

Sifting

The teaching and revelation of mysteries brings about a sifting. Those who were uncommitted and unsuitable to continue learning the deeper teachings were sifted out. This sifting process is a repeated pattern found throughout Scripture. By His teachings, Yeshua sifted and separated those who would follow Him from those who would not. When Yeshua taught the 5000 to eat His flesh and drink His blood, He lost thousands of followers:

> **For My flesh is food indeed, and My blood is drink indeed. He who eats My flesh and drinks My blood abides in Me, and I in him. . . . Therefore many of His**

> **disciples, when they heard this, said, "This is a hard saying; who can understand it?"… From that time *many* of His disciples went back and walked with Him no more (John 6:55-56, 60, 66).**

The word *many* is the word *polus*, meaning the *multitude* or *majority*. While the majority thought He was speaking about cannibalism, Yeshua was really teaching that He was the Passover Lamb of God, and one must consume the revelation of Him to obtain everlasting life. Those without the eyes to see were unable to understand the *sod* level and prophetic meaning of His teaching.

Only Pure Revelation

Even if some revelation is obtained, it cannot be mixed with carnal, dead, religious teachings. New wine cannot be placed into old wine skins:

> **And no one puts new wine into old wineskins; or else the new wine bursts the wineskins, the wine is spilled, and the wineskins are *ruined*. But new wine must be put into new wineskins (Mark 2:22).**

The word *ruined* is the word *apollumi*, the same word used to describe the wicked who will be destroyed and the lost who will perish. Those who are perishing are those who are unable to see the Torah on the spiritual, or *sod* level. In 2 Corinthians, Paul writes:

> **But even if our gospel is veiled, it is veiled to those who are *perishing*, whose minds the god of this age has blinded, who do not believe, lest the light of the gospel of the glory of Christ, who is the image of God, should shine on them (2 Corinthians 4:3-4).**

The word *perishing* is the same word *apollumi*. When the light and glory of God shines on these people – when they receive illumination from learning the discipline of the secret – they will no longer perish. From the word *apollumi* comes the name *Apollyon* (or in Hebrew, *Abaddon*), meaning *destroyer*, who is the angel of the bottomless pit (Revelation 9:11). Apollyon comes at the end of the age to release the final darkness and sealing of people in the bottomless pit. The word *bottomless* is the word *abussos*, consisting of the words *a* (without), and *bathos* (deep). *Buthos* comes from the word *bathos*, meaning *mystery*, or *secrets*. Thus, the bottomless pit is a place without secrets – a place without revelation.

Revelation cannot be placed into religion. New wine expands with fermentation. The old wine skin of religion will not be able to contain the new wine of revelation. If wine skins are not oiled regularly, they would not remain pliable. One must continually be infused with anointing and new revelations, otherwise one becomes stiff and eventually will crack and burst open. Revelation will either destroy the old fleshly nature or take one into the resurrected glorified body. However, transformation must first occur in the mindset (Romans 12:2).

Parables

The secrets that God has kept hidden since the beginning of creation are widely presented in the form of parables throughout the Scriptures. God spoke in parables, and Yeshua taught the people in parables. When Yeshua's disciples asked Him why He spoke to the masses in parables, He explained that, to those on the outside – those without eyes to see or ears to hear – the mysteries of the kingdom are presented in parables:

> **Because it has been given to you [the disciples] to know the *mysteries* of the kingdom of heaven, but to them it has not been given. . . . Therefore I speak to them in *parables*, because seeing they do not see, and hearing they do not hear, nor do they understand (Matthew 13:11, 13).**
>
> **And He said to them, "To you it has been given to know the *mystery* of the kingdom of God; but to those**

who are outside, all things come in *parables...*" (Mark 4:11).

But without a *parable* He did not speak to them. And when they were alone, He explained all things to His disciples (Mark 4:34).

All these things Jesus spoke to the multitude in *parables*; and without a *parable* He did not speak to them, that it might be fulfilled which was spoken by the prophet, saying: "I WILL OPEN MY MOUTH IN *PARABLES*; I WILL UTTER THINGS KEPT *SECRET* FROM THE FOUNDATION OF THE WORLD" (Matthew 13:34-35).

The Early Church emphasized the importance of the parables in Scripture. The "parables of the New Testament refuse to be handled like Aesop's fables; they were intended from the first to *shadow forth the 'mysteries of the Kingdom of Heaven,'* and they also have a double purpose which is attributed to Christ Himself" (Barry, 1911). The parables are necessary in order to convey the mysteries of the kingdom.

I will open my mouth in a *parable*; I will utter *dark sayings* of old (Psalm 78:2).

The nature of a riddle (or parable) has a light and a dark side, with the dark side associated with the dark sayings mentioned not only in Psalms, but also in the Book of Wisdom and Book of Sirach:

Or if wide knowledge be thy ambition, she can inform thee of what is past, make conjecture of the future; she is versed in the subtleties of debate, in the reading of all *riddles*; marvels and portents she can foretell, and what events time or season will bring (Wisdom 8:8).

But the wise man will be learning the lore of former times; the prophets will be his study. The tradition

> **handed down by famous men will be in his keeping; his to con the niceties of every *parable*, learn the hidden meaning of every *proverb*, make himself acquainted with *sayings hard to understand* (Sirach 39:1-3).**

The Hebrew word for *dark saying* (Psalm 78) is the word *chiydah*, which means *riddle, difficult question, parable, dark or obscure utterance*. In ancient Hebrew, *chiydah* is written חידה, which contains the root word *echad* (חד), meaning *unite, two or more coming together as a unity*. The letters *dalet* (ד, *door*) and *chet* (ח, *wall*) together depict a door in a wall. Through a door, the outside and inside are united. *Echad* can also mean *sharp*, describing the two edges of a sword that meet to form one point.

A riddle or dark saying begins by dividing the teller from the listener, and the answer unites the two. Pictorially, the understanding of the teller of the riddle (instructor, or catechist) is at a "higher" level than that of the listener (learner or catechumen), but as the instructor brings his knowledge to the learner, the learner's understanding increases until both become united in understanding the answer to the parable. In a similar matter, a good king comes down from his throne to teach his people. Those who do not understand the parable are those who are outside the door and need a removal of the veil. Thus, when Yeshua knocks at the door, He is asking us to come into His deeper teachings – to pass beyond the veil.

The word *parable* is the Hebrew word *maashaal* and the Greek word *parabolee*. The Fausset's Bible dictionary defines a *parable* as "placing side by side or comparing earthly truths, expressed, with heavenly truths to be understood. The basis of parable is that man is made in the image of God, and there is a law of continuity of the human with divine. The force of the parable lies in the real analogies impressed by the Creator on His creatures, the physical typifying the higher moral world." What is found on the Earth also exists in the heavenly kingdom. Parables answer to the parabolic characteristic of His own manifestation. The

Fausset's Bible dictionary further describes the purpose in using parables as being judicial and didactic "to discriminate between the careless and the sincere." The rabbis of Christ's time and earlier often used parables. Fausset's definition continues: "The untutored masses relish what is presented in the concrete and under imagery, rather than in the abstract. Even the disciples, through Jewish prejudices, were too weak in faith impartially to hear gospel truths if presented in naked simplicity; the parables secured their assent unawares." Similarly, Clement of Alexandria wrote as follows:

> **For many reasons, then, the Scriptures hide the sense. First that we may become inquisitive, and be ever on the watch for the words of salvation. Then it was not suitable for all to understand, so that they might not receive harm in consequence of taking in another sense the things declared for salvation by the Holy Spirit. Wherefore the holy mysteries of the prophecies are veiled in the parables – preserved for chosen men, selected to knowledge in consequence of their faith; for the style of the Scriptures is parabolic (Clement, *Stromata*).**

During the latter half of his ministry, when His teaching was rejected or misunderstood, Yeshua judicially punished the unbelieving by the parabolic veiling of the truth:

> **He answered and said to them, "Because it has been given to you to know the mysteries of the kingdom of heaven, but to them it has not been given. For whoever has, to him *more will be given*, and he will have abundance; but whoever does not have, even what he has will be taken away from him. . . . But *blessed* are your eyes for they *see*, and your ears for they *hear*" (Matthew 13:11-12, 16).**

It is clear that the process of revelation is not for everyone. The revelation of the Word is also judicial. Judgment comes through the deeper wisdom and maturity of the individual:

> **But from the fact that truth appertains not to all, it is veiled in manifold ways, causing the light to arise only on those who are initiated into knowledge, who seek the truth through love. The proverb, according to the Barbarian philosophy, is called a mode of prophecy, and the parable is so called, and the enigma in addition (Clement, *Stromata*).**

To those who have revelation of the kingdom mysteries, more will be given; but to those who do not, even the little revelation they do have will be removed. In fact, people who did not believe the parables of Christ were considered unbelievers. To the carnal, the parable is a veiling, as Paul writes in 2 Corinthians 4:3: "**But even if our gospel is veiled, it is veiled to those who are perishing.**" But to the receptive, it is a progressive revealing of the truth. Further, there was "a penalty of a blessing according to the hearer's state: a darkening to those who loved darkness; enshrining the truth (concerning Messiah's spiritual kingdom so different from Jewish expectations) from the jeer of the scoffer, and leaving something to stimulate the careless afterward to think over" (Fausset, 1878). While the parables bring light to those who see the deeper meanings, they bring further darkness to those who are spiritually blind.

The Sacrificial Lamb & Temple

The sacrificial Lamb mentioned throughout Scripture is the Messiah Himself, who was slaughtered before the foundations of the world.

> **All who dwell on the earth will worship him [the dragon, Satan], whose names have not been written in the Book of Life of the *Lamb slain from the foundation of the world.* If anyone has an ear, let him hear (Revelation 13:8-9).**

Yeshua was slain <u>before</u> He physically hung on the tree at Gethsemane. God had already atoned for Adam and Eve <u>before</u> they ate of the Tree of Knowledge of Good and Evil. God already had a plan that would create a greater Man than Adam. In fact, if Adam had realized that Yeshua had already atoned for his sin, he could have returned back to the glory after he fell.

The Lamb is closely associated with *blamelessness* and *holiness*, characteristics that were established in God's children before the foundations of the world. Paul, in his letter to the Ephesians, writes:

> **Just as *He chose us* in Him *before the foundation of the world,* that we should be *holy* and *without blame* before Him in love (Ephesians 1:4).**

Holy is the Greek word *hagios*, which fundamentally means *without blemish, pure, upright, set apart.* Another form of the word is *hagion*, which is used to describe structures set apart for God – in particular, the tabernacle (*hieron*) and more specifically, the Holy of Holies (*naos*) (Hebrews 9:3, 9:8, 9:24-25). In fact, the words *naos* and *heiron* are synonyms for the word *hagion*.

Without blame is the Greek word *amomos*, meaning *without spot or blemish, especially designating the absence of something amiss in a sacrifice or offering.* The Hebrew equivalent of the word *blemish* is the word *mum*, which means *defect, anything considered useless or without value*, and is used to describe imperfect offerings and sacrifices. The Hebrew equivalent of the phrase *without blame* is the word *tom,* meaning *integrity; completeness; someone or something that is whole, complete, full; one who is mature and upright.* In fact, maturity is directly linked to perfection. As shown when Paul, James, and other New Testament authors write about being *perfect*, the Greek word used is *teleios*, which means *complete, fullness of age (mature).* Another Hebrew equivalent of the word *without blame* is the word *tamiym*, which means *complete or entirely in accord with truth and fact.* Maturity is linked to having right understanding of truth.

In 1 Corinthians 2, Paul writes that the only way to become perfect or mature (*teleios*), is to learn the mysteries and secrets:

> **However, we speak wisdom among those who are mature, yet not the wisdom of this age, nor of the rulers of this age, who are coming to nothing. But we speak the wisdom of God in a mystery, the hidden *wisdom* which God ordained before the ages for our glory, which none of the rulers of this age knew; for had they known, they would not have crucified the Lord of glory (1 Corinthians 2:6-8).**

In Verse 7, Paul reveals that the hidden wisdom will bring us back into the glory. This was typified when the high priest entered through the veil to learn the secret teachings, mysteries of God to which the other priests did not have access. Yeshua paid the price for us to have this access, but we can only be part of this royal priestly office if we understand these wonderful truths for our time.

More on Blamelessness & Perfection

In ancient Hebrew, the word *tom*, meaning *without blame*, is written ᴍᴍ✝. The letter *mem* (ᴍᴍ) is a picture of water, or a river, and the letter *tav* (✝) is a cross, representative of the Tree of Life. The Tree of Life sits in the middle of the garden and is watered by a river flowing out of Eden (Genesis 2:10); likewise, the Tree of Life sits in the middle of the New Jerusalem and is watered by a river flowing from the throne of God (Revelation 22:1). Eden is one and the same as the New Jerusalem. From the spelling of the word *tom*, one may see that blamelessness – perfection – is in Eden, or the New Jerusalem. This is the ultimate habitation place of God found in His people.

Further, the water is symbolic of revelation, and the Tree is symbolic of Torah (see **The Tree**). Thus, blamelessness and perfection come with revelation of the Torah. A related word to ʍ† is ʍ♉†, meaning *double*. An apostle, represented by an ox (♉), teaching the revelation of the Torah – the prophetic and *sod*-level interpretation – yields *double portions*, such as the double portion anointing received by Elisha from Elijah. Another related word is ♆ʍ†, meaning *amazed, to bring out of confusion.* Confusion is connected to *Pharaoh*, whose name means *great double house*, or *double-minded.* Pharaoh ruled in Egypt; the Hebrew word for *Egypt* is *mitsrayim*, coming from the word *matsor*, meaning a *limit*, or essentially *limiting God.* Thus, to be blameless and perfect produces an exodus out of Egypt (*place of limiting of God*) whose ruler is Pharaoh (*double-mindedness, confusion*).

Yeshua is not the only sacrificial Lamb. God's children are called to be like Yeshua, which means we are likewise lambs for sacrifice.

> **I beseech you therefore, brethren, by the mercies of God, that you present your bodies a *living sacrifice, holy, acceptable* to God, which is your reasonable service. And do not be conformed to this world, but be *transformed by the renewing of your mind,* that you may prove what is that *good* and *acceptable* and *perfect* will of God (Romans 12:1-2).**

The word *mind* is the Greek word *nous*, and in Hebrew is equivalent to the word *leb*, meaning *heart*, which is the source of emotion or thought.

In Hebrew thought the *mind* and *heart* are synonymous. The sacrifice that Paul speaks about in Romans is that of the carnal, human mind to the will (mind) of Christ, which is *good*, *acceptable*, and *perfect*. These are the same qualities that describe an unblemished lamb suitable for sacrifice. Paul even plainly states that the fathers of the faith are sacrificial sheep:

> **As it is written: "FOR YOUR SAKE WE ARE KILLED ALL DAY LONG; WE ARE ACCOUNTED AS *SHEEP FOR THE SLAUGHTER*" (Romans 8:36).**

If the Lamb was slain before the foundations of the world, then a temple in which to slay the Lamb was also established before the foundations of the world. The Lamb and the temple began in the heavenly realm. The physical, earthly forms came afterwards as patterns pointing towards the heavenly version.

The Hebrew word for *lamb* or *sheep* is *seh*, written in ancient Hebrew, 𐤔𐤄. A related word is written 𐤔𐤅𐤄, meaning *veil*. Thus, a lamb is considered one who is veiled. When the Lord views His children as lambs, He sees a veiled people and desires to remove their ignorance. We must get rid of our ignorance to enter beyond the veil and understand the deeper facets of the kingdom of Yah. Our minds are still veiled in the Holy Place, so we must journey into the Holy of Holies to see these deeper secrets that Yahweh desires to reveal to His Body. Since *secret* in Hebrew is also associated with *intimacy*, learning the deeper teachings is a place of divine relationship with the Father in the secret chamber of His heart where He teaches us His language.

> **Give ear, O my people, to my law; incline your ears to the words of my mouth. I will open my mouth in a parable; I will utter dark sayings of old (Psalms 78:1-2).**

The language of Yah is a deeper place of intimacy and revelation, and Paul writes similarly about speaking in tongues, or languages:

> **For he who speaks in a *tongue* does not speak to men but to God, for no one understands him; however, in the spirit he speaks mysteries (1 Corinthians 14:2).**

The word *tongue* is the Greek word *glossa*, meaning *language*. The same word is used in 1 Corinthians 13:1 where Paul writes, "**Though I speak with the *tongues* of men and of angels. . . .**" Angels are *messengers* who bring the secrets out from behind the veil of the Holy of Holies, and so the tongues are *languages of secrets*. The highest form of speaking in tongues (languages) is speaking in mysteries. This is a new level of revelation that has come to the Church for the end time move to mature the Church for her purpose in the end time plan of Yah. Divine wisdom is required to handle the glory of the Father and partake in executing His divine plan.

The Temple

While a temple is required in which to sacrifice lambs, John, in the Book of Revelation describes the Lamb as the very temple itself:

> **But I saw no temple in it [the New Jerusalem], for the Lord God Almighty and the *Lamb* are its *temple* (Revelation 21:22).**

The Lamb, having existed before the foundations of the world, is the very temple, indicating that God's people are likewise the *temple*. Paul writes of us being the temple of God:

> **Do you not know that you are the *temple* of God and that the Spirit of God dwells in you? (1 Corinthians 3:16).**

> **Or do you not know that your body is the *temple* of the Holy Spirit who is in you, whom you have from God, and you are not your own? (1 Corinthians 6:19-20).**

The word *temple* is the Greek word *naos*, whose Hebrew equivalent is the word *devir*, meaning *oracle, inner most part of sanctuary*, or the Holy of Holies. Another word which translates to *temple* is the word *hieron*, but this word entails the entire building and surroundings (including the Outer Court, Holy Place, and the *naos* – Holy of Holies). Paul specifies that we are not the *hieron* but the *naos*. Only the high priest was allowed into the Holy of Holies to make atonement for the people's sins. As mentioned, the Early Church taught that the Holy of Holies was actually the garden of Eden, where God's glory resided. When the high priest entered into the Holy of Holies, he entered into the garden, where the mysteries of God are unveiled.

Malachi writes that the Lord will suddenly come to His temple:

> **"Behold, I send My messenger, and he will prepare the way before Me. And the Lord, whom you seek, will *suddenly come to His temple*, even the Messenger of the covenant, in whom you delight. Behold, he is coming," says the LORD of hosts (Malachi 3:1).**

The temple is God's people (1 Corinthians 3:16, 6:19), so if God will return into His temple, that means He will return into His people. God's return into His temple is directly reflected in the Feast of Tabernacles (Sukkot), during which God instructs His people to dwell in booths, or little tabernacles, but also is the appointed time and rehearsal for His final return into His people (see **Rains, Feasts & His Return**). Upon His return into His people, they become the Lamb and the light for the New Jerusalem. The Lamb is described by John in the Book of Revelation as being the light for the entire city.

> **The city [New Jerusalem] had no need of the sun or of the moon to shine in it, for the glory of God illuminated it. The *Lamb is its light* (Revelation 21:23).**

This light is that which existed before the foundations of the world – the light of Day One (see **The Beginning**).

Saving Grace

Yet another hidden foundation is God's *grace*:

> **[God] who has saved us and called us with a holy calling, not according to our works, but according to His own purpose and *grace* which was given to us in Christ Jesus *before time began* (2 Timothy 1:9).**

Grace was established since the beginning of the world. Grace was in the garden: the living water and the Tree of Life. The Tree of Life is in fact Torah, which is God's Word, so His Word is His grace. To grasp the spiritual understanding of the Word, we need God's grace:

> **Respecting which there is one opinion throughout the whole Church, that the whole law is indeed spiritual; but that spiritual meaning which the law conveys is not known to all, but to those only on whom the grace of the Holy Spirit is bestowed in the word of wisdom and knowledge (Origen, *De Principiis*).**

Since Genesis, there has been a battle between two seeds and ultimately two types of grace.

The word *grace* is the word *chen*, which has the meanings of *camp, beauty*. In ancient Hebrew, the word *chen* is written [illegible], a picture of a wall (𐤇) and a seed (𐤍), meaning the *wall continues*. As explained in the Ancient Hebrew Lexicon Bible, in Hebrew culture, nomadic camps consisted of several family tents placed in a circular configuration which formed a continuous wall around the camp. The camp is an enclosed community that contains *provision* and *covering*.

Receiving provision can be equated to receiving *profit*. Paul, in the Book of Hebrews, writes:

> **For indeed the *gospel* was preached to us as well as to them; but the *word* which they heard did *not profit* them, *not being mixed with faith* in those who heard it (Hebrews 4:2).**

The gospel was preached to the Hebrews in the wilderness in the same way that it was preached to us – *after* the Torah was given to Moses. However, because the Hebrews did not *believe* the good news, it profited them nothing. *Profit* is the word *opheleo*, which means *to prevail, better, advantage, profit, overcome*, and it comes from the word *opheleia*, meaning *advantage*. Profit extends beyond receiving finances (physical and spiritual) but includes prevailing and overcoming. To hear, believe, and take action upon the Word of God results in profit. God's Grace is also closely associated with rest:

> **For we who have believed do enter that *rest*, as He has said: "SO I SWORE IN MY WRATH, 'THEY SHALL NOT ENTER MY *REST*,'" although the works were finished from the foundation of the world. For He has spoken in a certain place of the seventh day in this way: "AND GOD RESTED ON THE SEVENTH DAY FROM ALL HIS WORKS" (Hebrews 4:3-4).**

The word *rest* is the word *katapausis*, which means *reposing down, abode, put to rest, calming of the winds*. This word comes from the word *katapauo*, which means *to settle down, colonize, desist, give rest.* Noah is a leading example of receiving *rest* through God's grace.

> **And the LORD was sorry that He had made man on the earth, and He was grieved in His heart. So the LORD said, "I will destroy man whom I have created from the face of the earth, both man and beast, creeping thing and birds of the air, for I am sorry that I have made them." But Noah found *grace* in the eyes of the LORD. This is the genealogy of *Noah*. Noah was a *just* man, *perfect* in his generations. Noah walked with God (Genesis 6:6-9).**

Noah had *grace*, and he was *just* and *perfect.* Perfection correlates to *maturity*, or rightly understanding God's divine plan and secrets (1 Corinthians 2:6). The term *perfect*, or *mature*, implies being *made ready for sacrifice* (see **The Sacrificial Lamb**). Just as Noah was perfect, mature, and ready for sacrifice, he had God's grace. So those who are ready for sacrifice, as Noah was, are also covered by God's grace. The word *just* is the word *tasaddiyq*, meaning *righteous*, which is *right understanding* - Noah had right understanding of God's divine plan. Noah's name in Hebrew, *noach*, means *rest.* Noah heard and understood God's Word, acted upon it, and therefore received God's grace and rest.

The term *perfect – tamiym –* is the same term used to describe a sacrificial lamb. Yeshua is the sacrificial Lamb, as are God's people (see **The Sacrificial Lamb**). When God describes Noah as being perfect, He describes Noah as a sacrificial lamb, and in turn a Messiah, or *savior.* Actually, Noah is just one of <u>many</u> saviors. In the Book of Obadiah it is written:

> **Then *saviors* shall come to Mount Zion to judge the mountains of Esau, and the kingdom shall be the Lord's (Obadiah 1:21).**

The word *savior* is the word *yasha*, meaning *to save, rescue, deliver*, and is a form of the word *yeshua*, meaning *deliverance or freedom from a trouble, salvation.* The word *yasha* is part of the name *Yehoshua*, the Hebrew name for Jesus. *Yehoshua* consists of the words *yehovah* and *yasha*, or "Yahweh is salvation."

These saviors mentioned in Obadiah are the sons of the kingdom in whom the fullness of Christ has manifested. God's grace not only entails provision, rest, maturity, and being made ready for sacrifice, but it also necessitates becoming one of many saviors.

Adam also experienced the same rest that Noah received while Adam was in the garden, the place where the mysteries of God's kingdom are fully understood. While in the garden, Adam ate out of the tree of grace – the tree of revelation – and was at rest with God. As soon as Adam sinned, he was removed from the garden and forced to toil with his hands for all his remaining days.

The removal of physical rest parallels the removal of spiritual rest. Adam lost the rest by giving way to the false glory offered by Satan and the carnal nature. In turn, Adam and Eve's senses became confined to the earthly realm. The loss of their original ability to see into the heavenly realm is depicted in the Forgotten Books of Eden:

> **And Adam said to Eve, "Look at thine eyes, and at mine, which afore beheld angels in heaven, praising; and they, too, without ceasing. But now we do not see as we did: our *eyes have become of flesh*; they *cannot see in like manner as they saw before.*" Adam said again to Eve, "What is our body today, compared to what it was in former days, when we dwelt in the garden?" (First Book of the Forgotten Books of Eden, 4:8-10).**

The loss of rest and provision resulted in an inability to see spiritually. Grace thereby entitles one to perceive the heavenly realm, allowing full comprehension of God's divine plan. Without grace – and without the corresponding provision, advancement, rest, and maturity – there is no ascension or ability to receive the revelation of God's mysteries.

Sweat Outside the Glory

It should be noted that the removal of rest came with toiling and *sweat*:

> **In the *sweat* of your face you shall eat bread till you return to the ground, for out of it you were taken; for dust you are, and to dust you shall return (Genesis 3:19).**

Once the glory was removed from Adam and Eve, they would experience labor with *sweat*. The high priest was allowed into the Holy of Holies once a year on Yom Kippur to atone for the sins of the people; however, the high priest could not enter in with sweat:

> **They shall have linen turbans on their heads and linen trousers on their bodies; they shall not clothe themselves with anything that causes *sweat* (Ezekiel 44:18).**

The Holy of Holies, a place of no sweat, was considered by the Early Church to be the garden of Eden. Hence, when Adam was removed from the garden, he was removed from the Holy of Holies and from his high priestly office. A residence outside of the garden was a place where he would not only need to labor but where he would also sweat.

In Genesis 3:19, the word *sweat* is the Hebrew word *zeah*, written in ancient Hebrew, . The word *sweat* in Ezekiel 44:18 is the Hebrew word *yeza*, written in ancient Hebrew, . Both words share the same root, which is the word *zah* (), meaning *tremble, sweat*. The letters *zayin* (, *weapon, cutting tool*) and *ayin* (, *eye, knowledge*), together can be read as "weapon seen," which causes fear, trembling, and sweat. Outside of the Holy of Holies is the realm of trembling and sweat due to lack of rest. On the other hand, in the Holy of Holies where God's glory resides, the mind is at complete rest, and there is no toil, labor, or sweat.

Adam's fall out of the garden is a picture of his demotion out of his original high priestly role. God's divine plan is for His people to come back into the Holy of Holies – the original garden – to rule and operate as high priests.

Grace & Faith

Grace is the fundamental *provision* that was established before the foundations of the world. Grace is one of several steps to redemption, another of which is *faith*. In the Book of Ephesians, Paul writes:

> **For by *grace* you have been *saved* through *faith*, and that not of yourselves; it is the gift of God, not of works, lest anyone should boast (Ephesians 2:8-9).**

To have faith is to understand and believe the Word of God. God's grace is His provision, His Word and His truth. Faith is belief and understanding of the truth, which leads to salvation and redemption. Grace is the provision itself while faith is the action associated with that provision. God's grace was the ark, and those who entered in were saved. God's grace was the blood on the door posts, and those who put the blood on the door were saved. Works (acting upon God's Word) are the proof of one's faith. In the Book of Revelation, Yeshua repeatedly says to the churches, "I know your works" (i.e., Revelation 2:2, 2:9, 2:19, 3:8, 3:15). Paul further writes that the promise of God comes through faith according to grace:

> **For the promise that he would be the heir of the world was not to Abraham or to his seed through the law, but through the *righteousness of faith*. . . . Therefore it is of *faith* that it might be according to *grace* [God's provision], so that the promise might be sure to all the seed, not only to those who are of the law, but also to those**

who are of the faith of Abraham, who is the father of us all (Romans 4:13, 16).

Faith necessitates action. Noah had to build the ark and bring his family into it. The Hebrews had to kill lambs and put the blood on the door posts. These actions of faith resulted in their salvation. In the Old Testament, sacrifices and offerings were required for redemption from mistakes. Noah sacrificed 120 years of his life to build the ark, and through his sacrifice, he brought others to salvation. There is a clear pattern throughout Scripture showing us that actions of sacrifice yield salvation. On the other hand, taking no action, or being lazy, yields sin and disbelief (ignorance and lack of understanding).

"For by grace we are saved:" not, without good works; but we must, by being formed for what is good, acquire an inclination for it. And we must possess the healthy mind which is fixed on the pursuit of the good; in order to which we have the greatest need of divine grace, and of right teaching, and of holy susceptibility, and of drawing the Father to Him (Clement, *Stromata*).

Grace For Those With Revelation

Paul writes to the Ephesian Church that one is saved by grace *through* faith (Ephesians 2:8). Faith requires action and *work*:

But do you want to know, O foolish man, that *faith without works* is *dead*? (James 2:20).

To not do work is to be lazy, and *laziness* is directly connected with a *lack of understanding*:

I went by the field of the *lazy* man, and by the vineyard of the man *devoid of understanding* (Proverbs 24:30).

The required work is not natural work but spiritual work. The word *work* is the word *malakah*, meaning *work: a message through action. Malakah* also contains the root *malak*, meaning *angel, messenger*. The required work is to bring messages out from behind the veil – the very action of the angels that ascended and descended the ladder into the Holy of Holies.

Grace comes through faith, which comes by hearing:

> **So then *faith* comes by *hearing*, and *hearing* by the *word of God* (Romans 10:17).**

However, *action* is required even after hearing the Word. James writes of being *doers*, not just hearers, of the Word:

> **But be *doers* of the *word*, and not *hearers* only, deceiving yourselves. For if anyone is a hearer of the word and not a doer, he is like a man observing his natural face in a mirror; for he observes himself, goes away, and immediately forgets what kind of man he was. But he who looks into the *perfect law* of liberty and continues in it, and is not a forgetful hearer but a *doer of the work*, this one will be blessed in what he does (James 1:22-25).**

The word *perfect* is *teleios*, meaning *mature*, and the word *law* is *nomos*, which translates in Hebrew to *Torah*. Those who understand the Torah by ascending into the Holy of Holies to learn the deeper secrets are those who have faith, who then in turn receive God's grace. Clearly, grace is given to those have access behind the veil – those who have revelation.

When Paul asked Yeshua to remove the thorn from his side, Yeshua said that His *grace* was sufficient for him (2 Corinthians 12:9). Paul *understood* the divine plan of God and the ascension into the glory through revelation of God's mysteries. The thorn held Paul back from ascension.

> **And lest I should be exalted above measure by the abundance of the revelations, a thorn in the flesh was given to me, a messenger of Satan to buffet me, lest I**

> **be *exalted above measure.* Concerning this thing I pleaded with the Lord three times that it might depart from me. And He said to me, "My *grace* is *sufficient* for you, for My strength is made perfect in weakness." Therefore most gladly I will rather boast in my infirmities, that the power of Christ may rest upon me (1 Corinthians 12:7-9).**

The term *exalted above measure* is the Greek word *huperairo*, which means *to raise, lift above, raise oneself over*, and consists of the words *huper* (*over*) and *airo* (*to lift, take up*). One of the Hebrew equivalent words is *alah*, which means *to ascend*, as well as *the rising of smoke from a burnt offering*. This is the same term used when the high priest ascended as he went into the Holy of Holies, when Moses went up Mount Sinai to receive the Torah, and also to describe the resurrection and enlightenment of the catechumen as they learned the secret teachings of God. The connection between ascension and a sacrificial offering illustrates that **one becomes a perfect sacrifice through revelation of the kingdom mysteries**. This ascension leads one back into the garden where God's glory resides.

Paul desired to enter into his glorified body. He described how he was *caught up* – how he *ascended* – into the third heaven. He did not know whether he was in or out of his body, because in the merging of the earthly and heavenly dimensions, there is no distinction between corporeal and supernatural states.

> **And I know such a man—whether *in the body or out of the body* I do not know, God knows—how he was *caught up* into *Paradise* and heard *inexpressible words*, which it is *not lawful for a man to utter* (2 Corinthians 12:3-4).**

Further, Paul heard mysteries that were *inexpressible*, similar to the secret teachings that were not written down or even verbally transmitted amongst the select group of disciples whom Yeshua taught.

Paul had a sin in his side, represented by the thorn, although nowhere is it mentioned what this sin was. On the other hand, after Noah became drunk with wine and became uncovered (considered a sin), Ham *exposed* his father (Genesis 9:22), and God put a curse on Ham and the descendants after him. Ham and his descendants were removed from the promises of kingdom inheritance. In Paul's case, the Church *covered* him, and he wrote two-thirds of the New Covenant with the sin in his life. Even so, Paul was a *perfect* man – he was *mature* and had *right understanding* of God's divine plan.

David is a similar example - he was considered *blameless* despite his actions. When David committed murder and adultery, his whole house grieved, mourned, and prayed for him. After committing adultery with Bathsheba and killing innocent lives to fulfill his own carnal lust, David states:

> **For all His judgments were before me; and as for His statutes, I did not depart from them. I was also *blameless* before Him, and I kept myself from my *iniquity*. Therefore the LORD has recompensed me according to my *righteousness*, according to my *cleanness* in His eyes (2 Samuel 22:23-25).**

God still considered David to be *righteous* because he never departed from Torah (God's teaching), and kept himself from iniquity (twisted teaching). *Purity* is determined by *rightly understanding* God's Word, not by performing good works. God's grace was already established before the foundations, and it is directly connected to faith. While God's Gospel leads to salvation from action filled faith, Satan offers a counterfeit gospel that leads to hell from actionless faith.

Wisdom

Wisdom also was established before the foundations of the world. In fact, Wisdom was present on Day One of Genesis assisting God in the creation of the world. Proverbs 8 depicts Wisdom as a woman, her existence before the foundations:

> **The LORD possessed me at the beginning of His way, before His works of old. I have been established from everlasting, *from the beginning*, before there was ever an earth (Proverbs 8:22-23).**

And her contribution to creation:

> **When He prepared the heavens, I was there, when He drew a circle on the face of the deep, when He established the clouds above, when He strengthened the fountains of the deep, when He assigned to the sea its limit, so that the waters would not transgress His command, when He marked out the foundations of the earth, then I was beside Him as a *master craftsman*; and I was daily His delight, rejoicing always before Him, rejoicing in His inhabited world, and my delight was with the sons of men (Proverbs 8:27-31).**

In her paper *Wisdom and the Stewardship of Knowledge*, Barker writes,

> When this passage [Proverbs 8:30] was translated into Greek, the word [master craftsman] chosen was 'the woman who holds things together' *harmozousa*, which can also mean 'the woman who keeps things in tune.' Wisdom, then, was understood to be the female figure who joined things together, kept things harmonious (Barker, 2004).

To the Early Church, the symbol of Wisdom was the Tree of Life, and Adam was intended to eat its fruit. As Barker states, Genesis 2-3 is an account of Adam and Eve rejecting Wisdom and the resulting consequences. Eden represents the original temple, in which Adam was the first high priest. While he was in Eden, Adam's vestment of glory was the high priestly garment, which included the Urim and Thummin (Levitus 8:7-8, Exodus 28:30), representative of Wisdom and Truth.

The rejection of Wisdom led to the removal of Adam's vestments of glory, his high priestly order, and a falling away – a departure from the truth. Adam was remembered as a glorious and wise figure whose priesthood upheld the creation. In fact, the Qumran text, the *Community Rule*, "shows that the people at Qumran hoped to regain all the glory of Adam, the knowledge of the Most High and the wisdom of the sons of heaven." Many non-canonical texts also depict Adam as being wise and glorious.

Paul also writes that those who are *mature* receive the wisdom of God, which was established before the foundations of the world:

> **However, we speak *wisdom* among those who are *mature*, yet not the wisdom of this age, nor of the rulers of this age, who are coming to nothing. But we speak the *wisdom of God* in a *mystery*, the *hidden wisdom* which God ordained *before the ages* for our glory (1 Corinthians 2:6-7).**

This word for *mature* is the same Hebrew equivalent *tamiym*, also meaning *perfect*. There is a company of people who are called the *perfected*, as written in Sirach:

> **He knew all things were ever they were created; so also after they were *perfected* he looked upon them all (Sirach 23:20).**

The divine wisdom spoken among the mature is taught by the Early Church to be the Tree of Life and they considered the anointing oil used by the high priests in the temple liturgy to be the perfume of the Tree of Life. Further, the high priest was anointed on his eyelids, a sign that his eyes were opened. Obtaining the divine wisdom of God opens our eyes spiritually, whereby we obtain the eyes to see His true plan. Wisdom and the revelation of God's mysteries, established since the foundations of the world, restores one's spiritual eyesight – the same glorified eyesight Adam had when he was able to clearly perceive the entire heavenly realm.

Tasting Wisdom

The word for *wisdom* in Hebrew is the word *chokmah*, written in ancient Hebrew חכמה. The first two letters, חכ, make the word *chek*, meaning *mouth, palate, taste*. The mouth is the portal for tasting food and drink. Job asks, "**Does not the ear test words and the mouth taste its food?**" (Job 12:11). This illustrates the mouth as the gateway to discern the type of food and drink – the type of teaching – being fed to the rest of the body. The meat of the Word is for the mature, while milk is for babies (1 Corinthians 3:2). The mouth is able to taste and discern between living water and bitter waters. After tasting the bitterness of gall, Yeshua rejected the sour wine:

> **They gave Him sour wine mingled with gall to drink. But when He had *tasted* it, He would not drink (Matthew 27:34).**

Gall, meaning *bile* or *poison*, is used to describe bitter things and depicts counterfeit and false teachings. Likewise, the sour wine depicts false revelation and understanding. Wisdom thus entails the discernment of the type of teachings and messages one receives. By wisdom, one must be able to discern between the living waters (מ) of revelation (ה) that yield eternal life from the bitter waters that bring death.

Royal Priesthood

As the heavenly temple was established before the foundations of the world, so were all the temple elements, including the priesthood. Those from the tribe of Levi were allowed to be priests, but the high priestly office was reserved only for those from the bloodline of Aaron:

> **Now take Aaron your brother, and his sons with him, from among the children of Israel, that he may minister to Me as priest, Aaron and Aaron's sons: Nadab, Abihu, Eleazar, and Ithamar. And you shall make holy garments for Aaron your brother, for glory and for beauty (Exodus 28:1-2).**

Only the high priest could enter the Holy of Holies to atone for the people's sins on Yom Kippur (Leviticus 16:2-3), and at thirty years old, one could begin in ministry:

> **Take a census of the sons of Kohath from among the children of Levi, by their families, by their fathers' house, from thirty years old and above, even to fifty years old, all who enter the service to do the work in the tabernacle of meeting (Numbers 4:2-3).**

John the Baptist, the son of Zacharias and Elizabeth, was from the line of Aaron. Elizabeth was a daughter of Aaron:

> **There was in the days of Herod, the king of Judea, a certain priest named Zacharias, of the division of Abijah. His wife was of the daughters of Aaron, and her name was Elizabeth (Luke 1:5).**

Zacharias was of Abijah, who was also from the bloodline of Aaron:

> **Now these are the divisions of the sons of Aaron. The sons of Aaron were Nadab, Abihu, Eleazar, and Ithamar. And Nadab and Abihu died before their father, and had no children; therefore Eleazar and Ithamar ministered as priests. . . . Thus they were divided by lot, one group as another, for there were officials of the sanctuary and officials of the house of God, from the sons of Eleazar and from the sons of Ithamar. . . Now the first lot fell to Jehoiarib, the second to Jedaiah . . . the seventh to Hakkoz, the eighth to *Abijah* (1 Chronicles 24:1-2, 5, 7, 10).**

As both Zacharias and Elizabeth came from the house and bloodline of Aaron, John the Baptist, conceived from the barren womb of Elizabeth, was part of the high priesthood of the Aaronic lineage. However, while the descendants of Aaron were high priests, they were not kings.

The high priestly office was already in place with Adam, a king to whom God gave dominion, and a priest who offered sacrifices to God. The act of God bringing all the living creatures to Adam to see what he would name them (Genesis 2:19) directly parallels the role of the Hebrews bringing their sacrificial animals to the high priest who would atone for the sins of the people. Just as the high priest inspected each animal to determine whether it was an unblemished and worthy sacrifice, Adam likewise inspected each creature to determine its sacrificial worthiness. Adam was a high priest in the garden before he fell.

After the fall, Adam lost his high priestly role, and man moved further from the Lord because of sin – ignorance of His Word. Simultaneously, the understanding of the high priestly office began to fade. However, God restored the royal high priestly office through Yeshua. God also calls His children *kings* and *priests*, His *royal priesthood*:

> **But ye are a chosen generation, a *royal priesthood*, an holy nation, a peculiar people; that ye should shew**

> **forth the praises of him who hath called you out of darkness into his marvelous light (KJV, 1 Peter 2:9).**

Therefore, there is yet a higher priesthood above the Levitical and high priesthoods. This royal priesthood comes from a bloodline different than that of Aaron; it comes from the order of Melchizedek, the royal bloodline belonging to Yeshua.

Melchizedek

Yeshua is a high priest of the order of Melchizedek.

> **The LORD has sworn and will not relent, "You are a priest forever according to the order of Melchizedek" (Psalm 110:4).**

> **Where the forerunner has entered for us, even Jesus, having become High Priest forever according to the order of Melchizedek (Hebrews 6:20).**

However, the priestly order of Melchizedek is a royal priesthood, as Melchizedek was a king. Melchizedek first appears to Abram:

> **Then Melchizedek king of Salem brought out bread and wine; he was the priest of God Most High (Genesis 14:18).**

Melchizedek is composed of two words: *melek* (meaning *king*), and *tsaddiyq* (meaning *righteous*). The word *melek* in ancient Hebrew is written ШJ𝓂, which is also the same spelling for the word *malak*, meaning *angel*, or *messenger*. The Early Church taught that when the high priest entered the Holy of Holies, he was transformed into an angel in the glory of God, and he came out as *Immanuel* (*God is with us*), bringing the glory out with him. The order and priesthood of Melchizedek is of the order of the angelic realm – the messengers of God. Since learning the secret discipline in the Early Church was considered an enlightenment and ascension, the revelation of kingdom mysteries changes one's bloodline into that of Melchizedek.

The word *salem* is the word *peace*, which is the second part of the word *Jerusalem*. Hence, Melchizedek came from the very place to which God will restore His people *(the New Jerusalem)* in the Book of Revelation. As written in the Book of Hebrews, Melchizedek is not only the king of righteousness, but also the king of peace, who has no beginning or end, a very depiction of Yeshua the Son of God:

> **For this Melchizedek, king of Salem, priest of the Most High God, who met Abraham returning from the slaughter of the kings and blessed him, to whom also Abraham gave a tenth part of all, first being translated "king of righteousness," and then also king of Salem, meaning "king of peace," without father, without mother, without genealogy, having neither beginning of days nor end of life, but made like the Son of God, remains a priest continually (Hebrews 7:1-3).**

Melchizedek brought bread and wine to Abram; He had communion with Abram, indicating that communion is a royal, priestly act. Yeshua had communion of bread and wine with His disciples and instructed them to eat His flesh and drink His blood – a spiritual communion for them to consume the Word of God and the revelation of the Word. Thus, Yeshua's act of communion displays His royal priestly role and further indicates that God calls His people to be royal priests, whose job it is to have communion through teaching the revelation of His Word.

Unlike Aaron, Melchizedek was a *king* and a priest. Thus, in order to fulfill the statement that God's people would be a *royal* priesthood (1 Peter 2:9), the priesthood had to change from Aaron's bloodline to that of Melchizedek. This could only be done by a transfer of priesthood.

> **Therefore, if perfection were through the Levitical priesthood (for under it the people received the law), what further need was there that another priest should**

> **rise according to the order of Melchizedek, and not be called according to the order of Aaron? For the priesthood being changed, of necessity there is also a change of the law (Hebrews 7:11-12).**

This transfer of priesthood occurred when Yeshua came to John the Baptist at the Jordan River seeking to be baptized.

> **Then Jerusalem, all Judea, and all the region around the Jordan went out to him and were baptized by him in the Jordan, confessing their sins. . . Then Jesus came from Galilee to John at the Jordan to be baptized by him. And John tried to prevent Him, saying, "I need to be baptized by You, and are You coming to me?" But Jesus answered and said to him, "Permit it to be so now, for thus it is fitting for us to fulfill all righteousness." Then he allowed Him (Matthew 3:5-6, 13-15).**

Yeshua did not come to John the Baptist to be baptized for the remission of sin since Yeshua had no sin in Him (He fully understood the Torah and the divine plan of God). The act of baptism was a transfer of the Levitical priesthood over to the Melchizedek priesthood. Yeshua said that this act would be to "fulfill all righteousness," meaning that the transfer to the *royal* priesthood would bring about right understanding:

> **It is the glory of God to conceal a matter, but the glory of *kings* is to *search out* a matter (Proverbs 25:2).**

The transfer of priesthood has given us access back into the Holy of Holies as royal high priests, an access that even the Levitical high priests did not truly have. Paul writes that the way into the Holy of Holies was not yet made manifest with the first tabernacle:

> **But into the second part the high priest went alone once a year, not without blood, which he offered for himself and for the people's sins committed in ignorance; the Holy Spirit indicating this, that the way into the Holiest of All was not yet made manifest while the first tabernacle was still standing (Hebrews 9:7-8).**

Even though the high priests physically went into the Holy of Holies, they did not truly come into the full glory of God. The act of going into the Holy of Holies was only symbolic, or parabolic, of the present time (Hebrews 9:9). It was a type and shadow of the royal priesthood – the true sons of God – in the full glory of the kingdom. This full manifestation of revelation, or *apocalypse* of the heavenly Holy of Holies, was made possible with the perfect, unblemished sacrifice of Yeshua's *royal* blood. It is the *royal* bloodline that has access behind the veil. Through revelation of the secrets behind the veil, we obtain access to restore the original creation that was lost by Adam to a greater magnitude, for Yeshua said, "**He who believes in Me, the works that I do he will do also; and *greater works* than these he will do, because I go to My Father**" (John 14:12). The royal bloodline is imparted by the living Word of God, the divine seed.

> **But Christ came as High Priest of the good things to come, with the greater and *more perfect tabernacle* not made with hands, that is, not of this creation. Not with the blood of goats and calves, but with His own blood He entered the Most Holy Place once for all, having obtained eternal redemption (Hebrews 9:11-12).**

Yeshua brought a more perfect tabernacle and now God seeks for us to be that tabernacle. We are called to be the Most Holy Place, the garden of Eden, the New Jerusalem – these things are to be within us, because the true kingdom is an <u>internal kingdom</u>:

> **Now when He was asked by the Pharisees when the kingdom of God would come, He answered them and**

> **said, "The kingdom of God does *not come with observation*; nor will they say, 'See here!' or 'See there!' For indeed, the kingdom of God is *within you*" (Luke 17:20-21).**

Paul writes in 1 Corinthians 2 that perfection is for the mature sons who know the secrets of the kingdom which Yeshua established on Earth. The glory of God is accessible by going through the veil to learn these mysteries and secrets.

Priests and Prophets

The next move of God will take place with the final restoration of the high priestly office, which is also a *prophetic* office. The word *priest* in Hebrew is *kohen*, and in ancient Hebrew *kohen* is written כהן. The root word is כן, where the *kaph* (כ, *open palm*) and the *nun* (נ, seed) together mean "opening of a seed." The letter *hey*, ה, depicts a *revealing*, or *revelation*. Thus, a priest is one who opens a seed of revelation by uncovering the hidden secrets within the Word of God. The priestly office is one that breaks open the dead letter – the *logos* – to reveal the hidden, living Word – the *rhema* (see **The Dead Letter & The Living Word**).

The word *prophet* in Hebrew is *nabiy*. In ancient Hebrew, *nabiy* is written נביא, where the root word נב means "the seed inside," and seeds are contained within fruit. The Ancient Hebrew Bible Lexicon defines *nabiy* (נביא) as *one who brings forth the inner fruit*. The Complete Word Study Dictionary defines a prophet as "one who was raised up by God and, as such, could only proclaim that which the Lord gave him to say. A prophet could not contradict the Law of the Lord or speak from his own mind or heart." A prophet is further defined as "an interpreter of oracles or of other hidden things." Like apostles, prophets reveal the secrets of the kingdom.

The high priestly and prophetic office is for those who have spiritual eyes to see and understand God's divine plan. Prophets do not merely foretell events without revealing the Word of God. John the Baptist was a high priest and carried a prophetic office.

> **For I say to you, among those born of women there is not a greater *prophet* than John the Baptist . . . (Luke 7:28).**

Access behind the veil gives us understanding of good and evil and of the consequences of sin – this is understanding that Adam did not have. The deeper *sod*-level of understanding of God does not come plainly but hidden in mysteries and given to those who are mature:

> **However, we speak wisdom among those who are *mature*, yet not the wisdom of this age, nor of the rulers of this age, who are coming to nothing. But we speak the wisdom of God in a *mystery*, the hidden wisdom which God ordained before the ages for our glory (1 Corinthians 2:6-7).**

This next move will take the Church behind the veil, ushering in the kingdom of God, which was hidden from the foundations of the world, but is destined to be brought back into the Earth for eternal glory. Ultimately the Lord's plan of complete restoration will be fulfilled when heaven comes to Earth.

> **In this manner, therefore, pray: Our Father in heaven, hallowed be Your name. Your kingdom come. Your will be done on earth as it is in heaven (Matthew 6:9-10).**

Chapter Three

Torah

But well knowing that the Savior teaches nothing in a merely human way, but teaches all things to His own with divine and mystic wisdom, we must not listen to his utterances carnally; but with due investigation and intelligence must search out and learn the meaning hidden in them.

Clement,
153-215 A.D.

The Torah is the first five books of the Old Covenant; it is the 613 mitzvahs given to Moses on stone tablets at Mount Sinai. However, the Torah extends far beyond just these five books – it is a mystery of God, containing His divine plan. It is a pattern of creation and restoration and it encompasses all of God Himself.

The Mystery of Torah

Often overlooked and not fully understood in English Bibles is the word *law*. The word *law* appears over 400 times in more than 400 verses in the Bible. In the Old Testament, 91% of the time the word *law* appears it is the Hebrew word *torah.* In the New Testament (New Covenant), 88% of the time the word *law* appears it is the Greek word *nomos*, whose Hebrew counterpart is the very word *torah*. The other 12% of the time that the word *law* appears in the New Testament, *nomos* (*torah*) is still the root word as in anomia, anomos, and ennomos. Torah appears all throughout the Bible, not just in the Old Testament.

A deeper meaning is hidden in the very spelling of the word *Torah* itself and the meaning behind each letter. In Hebrew thought, a person's future is behind him while his past is in front of him. A person can look at events that have occurred in the past, just as he can plainly see something in front of him, but he cannot see what lies in the future, just as he cannot see something that is behind him. Unlike English, Hebrew is read from right to left, but the hidden meaning in a word can be discovered by reading the letters from the end of a word to the beginning. Recall what God told the prophet Isaiah to tell the people:

> **Remember the former things of old, for I am God, and there is no other; I am God, and there is none like Me, declaring the *end from the beginning*, and from ancient times things that are not yet done, saying, 'My counsel shall stand, and I will do all My pleasure' (Isaiah 46:9-10).**

In ancient Hebrew, *Torah* (TWRH) is written 𐤕𐤅𐤓𐤄. The 𐤕 (*tav*) is a cross, the 𐤅 (*vav*) is a nail or tent peg, the 𐤓 (*resh*) is a man's head, and the 𐤄 (*hey*) is a man with arms raised in wonder and signifying, "Behold!" Upon deciphering the word *Torah* from the end to the beginning, the hidden meaning becomes clear: **Behold, the Man nailed to the cross**. The Man nailed to the cross is Yehoshua. **The Torah is Yehoshua**.

The word *Torah* appears over 200 times in each the Old and New Testaments. When Torah is mentioned in the New Testament, it is never implied that it should be done away with or destroyed, as is commonly but incorrectly taught in many churches. In the Book of Matthew, Yeshua clearly states that He did not come to destroy the Torah but to *fulfill* it:

> **"Do not think that I came to *destroy* the Law (*Torah*) or the Prophets. I did not come to destroy but to *fulfill*. For assuredly, I say to you, till heaven and earth pass away, one jot or one tittle will by no means pass from the law (*Torah*) till all is fulfilled" (Matthew 5:17-18, emphasis added).**

The saying "destroying" or "fulfilling" the Torah is a Hebrew idiom used to describe one's understanding and interpretation of the Torah. One was said to "destroy" the Torah if one did not interpret it correctly, while one was said to "fulfill" the Torah if one interpreted it correctly. In fact, misinterpreting and misunderstanding the Torah is considered *sin*.

Sin

Many people think that the Torah is a book of do's and don'ts, delineating how to live a life without sin, and most would say that sin has to do with committing a morally wrong action or thought. However, by returning to the original Hebrew one can see that these are misconceptions. The word *sin* in Hebrew is *chattah*, which actually means *to miss the target*.

The word *chattah* in ancient Hebrew is written **†ᐅ⊗ш**. The word **⊗ш** means *measure, cord, miss*. Pictorially, **⊗ш** depicts a knot in a cord or rope; cords with incremental knots were used to measure distances, and when shooting an arrow at a target, the distance by which the arrow missed the target was measured by stretching a cord between the two points and counting the number of knots in the cord. The **†ᐅ** is Yahweh Himself, as He said, "I am the *aleph* and *tav*" (Revelation 1:8). So, *sin* is *missing Yahweh*. If Yahweh is Yeshua, and Yeshua is the Torah, then the target is Torah, and to *sin* is actually to **not fully understand the Torah**.

An archer shoots at a target. In fact, the word *shoot* is the word *yara*, which means to throw, as in throwing an arrow. It also means *to throw* in the sense that the throwing of the finger shows a direction to walk or live. It also means to teach, or to point the way one is to walk in life. One who hits the mark has authority, and to have authority, one must understand Torah.

When Adam ate from the Tree of Knowledge of Good and Evil, he decimated his understanding of truth by introducing mixture. The same problem occurs with the harlot Church in the Book of Revelation, where she is called Babylon (Revelation 17:5). The name *Babylon* comes from the word *babel*, meaning *confusion. Babel* comes from the word *babal*, meaning *to overflow specifically with oil, mix, anoint, confound, mingle, confuse*. Babylon is therefore a mixture in the anointing or teaching. In the Hebrew mindset, every name speaks of character and function, so Babylon is a people who are confused in their speech due to mixed teaching. Babylon is the Church, whose fruit comes from a mixed, confused seed.

Part of the confused speech and twisted teaching in the Church today is that many churches incorrectly believe that the law (Torah), or even the Old Testament, is no longer applicable. In the New Testament, Timothy clearly states otherwise:

> **All Scripture is given by inspiration of God, and is profitable for *doctrine*, for *reproof*, for *correction*, for instruction in *righteousness*, that the man of God may be complete, thoroughly equipped for every good work (2 Timothy 3:16-17).**

All Scripture is for righteousness, reproof, correction, and instruction in righteousness. *Righteousness* in Hebrew means *straight* or *one who walks a straight path* - one walks a straight path with correct understanding. Correspondingly, having right understanding eliminates incomplete or false understanding, which is sin.

The Pattern

When Moses was on Mount Sinai in the presence of God, he was instructed to build a tabernacle on Earth:

> **And let them make Me a *sanctuary*, that I may dwell among them. According to all that I show you, that is, the *pattern* of the *tabernacle* and the *pattern* of all its furnishings, just so you shall make it (Exodus 25:8-9).**

Various sources indicate that Moses did not see a vision of the heavenly tabernacle on Mount Sinai, but actually a vision of heaven and Earth. The Book of Jubilees, which records an ancient version of Genesis, states that Moses was told to record the six days of creation, so the earthly tabernacle was a pattern of the Genesis 1 creation which God showed Moses on Mount Sinai. While the word *tabernacle* (the Hebrew word *mishkan*) means *dwelling place*, the tabernacle is also a *miniature model of the Earth*, as Israel was a pattern to all nations. Upon the restoration of Genesis creation, God will dwell in His tabernacle of glory:

> **And I heard a loud voice from heaven saying, "Behold, the *tabernacle* of God is with men, and He will *dwell* with them, and they shall be His people. God Himself will be with them and be their God" (Revelation 21:3).**

The tabernacle is seen as the copy and shadow of the heavenly realm, and the Torah is the living Word of God that captures this pattern:

> **For if He were on earth, He would not be a priest, since there are priests who offer the gifts according to the *law* [Torah]; who serve the *copy and shadow of the heavenly things*, as Moses was divinely instructed when he was about to make the *tabernacle*. For He said, "SEE THAT YOU MAKE ALL THINGS**

> **ACCORDING TO THE *PATTERN* SHOWN YOU ON THE MOUNTAIN" (Hebrews 8:4-5).**

The equivalent Hebrew word for *pattern* is *tabniyth*, which is written in ancient Hebrew, תבנית. The root of the word is *ben*, בן, which means *build, tent panel, intelligence, son* (the "continuing of the house"). The נ (*nun*) is the *seed, sperm* (DNA of God), and the ב (*bet*) is the *house*. This is the same root word for *stone* (*eben*, אבן), representative of the secrets of the kingdom – the stones are the foundation (*sod*) of God's house.

God desires for His seed to be in His house. The seed is the Word of God (Luke 8:11), and God's people are His house, or tabernacle (1 Corinthians 3:16, 6:9). God seeks to impregnate His children with His seed – His DNA, His character – to create sons of the kingdom.

> **The field is the world, the *good seeds* are the *sons of the kingdom*, but the tares are the sons of the wicked one (Matthew 13:38).**

> **He who overcomes shall inherit all things, and I will be his God and he shall be My *son* (Revelation 21:7).**

Even the Hebrew word for *son* is the word *zera*, meaning *seed*. Hence, God's pattern entails imparting His seed, or nature, into His people.

> **For the *law*, having a *shadow* of the *good things to come*, and not the very image of the things, can never with these same sacrifices, which they offer continually year by year, make those who approach *perfect* (Hebrews 10:1).**

The Torah is only a shadow of the good things to come; it is thus a parable. It is a pattern of the heavenly realm, and if followed, provides complete access to that supernatural realm. If read as a history book, the deeper meaning is never discovered. It is only through the deeper understanding that we become spiritual:

> **Now a "spiritual" interpretation is of this nature: when one is able to point out what are the heavenly things of which these serve as a pattern and shadow, who are Jews "according to the flesh" and of what things future the law contains a shadow, and any other expressions of this kind that may be found in Holy Scripture; or when it is a subject of inquiry, what is that wisdom hidden in a mystery which "God ordained before the world for our glory, which none of the princes of this world knew;" (1 Cor. 2:7) or the meaning of the apostle's language, when, employing certain illustrations from Exodus or Numbers, he says: "These things happened to them in a figure, and they are written on our account, on whom the ends of the ages have come…" (Origen, *De Principiis*).**

The word *pattern* found in Hebrews 8 is the Greek word *tupos*, which means *a die (a mold that is struck), a stamp or scar, shape, statue, style or resemblance, sampler, model (for imitation) or instance (for warning), example, print*. It also means *an image of something being created, mark of a stroke or blow, figure formed by a blow or impression: of a figure or image of gods (idols)*. A pattern encompasses *markings* and *warnings*. The notion of being marked is found throughout Scripture. There are only two marks – the mark of God and the mark of the enemy (the mark of the beast). There are people being marked to look like Yeshua, and others who are marked as beasts and stamped with the carnal nature. In the Book of Ecclesiastes, Solomon clearly indicates that the people themselves are beasts:

> **I said in mine heart concerning the estate of the sons of men, that God might manifest them, and that they might see that they themselves are *beasts* (KJV, Ecclesiastes 3:18).**

The mark of the beast – the carnal nature – is already in humanity. It is the mark of God, or mindset of God, for which we should all be striving. A *pattern* further implies a *warning* to those who are not being marked properly. Therefore, the Torah itself is meant to mark and warn us.

Within the Ten Commandments (and 613 mitzvahs) given to Moses is a mitzvah that states that one is not to make any *graven images* of God.

> **You shall not make for yourself a *carved image*—any likeness of anything that is in heaven above, or that is in the earth beneath, or that is in the water under the earth (Exodus 20:4).**
>
> **You shall not make *idols* for yourselves; neither a *carved image* nor a sacred pillar shall you rear up for yourselves; nor shall you set up an engraved stone in your land, to bow down to it; for I am the LORD your God (Leviticus 26:1).**

The term *carved image* is the word *pesel*, meaning *idol*, and comes from the word *pasal*, meaning *to carve* and is usually used to describe the cutting of stone. *Pasal* is the same word describing Moses' cutting of the stone tablets on which God wrote the Torah. As Torah is the pattern, this mitzvah commands that one must not make any false patterns of God. We must be attentive to not follow a counterfeit Torah – one that offers a false glory.

Satan offered the counterfeit glory to Adam and Eve in the garden, and once they ate of the wrong tree, they began to follow the wrong pattern. Thus, Adam lost the *image* of God. We will see God restore His image in the Earth again following the *pattern* outlined in His Torah. The word *pattern* also means *example, warning to others, an example to be imitated (of men worthy of initiation), a type of person that prefigures a future (Messianic) person*. The word *pattern* (*tupos*) comes from the word *tupto*, meaning *to strike, beat, whip, smite, create wounds, disquiet one's conscious, pummel, offend.* The pattern of creation, when released from the heavens, brings about a beating, the same way that Yeshua went through a beating when He went to the cross. All throughout Scripture, scourging and fighting come with receiving revelation. For example, Jacob fought the angel all night to retrieve the message. There is a battle for true teaching and revelation, and this battle is fought with a sword – the Word of God:

> **For the *word of God* is living and powerful, and *sharper than any two-edged sword*, piercing even to the division of soul and spirit, and of joints and marrow, and is a discerner of the thoughts and intents of the heart (Hebrews 4:12).**

The war is a war of words, or a war of Torahs (see **War of Seeds**). The battle is between those who through revelation understand the true pattern and those who follow the counterfeit pattern through carnal reasoning.

The Torah contains the mystery of the tabernacle, the earthly pattern of the hidden, heavenly counterparts:

> **. . .the Holy Spirit indicating this, that the way into the Holiest of All was not yet made manifest while the first tabernacle was still standing. It was *symbolic* for the present time in which both gifts and sacrifices are offered which cannot make him who performed the service perfect in regard to the conscience (Hebrews 9:8-9).**

Paul depicts that the tabernacle and its offerings were symbolic, or parables, for the present time. The tabernacle of Moses was thus only a parable of the kingdom that Yeshua spoke of in Matthew 13. The tabernacle was established to fulfill the Torah – to atone for one's sin, or ignorance of truth. Just as the tabernacle is symbolic, the Torah is likewise symbolic, as depicted in Deuteronomy 29:29:

> **The secret things belong to the LORD our God, but those things which are revealed belong to us and to our children forever, that we may do all the words of this *law* [Torah] (Deuteronomy 29:29).**

The Torah is a secret that must be revealed by God to His people. However, it must be understood in the right manner, because the true Torah brings life and the counterfeit brings death.

The Dead Letter & The Living Word

The war of Torahs is between the dead letter of the law and the living Word. The dead letter is the natural and literal interpretation of the Word, which is the *pshat* level, whereas the living Word is the spiritual and prophetic interpretation, or the *sod*, secret level.

> **For the *law of the Spirit of life* in Christ Jesus has made me *free* from the *law of sin and death* (Romans 8:2).**

The prophetic Torah (the law of the Spirit of life and the living Word) brings freedom from the dead letter of the Torah (the law of sin and death). Just as there are two Torahs, there are two trees: The Tree of Life and The Tree of the Knowledge of Good and Evil. The Tree of Life is the living Word – the spiritual Torah – while The Tree of Knowledge of Good and Evil is the dead letter – the literal and carnal interpretation of the Torah.

The living Word brings one through the veil into the Holy of Holies, and back into Eden, where creation will be restored. In Matthew 19, Yeshua speaks to the disciples about returning to the original state of creation:

> **So Jesus said to them, "Assuredly I say to you, that in the *regeneration*, when the Son of Man sits on the throne of His glory, you who have followed Me will also sit on twelve thrones, judging the twelve tribes of Israel" (Matthew 19:28).**

The word *regeneration* is the word *paliggenesia*, made up of the words *pali* (*again*) and *genesis* (*birth*), or "Genesis again." God is bringing His people back into the garden, where Genesis is restored during this end time move. The root to the word *genesis* is the word *genos*, meaning *genes*, the fundamental building blocks of one's heredity, which are made up of DNA. The seed is the Word of God (Luke 8:11), and the word *seed* (the Greek word *speiro*) also means *sperm*, which contains DNA. The Word of God, His Torah, contains His very DNA – His genes and character.

A seed contains two portions: the shell and the hidden inner portion. The shell is considered the *logos* and the hidden inner part the *rhema*. Both *logos* and *rhema* are Greek words meaning *word*. However, the *logos* is the shell – the dead letter, or natural interpretation of the Torah – and the *rhema* is the hidden seed inside – the living Word, or spiritual interpretation of the Torah. Yeshua and the Early Church taught the living, *rhema* Word.

In Scripture, *rhema* is the living substance of eternal life (i.e., Luke 4:4, Matthew 4:4, John 6:63, John 6:68) and hidden sayings (i.e., Luke 9:45, Luke 18:34). The *rhema* word is also one of the seven elements of the armor of God mentioned by Paul in Ephesians 6:

> **And take the helmet of salvation, and the sword of the Spirit, which is the *word* [*rhema*] of God (Ephesians 6:17).**

Just as the nutrition of a loaf of bread is contained in the soft inner part and the nutrition of a seed is contained in the hidden inner portion, the *rhema* contains the true substance of the Torah. On the other hand, the crust of bread and the shell of a seed contain no nutrition, just as the *logos* cannot bring everlasting life.

As such, one must look beyond the surface of the words of the Torah. The 613 commandments, or *mitzvahs*, do not all make sense if taken literally. But upon spiritual interpretation, the commandments point to a restoration of the secret teachings of the Early Church, which ultimately bring restoration of creation as it was meant to be in the garden.

A clear depiction of the dead letter in contrast to the living Word is the physical temple and the heavenly temple. Paul states that even all the ordinances which the priests performed never really got them through the veil:

> **. . .the Holy Spirit indicating this, that the w*ay into the Holiest of All was not yet made manifest* while the first tabernacle was still standing. It was *symbolic* for the present time in which both gifts and sacrifices are offered which cannot make him who performed the service perfect in regard to the conscience—concerned only with foods and drinks, various washings, and fleshly ordinances imposed until the time of *reformation* (Hebrews 9:8-10).**

Paul clearly indicates that the entrance into the Holy of Holies, which required access behind the veil, did not actually take place with the first tabernacle. This statement seems contradictory because the high priests were indeed physically translated through the thick curtain that separated the Holy Place from the Holy of Holies; however, Paul is stating that the true *apocalypse* and entrance into God's glory did not occur because the priests at that time did not receive the full revelation and secret teachings of the kingdom. Paul further writes:

> **But Christ came as High Priest of the good things to come, with the greater and more perfect tabernacle not made with hands, that is, not of this creation. Not with**

> **the blood of goats and calves, but with His own blood He entered the Most Holy Place once for all, having obtained eternal *redemption* (Hebrews 9:11-12).**

Yeshua came as the ultimate perfect sacrifice, having truly entered into the Holy of Holies – He ascended and became transfigured in the glory. The word *reformation* is the word *diorthosis*, whose definition is *in a physical sense, a making straight, restoring to its natural and normal condition something which in some way protrudes or has gotten out of line, as broken or misshapen limbs*. The reformation is a restoration back to a natural condition – the garden at creation in Genesis.

The Tree

Torah is a tree; in fact, it is the Tree of Life. Just as the Torah is a pattern, the fruit from the tree – the fruit of the Spirit – must fit the pattern.

> **So the LORD God said to the serpent: "Because you have done this, you are cursed more than all cattle, and more than every beast of the field; on your belly you shall go, and you shall eat *dust* all the days of your life. And I will put enmity between you and the woman, and between your *seed* and her *seed*; he shall bruise your head, and you shall bruise his heel" (Genesis 3:14-15).**

In the beginning, God told Satan that he would crawl on his belly and eat the dust of the Earth. Dust, coming from the Earth (*adam*), is representative of man's carnality and beastly nature. Satan's dominion is carnality.

Since the beginning, God predetermined a war of seeds – a war of *words*. The only way for a war to exist would be for Satan to put his seed above

God's Seed. The Church has submitted to Satan through sin, the ignorance of Torah, and staying ignorant gives Satan more authority. While Satan is a serpent on the ground in Genesis, he is a dragon in the air in the Book of Revelation. It is the ignorant Church that put Satan in the air, giving him an authority that he was not originally given.

The seed is the word (Luke 8:11), and in the beginning was the Word (John 1:1-2). The Word (Torah and Yeshua) is God and was with God since the beginning.

> **In the beginning was the Word, and the Word was with God, and the Word was God. He was in the beginning with God (John 1:1-2).**

The Torah is God so to say that Torah is done away with is to say that God is done away with. Everything was created from Him, and all things were already established before He even began speaking and unveiling matter.

The seed is the Word, the Word is God, and God is light (1 John 1:5):

> **This is the message which we have heard from Him and declare to you, that *God is light* and in Him is no darkness at all (1 John 1:5).**

Therefore, the *seed* is *light. Revelation* of the kingdom secrets is *illumination*, which is exactly what the Early Church believed and taught. The Early Church knew that redemption came through revelation of the secrets of the kingdom.

In contrast to this revelatory illumination, to be in darkness is to not understand, misunderstand or to be blind to truth. Behind the veil, where the secrets of the kingdom reside, is the light of Yah – the same light from the first day of creation (see **The Light**). What is not yet understood is hidden behind the veil and still in darkness until one obtains revelation, or an *apocalypse*, of the truth. The journey and race that we run is a progression from understanding the Way – the teachings of the Early Church Fathers, who called themselves *the Way* – to the Truth, and ultimately to everlasting Life. The progression through these three positions is the advancement through the temple: from the Outer Court (the Way) to the Holy Place (the Truth) to the Holy of Holies (the Life) (see Table 2). To be ignorant of the divine secrets behind the veil is to remain in darkness and in the realm of Satan. The Early Church taught that the power was in the hidden, or secret, meaning of the Word:

> **Moreover, if the law of Moses had contained nothing which was understood as having a secret meaning, the prophet would not have said in his prayer to God, "Open Thou mine eyes, and I will behold the wondrous things out of Thy Law;" whereas he knew that there was a veil of ignorance lying upon the heart of those who read but do not understand the figurative meaning, which veil is taken away by the gift of God, when He hears him who has done all that he can, and who by reason of habit has his senses exercised to distinguish between good and evil, and who continually utters the prayer, "Open thou mine eyes, and I will behold the wondrous things out of Thy law" (Origen, *Against Celsus*).**

God seeks for His people to return to the fundamental foundation of truth. In the Book of Revelation, Yehoshua said to the Church of Ephesus:

> **Nevertheless I have this against you, that you have left your *first love* (Revelation 2:4).**

This *love* is the *agape* love of God, not the *phileo* love of man. If love is the fullness of the fruit of the Spirit, and fruit comes from a tree, which comes from a seed (the Word of God), then Yehoshua actually tells the

Ephesian Church that they have left the first seed, or the first Torah. That is, the Church has left the foundational teaching of the secrets. The *agape* love is a *passion* for the *truth*, but because the Church has lost its passion for the truth, it has fallen away. Paul writes to the Thessalonian Church that God will send a strong delusion to those who do not love the truth:

> **The coming of the lawless one is according to the working of Satan, with all power, signs, and lying wonders, and with all unrighteous deception among those who perish, because they did not receive the *love of the truth*, that they might be saved. And for this reason God will send them strong *delusion*, that they should believe the lie, that they all may be condemned who did not believe the truth but had pleasure in unrighteousness (2 Thessalonians 2:9-12).**

In Verse 10, the word *love* is *agape*. With the *agape* love of God, there must be a love of the truth, where an intimate pursuit occurs to obtain His Word or His seed. The word *delusion* is the Greek word *plane*, meaning *a straying from orthodoxy*, or a straying from right teaching. The equivalent Hebrew words for *plane* include *mirmah* (*deceiving, fraud*), *pasha* (*revolt, as in sin, rebellion, transgression*), and *sherirut* (*twisted, obstinacy*). Scripture tells us that God will send lies and twisted teachings to those who do not love the truth – choosing not to pursue truth is ultimately what results in falling away.

Sincere repentance is required for those who have fallen away. God has faced the same battle with His children throughout all the generations – they kept moving away from His truth. Yeshua came to reestablish the truth in the Earth by teaching the mysteries and revelations behind the veil to His new royal priesthood, the apostles and prophets, who have the ability to break open the Word. While His teachings were parables to the masses, they were revelatory secrets to the apostles. His apostles likewise taught the secrets and sowed seeds to those who had eyes to see.

The seed is light. The seed is likewise Christ:

> **Now to Abraham and his Seed were the promises made. He does not say, "And to seeds," as of many, but as of one, "AND TO YOUR SEED," who is Christ (Galatians 3:16).**

Christ is the word of life:

> **...holding fast the *word of life*, so that I may rejoice in the day of Christ that I have not run in vain or labored in vain (Philippians 2:16).**

God is love:

> **He who does not love does not know God, for *God is love* (1 John 4:8).**

Love is one (and the fullness) of the fruit of the Spirit. But there cannot be **fruit** unless a **seed** first enters into the ground. However, counterfeit versions of God's creation and His seed exist. In fact, there are two seeds: one yielding the sons of God and one yielding the sons of Satan. Just as there are two laws (two words, two Torahs): one of life and one of sin and death. Ultimately, there are even two gods: the God of heaven and the god of the carnal world. Yehoshua said, "**Therefore take heed that the light which is in you is not darkness**" (Luke 11:35). The battle is between light and darkness – following the truth or following the counterfeit.

The dichotomy is obvious: Christ is life and love. The anti-Christ is death and hatred. One cannot know, embrace, and exhibit love until one has the correct seed. God ordained a law stating that every seed will produce according to its kind (Genesis 1:11-12), which applies to both the physical and spiritual realms. The seed must produce that which it is *intended* to produce.

Seed is imparted through an intimate, love-making process. The true love of God is an impregnation of His Word. Just as the Holy Spirit hovered over Mary and impregnated her with Yeshua, the Holy Spirit hovers over us to impregnate us with His Seed, which is the living Word. From that seed comes the tree that produces fruit, which is also indicative of offspring.

In Galatians 5:22-24, Paul the Apostle lists nine fruits of the Spirit:

> **But the fruit of the Spirit is *love, joy, peace, longsuffering, kindness, goodness, faithfulness, gentleness, self-control.* Against such there is no law. And those who are Christ's have crucified the flesh with its passions and desires (Galatians 5:22-24).**

Two more are listed in Ephesians 5:9:

> **...for the fruit of the Spirit is in all goodness, *righteousness*, and *truth*... (Ephesians 5:9).**

And one more in Hebrews 13:15:

> **Therefore by Him let us continually offer the sacrifice of *praise* to God, that is, the fruit of our lips, giving thanks to His name (Hebrews 13:15).**

The seed bears the tree that bears the fruit. The Torah encompasses each stage of this cycle – from the seed to the tree to the fruit.

Opening the Seed

Essentially, only water can break open a seed. As water is representative of revelation, once the revelation hits the seed, the hidden *rhema* (inside) emerges out of the *logos* (shell). However, it is flowing water that constitutes revelation. Stagnant water is considered bitter. The word *bitter* is the Hebrew word *mar*, written in ancient Hebrew, 𐤌𐤓. The letters *resh* (𐤓, *head*) and *mem* (𐤌, *water*) together mean "head water," or the headwaters of a river, where water is stagnant or just a trickle and therefore bitter to the taste. It takes *moving* water to break open a seed.

At the Pool of Bethesda, it was only when the angel *stirred* the water, causing it to be *moving*, that healing occurred for those who entered the water (John 5:4). The angel was the messenger that brought forth revelation, thereby bringing resurrection life through the release of kingdom mysteries. This resurrection life is the true healing. Once the water was stirred and revelation came forth, those who were originally hindered by disease – those deficient in understanding – were then healed and resurrected through enlightenment.

The amount of force required for a seed to open is comparable to that of a nuclear blast. In studies on seed germination, it was found that the force required to break open the seed coat (the shell, or *logos*), ranges from 9.9 MPa to 133.2 MPa for various seed types (Blumenthal, 1986). This range of pressure falls within the range required in realistic calculations to design blast doors to protect against penetrations from weapon effects, as calculated in a technical manual from the Department of the Army.

Thus, the power of the Word and of revelation can literally be measured - every revelation that opens up is equivalent to a nuclear explosion. Without revelation, seeds remain dormant. In Hebrew thought, being *dormant* is equivalent to being *dead*. The sleeping virgins in Matthew 25 are illustrative of the sleeping, or dead, Church that has no revelation of Yeshua and are at risk of missing His arrival.

The twelve fruits of the Spirit are as follows:

Love	*Agape – unconditional love of God*	Galatians 5:22
Joy	*Chara – cheerfulness, delight, gladness, fullness*	Galatians 5:22

Peace	*Eirene – prosperity, quietness, rest, security, safety, harmony, blessed state of upright men after death*	Galatians 5:22
Longsuffering	*Makrothumia – patience, endurance, constancy, steadfastness, perseverance, slowness in avenging wrongs*	Galatians 5:22
Kindness	*Chrestotes – moral goodness, integrity, useful*	Galatians 5:22
Goodness	*Agathosune – uprightness of heart and life, goodness, kindness, having right understanding and living it out*	Galatians 5:22
Faithfulness	*Pistis – conviction of the truth, conviction of man's relationship to God and trust in God*	Galatians 5:22
Gentleness	*Praotes – mildness, meekness, humbleness*	Galatians 5:23
Self-Control	*Egkrateia – virtue of one who masters his desires and passions, especially his sensual appetites*	Galatians 5:23
Righteousness	*Dikaiosune – correctness of thinking, feeling and acting; doctrine concerning the way in which man may attain approval from God*	Ephesians 5:9
Truth	*Aletheia – respecting the duties of man, opposing superstitions of the Gentiles and inventions of the Jews, and corrupt opinions of false teachers even among Christians*	Ephesians 5:9
Praise	*Ainesis – offering of thanks*	Hebrews 13:15

Besides the first nine fruits listed in Galatians 5, **righteousness** (right understanding) and **truth** are part of the twelve fruits. Love contains right understanding. One cannot truly love God without rightly understanding His plan and truth, which comes from revelation. A counterfeit exists for everything, so a **love *without* revelation is a counterfeit and false love**. Love without revelation is not true agape love.

The twelfth fruit is **praise**. It is praise that counters the spirit of heaviness:

> **To console those who mourn in Zion, to give them beauty for ashes, the oil of joy for mourning, the garment of *praise* for the spirit of *heaviness*; that they may be called trees of *righteousness*, the planting of the LORD, that He may be glorified (Isaiah 61:3).**

In Isaiah 61:3, the word praise is the Hebrew word *tehillah*, meaning *praise, adoration, thanksgiving*. In ancient Hebrew, it is written [illegible], and means *folly: in the sense of shining*, where the root word [illegible] means *shine, star*. The Hebrew letters, when read from right to left, can be read, "Behold the teaching of the revelation of the cross." The cross is in fact the Tree of Life – the Torah. Therefore, the teachings of the Early Church – the mysteries of the kingdom – reveal the divine plan regarding the Tree of Life. We are called to become the Tree of Life back in the New Jerusalem, which is the garden.

The word *heaviness* is the word *keheh*, meaning *dim, dull, colourless, dark, faint*. In ancient Hebrew, *keheh* is written [illegible], where the root word [illegible] means *burn, brand (such as the branding of the skin)*. Heaviness is thus associated with a burning. In the end of the age, everything must pass through fire and a burning. The gold, silver, and precious stones will be refined, while the wood, hay, and stubble will be destroyed:

> **Now if anyone builds on this foundation with gold, silver, precious stones, wood, hay, straw, each one's work will become clear; for the Day will declare it, because it will be *revealed by fire*; and the fire will test each one's work, of what sort it is (1 Corinthians 3:12-13).**

To avoid burning, or heaviness, one must have praise, which is receiving the revelation of the Tree of Life, the Torah. Having the revelation of Yeshua (the Torah, the Tree of Life) inevitably produces an offering of thanks, which is the essence of praise. Revelation of the truth reverses all wrong understanding, or unrighteousness. A reversal of a wrong mindset is the equivalent of repentance. John the Baptist clearly stated that those without the proper *fruit worthy of repentance* will be cut down:

> **Therefore bear fruits *worthy of repentance* . . . . And even now the ax is laid to the root of the trees. Therefore every tree which does not bear good fruit is cut down and thrown into the fire (Matthew 3:8, 10).**

The fruit of the Tree of Life are worthy of repentance, meaning the revelation of truth will produce the fruit that allows the *reversal of wrong understanding*. It is out of God's love that He offers repentance of sin, the missing of the mark, or the missing of His Torah. But the love of God cannot exist without the revelation of His Word. The revelation starts as a seed that ultimately produces the tree and the fruit. In Revelation 22, John writes of two trees of life each bearing twelve fruits:

> **And he showed me a pure river of water of life, clear as crystal, proceeding from the throne of God and of the Lamb. In the middle of its street, and on either side of the river, was the *tree of life*, which bore *twelve fruits*, *each tree* yielding its fruit every month. The leaves of the tree were for the healing of the nations (Revelation 22:1-2).**

The twelve fruits are the twelve fruits of the Spirit, and the two trees are Yehoshua and His Bride. Yehoshua already bears these twelve fruits, and He is waiting for His Bride to bear those same twelve fruits in order to come into full marriage with Him.

All fruit have the ability to produce seed, an important concept in Judaism. Once God gives us seeds of revelation, we have the ability to reproduce more seeds, ultimately yielding an abundant harvest. The concept of multiplication is mandated by God not only regarding fruit, but also *talents,* which are indicative of His Secret teachings.

Bad Fruit from False Prophets

As a tree continually bears fruit, God's children are called to constantly bear and multiply fruit. However, the fruit must be tested. Those who bear good fruit are good, life-giving trees, and they become the Tree of Life back in the garden. But those who bear bad fruit are cut down and thrown in the fire. Yeshua warns us of the false prophets who bear bad fruit:

> **"Beware of *false prophets*, who come to you in sheep's clothing, but inwardly they are ravenous wolves. You will know them by their fruits. Do men gather grapes from thornbushes or figs from thistles? Even so, every good tree bears good fruit, but a bad tree bears bad fruit. A good tree cannot bear bad fruit, nor *can* a bad tree bear good fruit. Every tree that *does not bear good fruit* is *cut down* and *thrown into the fire.* Therefore by their *fruits* you will know them. . ." (Matthew 7:15-20).**

These false prophets will come looking like real prophets but are in every way counterfeit. In the Old Testament, true prophets were those who could interpret the secrets of the Scripture and were often despised by the children of God. True prophets bring the Word of God, which is sharper than a double-edged sword and brings correction and circumcision. Those with the seed of revelation and the ability to unveil the secrets were those with true power and authority, which is depicted with Daniel, Joseph, Solomon, and many others. These individuals became governmental leaders because they could interpret the secrets of the Scripture.

The bad fruit of false prophets comes from not loving the truth. Paul indicates in 2 Thessalonians that those who do not love the truth have no access behind the veil, and Yeshua reiterates that not everyone will obtain access:

> **"Enter by the *narrow gate*; for wide is the gate and broad is the way that leads to destruction, and there are many who go in by it. Because narrow is the gate and difficult is the way which leads to life, and there are *few* who find it". . . . "Not everyone who says to Me, 'Lord, Lord,' shall enter the kingdom of heaven, but he who does the will of My Father in heaven. Many will say to Me in that day, 'Lord, Lord, have we not prophesied in Your name, cast out demons in Your name, and done many wonders in Your name?' And then I will declare to them, 'I never *knew* you; depart from Me, you who practice *lawlessness*!'" (Matthew 7:13-14, 21-23).**

The narrow gate is the doorway into the Holy of Holies, a gate through which only one individual could enter at a time. The numbers become fewer when one approaches the glory, just as the numbers allowed in the three sections of the temple decrease from the Outer Court to the Holy Place to the Holy of Holies. Only a few – a remnant – will obtain the ultimate promise. Recall that that the word *mystery* means *to be initiated* (**Revelation of Mysteries & The Veil**), indicating that only few obtain access behind the veil to learn the kingdom secrets.

Yehoshua said, "I never *knew* you," where the word *knew* is the Greek word *ginosko*, which is an idiom meaning *to have intercourse*. Thus, He was saying, "I never had intercourse with you. I never *impregnated* you." Even though false prophets move in miracles, signs, and wonders, they are not impregnated with truth. While false teachers will direct people away from the law, even saying that it is done away with, God's true prophets will teach the Torah and the secrets of the kingdom:

> **Some of the heretics simply deny the Law and the Prophets for the sake of their own doctrine. And under**

> **the pretense of grace, they have sunk down to the lowest abyss of perdition (Caius, *Ante-Nicene Fathers*).**

In Matthew 7:23, Yehoshua says these false prophets practice *lawlessness*, meaning they lack understanding of Torah. Jeremiah writes of God's anger toward false and lying prophets…

> **Also I have seen a horrible thing in the prophets of Jerusalem: they commit *adultery* and walk in *lies*; they also strengthen the hands of evildoers, so that no one turns back from his wickedness. All of them are like Sodom to Me, and her inhabitants like Gomorrah. "Therefore thus says the LORD of hosts concerning the prophets: 'Behold, I will feed them with *wormwood*, and make them drink the *water of gall*; for from the prophets of Jerusalem profaneness has gone out into all the land.'" Thus says the LORD of hosts: "Do not listen to the words of the prophets who prophesy to you. They make you *worthless*; they speak a vision of their own heart, not from the mouth of the LORD. They continually say to those who despise Me, 'The LORD has said, "You shall have peace"'; And to everyone who walks according to the dictates of his own heart, they say, 'No evil shall come upon you.'" For who has stood in the *counsel* of the LORD, and has perceived and heard His word? Who has marked His word and heard it? Behold, a whirlwind of the LORD has gone forth in fury— a violent whirlwind! It will fall violently on the head of the wicked. The anger of the LORD will not turn back until He has executed and performed the thoughts of His heart. In the latter days you will understand it perfectly. "I have not sent these prophets, yet they ran. I have not spoken to them, yet they prophesied. But if they had stood in My *counsel*, and had caused My people to hear My words, then they would have turned them from their evil way and from the evil of their doings…" (Jeremiah 23:14-22).**

The latter days (Verse 20) indicates the end of the age. As the prophetic office is part of the priestly office, the false prophets are also false and counterfeit priests. Those who listen to the false prophets will drink gall (Jeremiah 23:15), which is bitter waters. Water turns bitter when it is stagnant, and it takes living and *moving* water – revelation – to bring restoration. Stagnant and bitter water is false teaching that brings death. Wormwood is also released onto the false prophets (Jeremiah 23:15). Wormwood appears again in the Book of Revelation as one of the plagues; the curses are released on both those who give and receive false teachings.

However, if the false prophets would have stood in His *counsel*, they would have turned from their evil ways (Jeremiah 23:22). The word *counsel* is the word *sod*, or secrets. These false prophets have no understanding of God's secrets, they don't hear His voice, and they make people worthless (Jeremiah 23:16). The word *worthless* is the word *habal*, meaning *to lead astray.* The equivalent Greek words all include the definition of *empty*. As Satan is the son of perdition, or the son of *emptiness*, those who follow false prophets become sons of Satan. Those who despise the Lord listen to the false prophets (Jeremiah 23:17); they offer a false peace. Peace is one of the fruits of the Spirit, so those who don't have a love for the truth inevitably bear counterfeit (bad) fruit.

Fullness of the Fruit is Love

The tree grows from a seed, which requires light and water – revelation of the Word of God. The seed, which brings life, needs to be watered with the Word. The whole process of revelation is to bear fruit. The *fullness* of the fruit is *love*, so the fullness of revelation is God's *love*. The unveiling of the mysteries of the kingdom leads to the *agape*, or *ahavah*, love of God.

> **And though I have the gift of prophecy, and understand all *mysteries* and all knowledge, and though I have all faith, so that I could remove mountains, but have not *love*, I am nothing (1 Corinthians 13:2).**

The well-known love chapter that Paul wrote in 1 Corinthians 13 contains an understanding that extends beyond people merely loving one another in the natural sense. Recall that the word for *love* is the Greek word *agape*, the unconditional love of God. *Agape* translates to the Hebrew word *ahavah*, written in ancient Hebrew, אהבה. The root word *hab*, הב, means *love, gift*, with the combination of letters reading, "Look towards the house." God instilled the foundation that His house – His lineage and bloodline – is His gift to humanity. Adding the *aleph* (א, *God*) and another *hey* (ה, *revelation*) to the word הב yields, "God's gift of revelation." This is the *ahavah* – the *agape* – love of God: His gift of revelation. The love of God is a love for truth, which is embodied in Yehoshua.

When the seed of the Word is planted in one's life, there comes a knowledge that must be cultivated from head knowledge (information) to heart knowledge (passion, *agape* love). This is the point where the Word becomes engrafted in the soul, transformation takes place, and the soul becomes His Spirit. To withstand sifting, the revelation must proceed from the head (*logos* understanding) and into the heart (*rhema* understanding) – if the seed is shallowly planted, it will result in an uprooted tree. As the seed is the Word (Luke 8:11), which is also the sperm, the love of God is an intimate love-making process involving God's Word, which produces the fullness of the spiritual fruits all coming from His holy seed.

The enemy seeks to fight those who have the holy seed. Only the remnant will have the holy seed at the end of the age. God said that the enemy's seed would be at war with His Seed (Genesis 3), and this is the same seed mentioned in Revelation 12:

> **And the dragon was enraged with the woman, and he went to make war with the *rest* [remnant] of her *offspring* [seed], who *keep the commandments of God* [keep Torah] and have the testimony of Jesus Christ (Revelation 12:17, emphasis added).**

The woman who produces the seed is the personification of Wisdom. Those who are born of Wisdom and keep the Torah are God's remnant. In the same chapter of the Book of Revelation, the man-child being caught up into the heavens is representative of the sons of God ascending into the Holy of Holies and into His glory. The catching up of the man-child is also a picture of those who become a sacrifice, die to themselves, and are used in the end time move for the final glory. At the same time, Satan and the fallen angels are cast down to the Earth.

Holy Seed and Persecution

Where the true seed is, there will be persecution. For the first three centuries, the Early Church faced persecution. Many refused to deny the Lord and therefore died as martyrs. Prior to the ruler Constantine becoming emperor, the Early Church experienced some of the heaviest and most gruesome persecutions by the Roman government. Constantine issued the Edict of Milan in 313, declaring Christianity to be a legal religion. However, Constantine also began to pervert the Early Church teachings by accepting many pagan beliefs and doctrines.

Constantine engrafted other pagan religions and holidays into Christianity. At the same time, he ceased persecuting Christians, resulting in a drastic increase in numbers of people joining Christianity. However, Constantine's massive evangelism of this "Christian" faith was none other than a false seed. False doctrine and teachings correlate to lack of persecution. The toleration of all types of teaching is clearly seen in the present-day system, where there is little to no persecution or chastisement.

The true Christians, those who continued to learn the secrets of the Early Church Fathers, didn't associate with the newly perverted "Christian" faith and remained segregated from them. The followers of the true and holy seed faced persecution, martyrdom, and death. Yeshua told His disciples:

> **Blessed are those who are persecuted for righteousness' sake, for theirs is the kingdom of heaven. Blessed are you when they revile and persecute you, and say all kinds of evil against you falsely for My sake. Rejoice and be exceedingly glad, for great is your reward in heaven, for so they persecuted the prophets who were before you (Matthew 5:10-12).**

Those who are righteous, or have right understanding and the holy seed, are persecuted. Yet they will be blessed for pursuing access behind the veil to learn the deeper teachings of God. Persecution comes with the holy seed - this battle of seeds still exists today.

The enemy's strength is ignorance and darkness. Paul prayed that the Church would have the spirit of wisdom and revelation. Yeshua taught His disciples that those who love Him will keep His doctrine:

> **"If anyone loves Me, he will keep My word; and My Father will love him, and We will come to him and make Our home with him. He who does not love Me does not keep My words; and the word which you hear is not Mine but the Father's who sent Me" (John 14:23-24).**

Essentially, He was saying, "Why do you say you love Me but do not obey My commandments?" Disobedience is being ignorant of God's Torah which is the opposite of love (the fullness of the fruit of the Spirit).

The Torah, the Tree of Life bearing twelve fruits of the Spirit, is found in both the garden in Genesis and in the New Jerusalem in the Book of Revelation. In the New Jerusalem, the tree is on both sides of the river:

> **In the middle of its [the New Jerusalem's] street, and on either side of the river, was the tree of life, which bore twelve fruits, each tree yielding its fruit every month. The leaves of the tree were for the healing of the nations (Revelation 22:2).**

The word *tree* is the word *xulon*, whose Hebrew equivalent includes the word *ets*, a collective noun representing *multiple trees*. Thus, the tree is indicative of a *forest of trees* bearing fruit, and so the Tree of Life can be seen as a whole forest of Trees of Life. Those with the Torah written in their hearts become the living Word of God – they are the forest of Trees of Life in the New Jerusalem. These trees are planted by God Himself.

> **To proclaim the acceptable year of the LORD, and the *day of vengeance* of our God; to comfort all who mourn, to console those who mourn in Zion, to give them beauty for ashes, the oil of joy for mourning, the garment of praise for the spirit of heaviness; that they may be called trees of righteousness, the *planting of the LORD*, that He may be glorified (Isaiah 61:2-3).**

These trees are planted during the *day of vengeance* of our God. This day is the Great and Terrible Day, the Day of Atonement, *Yom Kippur*. The garden thus comes back into existence during the fall feasts, when the ingathering of the harvest occurs (see **Rains, Feasts & His Return**). The trees depicted in the Book of Revelation are fruit-bearing, righteous people who understand Torah at the end of the age.

Each tree gives fruit every month, indicating that the trees produce unceasingly, all year long. A fruit of the Spirit is associated with each month of God's calendar. Further, the leaves carry healing for the nations. Thus, it is from the Tree of Life – the Torah – that the nations under the curse of Adam will be healed and restored. The Torah is the source of restoration life.

The Marriage Covenant

The Torah is additionally a marriage covenant. A traditional Hebrew wedding involves several stages and processions. The foremost stage requires a covenant, the *ketubah* (marriage contract), which is a written document of the promises of the groom and the rights of the bride. This wedding covenant outlines the fundamental conditions set forth by the Torah upon the husband: providing his wife with food, clothing, and conjugal rights, which are inseparable from marriage. The *ketubah* also includes the guarantee that the husband will pay a certain sum in the event of divorce and provide inheritance rights to his heirs.

The three main conditions of the *ketubah* are provision of food, clothing, and conjugal rights, which shall not be denied, as written in Exodus 21:10-11:

> **If he takes another wife, he shall not diminish her *food*, her *clothing*, and her *marriage rights*. And if he does not do these three for her, then she shall go out free, without paying money (Exodus 21:10-11).**

The word *food* is the Hebrew word *sheer*, meaning *flesh, body, meat*. A related word is *basar*, which means a *feast of meat*, used to describe the Gospel, the Torah, and the secret teachings. In ancient Hebrew, the word *sheer* is written 𐤔𐤀𐤓, and means *remnant, kin*. The letters *shin* (𐤔, *anointing, pressure*), *aleph* (𐤀, *apostle, God*), and *resh* (𐤓, *mind*), depict that the anointing of the apostolic mindset is for the remnant, or those who understand the mysteries. The apostles' job is to provide the food, the meat of the Word, through teaching the secrets and mysteries of the kingdom.

Manna, Bread, and Meat

God provides His people, the Bride, with the meat of the living Word. This precept is clear in John 6:53, where Yehoshua teaches that His body is flesh (meat). He further states that He is the living bread (John 6:51), and the manna that came down from heaven (John 6:31-33). Hence, the manna is the bread, the bread is the meat, and the meat is His body, which is also the manna from heaven. Manna appears again at the end of the age:

> **"He who has an ear, let him hear what the Spirit says to the churches. To him who overcomes I will give some of the hidden *manna* to eat. And I will give him a white stone, and on the stone a new name written which no one knows except him who receives it" (Revelation 2:17).**

The overcomers eat the hidden manna or meat, the food of angels. The word *hidden* is the Greek word *krupto*, meaning *to be veiled.* As only the royal high priests have access behind the veil, the overcomers are part of the holy royal priesthood who have moved beyond the carnal, or natural, understanding of the Word of God. One is considered to become an angel upon receiving revelation of the secret teachings of God; it is then that one partakes of angel food – the hidden manna. The overcoming of the flesh (obtaining access behind the veil) provides true sustenance that yields eternal life.

The second condition of the *ketubah* outlined in Exodus 21:10-11 is to provide clothing. The word *clothing* is the Hebrew word *kesuth*, meaning *covering, raiment.* In ancient Hebrew, *kesuth* is written †Y⋛Ш. The root word is [ancient Hebrew script], meaning *cover, cup, seat.* The mercy seat, the *kapporeth* ([ancient Hebrew script]), sat on top of the ark of the covenant and was the covering and atonement of God over His people. This covering is also the glory that covered Adam and Eve in the garden; thus, the raiment is the glory that God will put upon those who receive the feast of meat (the secrets) from Him.

The marriage covenant thus calls for a transfiguration of God's people, who will ultimately become His mercy seat through the revelation of Torah. The remnant will become the ark, which is His very throne. Only the high priest could be in the presence of the ark, the container of the supernatural light of Day One (see **The Light**) and the secrets hidden before the foundations (see **Secrets**). Early Church Father Ignatius wrote that it was Yehoshua the High Priest "to whom the Holy of Holies has been committed, and who alone has been entrusted with the secrets of God. He [Yehoshua] is the door of the Father, by which enter in Abraham, and Isaac, and Jacob, and the prophets, and the apostles, and the church." As Yehoshua is the living Word, it is through a marriage with Him – a marriage with the Torah, the marriage contract itself – that we obtain access behind the veil to become the ark. In fact, the Early Church taught that a marriage had to take place in order to enter through the veil into the Holy of Holies (Barker, 2000).

The third condition of the *ketubah* is to provide marriage rights. The phrase *marriage rights* equates to the Hebrew word *onah*, written in ancient Hebrew as [ancient Hebrew script], meaning *habitation*. The first three letters form the word [ancient Hebrew script], meaning *watch, abode (a home is a place closely watched)*. The home is considered protected by keeping a close eye on it. The *marriage rights* are a habitation – that is, the place of dwelling prepared by the husband. In the customs of a Hebrew wedding, after the *ketubah* is written, the husband leaves to build a house for the bride. In the Book of John, Yehoshua said:

> **In My Father's *house* are many mansions; if it were not so, I would have told you. I go to *prepare a place* for**

> **you. And if I go and prepare a place for you, I will come again and receive you to Myself; that where I am, there you may be also (John 14:2-3).**

This statement is a direct reference to the stage of marriage when the bridegroom (Yehoshua) prepares a house for the bride (His Church). In John 14:2, the word *mansion* is the Greek word *mone*, whose definition is a *dwelling of God in believers.* It is further the duty of the apostles to prepare the Church for the marriage.

> **For I am jealous for you with godly jealousy. For I have betrothed you to one husband, that I may *present you as a chaste virgin to Christ* (2 Corinthians 11:2).**

Paul was stating that his job was to prepare the Church to be ready for marriage with Christ. The marriage covenant outlines the requirement to provide the meat of the Word (the secrets of the kingdom), which will produce a covering of glory, and ultimately a dwelling place – a tabernacle ready for God to dwell in.

It should be noted that Yehoshua specifically mentioned these three elements (food, clothing, and a dwelling place) were being provided by those who will inherit the kingdom:

> **Then the King will say to those on His right hand, 'Come, you blessed of My Father, inherit the kingdom prepared for you from the foundation of the world: for I was *hungry* and you gave Me *food*; I was *thirsty* and you gave Me *drink*; I was a *stranger* and you *took Me in*; I was *naked* and you *clothed* Me; I was sick and you visited Me; I was in prison and you came to Me.' . . . And the King will answer and say to them, 'Assuredly, I say to you, inasmuch as you did it to one of the least of these My brethren, you did it to Me' (Matthew 25:34-36, 40).**

His statement regarding feeding, clothing, and providing a dwelling place directly relates to the requirements of a marriage. Providing these key elements is equivalent to agreeing to a marriage covenant with Yehoshua and obtaining a place at His right hand – the position for the Bride.

The *ketubah* contains five main parts:

1. **Combined Lineage** – a family history of the bride and groom
2. **Bride's History**
3. **Groom's History**
4. **Bride and Bridegroom's Story** – an account of how they met
5. **Responsibilities** – those of both the bride and bridegroom

The Torah, similarly, contains five main parts, distinguished in the five books of Moses:

1. **Genesis** – a history of Yehoshua, the Light that existed before the foundations of the Earth, and the Bride (God's chosen people)
2. **Exodus** – personal history of the Bride, God's chosen people
3. **Leviticus** – history of God's lineage, the Levites
4. **Numbers** – the love affair of God and His people in the wilderness, including the sorrows as He reaches out to His Bride
5. **Deuteronomy** – the responsibilities from both the Bride and the Bridegroom, in the form of mitzvahs

Hence, the *Torah* is the *ketubah*, the marriage covenant, between God and His people. When Moses ascended Mount Sinai, he was not only shown all of creation and told to build the tabernacle as a pattern - he also received the marriage covenant between God and His people. Receiving the covenant on Mount Sinai was only the beginning of the process of a marriage whose key elements are timed and fulfilled according to God's appointed feasts (see **Rains, Feasts & His Return**).

It should be noted that according to Hebrew law, there are only two ways out of the marriage covenant: **death** or **adultery**, the latter which constitutes a right for divorce. After God's children left Egypt and were in the wilderness, they committed adultery by complaining to Moses to return to Egypt, where they deemed had better food and provision. God's children turned their eyes to the idols of Egypt, thereby serving other idols above God. The Hebrews essentially committed adultery against God and entered into a false marriage.

God used the Red Sea to kill the Egyptian army in order to release His people out of this wrong marriage. Leading up to the crossing of the Red Sea, God released the plagues into Egypt *(Egypt means to limit God)* with the sole purpose of setting His people free – releasing His Bride from the wrong bridegroom and the bondage of Pharaoh *(Pharaoh means double minded).*

The same adultery occurs with the Church in the Book of Revelation:

> **And upon her forehead was a name written, MYSTERY, BABYLON THE GREAT, THE MOTHER OF HARLOTS AND ABOMINATIONS OF THE EARTH (Revelation 17:5).**

The Church has become the harlot by taking in the wrong seed and wrong doctrine, becoming entranced with a false glory. Plagues are poured onto her:

> **In the measure that she glorified herself and lived luxuriously, in the same measure give her torment and sorrow; for she says in her heart, 'I sit as queen, and am no widow, and will not see sorrow.' Therefore her *plagues* will come in one day—death and mourning and famine. And she will be utterly burned with fire, for strong is the Lord God who judges her (Revelation 18:7-8).**

The release of plagues is not to destroy the harlot but to bring restorative change. Just as God sent the plagues into Egypt to set His children free, He once again sends the plagues at the end of the age to set His children free from double mindedness. In Hebrew, the word *deber* translates to *plague*, which means *to reorder society*. Plagues are sent to reorder the mindset and bring about a single, unified mind – the mind of Christ.

The *ketubah* was also required to be signed by seven witnesses. Isaiah depicts seven spirits of God:

> **The Spirit of the LORD shall rest upon Him, the Spirit of wisdom and understanding, the Spirit of counsel and might, the Spirit of knowledge and of the fear of the LORD (Isaiah 11:2).**

These seven spirits compose the seven-branched lamp, the *menorah*, representative of the seven churches in the Book of Revelation (Revelation 1:20). The menorah is in fact also representative of the Tree of Life, which appears again in Revelation 22.

The Marriage Process

The writing and signing of the *ketubah* was the first part of the Hebrew wedding process. After the *ketubah* was created, agreed upon and signed, the bride's and bridegroom's families would share a meal of bread and wine. Similarly, Yehoshua shared communion with His disciples, representative of the wedding process. Then the bridegroom would begin to build a house for the bride, which was in fact an extension of his father's house.

Upon completion of the abode, with the process taking up to several years, the bridegroom would come to the bride's city in the middle of the night with his groomsmen, loudly notifying the entire town along the way that he was coming to take his bride. This procession followed that of a thief; unlike today's concept of a sly individual keeping quiet to steal items, in the early days a thief induced a loud commotion to notify the entire city that it was about to be pilfered. Thus, the saying "as a thief in the night" points to Yehoshua the Bridegroom coming to take His Bride.

While the bride waited for her bridegroom, she would keep a lamp burning in her window so that her bridegroom would know from which house to retrieve her. Once the bridegroom arrived at her house, he would take her directly to the wedding ceremony. During the ceremony, the bride and bridegroom entered a *chuppah*, a covered bed chamber, and consummated. They were not officially married until the bride was no longer a virgin – that is, until the flesh was removed.

The parable of the virgins depicts the waiting period leading up to, and the beginning of, the wedding ceremony. The bride had to have enough oil to keep her lamp burning. The Church must have enough anointing oil – teaching – before the return of the Bridegroom. Otherwise, upon His return, He will pass by those whose lamps aren't burning (those without the correct teaching and doctrine). All the virgins were asleep when the bridegroom arrived, and so the Church is asleep, or dead. The door being shut on the virgins who did not have enough oil is illustrative of those who do not make it into the bed chamber. This is also stated in the Constitutions of the Apostles:

> **Lest some of the things necessary to thy journey be wanting; as the oil of piety was deficient in the five foolish virgins (Matt. 25: 1-46) mentioned in the gospel, when they, on account of having extinguished their lamps of divine knowledge, were shut out of the bride chamber (*Constitutions of the Apostles*, Bk. 8).**

Paul writes that the veil is the flesh (Hebrews 10:20), so a piercing of the flesh during consummation was a type and shadow of the high priest going through the veil to enter the Holy of Holies; it is also symbolic of the remnant ultimately returning to the glory Adam lost in the fall. The Early Church taught that during the process of receiving revelation and learning the secret teachings of God, ascension occurred, transforming one into an angel. Thus, learning the mysteries is an impregnation process during which God imparts His DNA, which is His character. As a name comprises of character and function, a change in character is a change in name. During marriage, the bride receives a new name, which can only occur if consummation – revelation of the secret teachings – has occurred.

Chapter Four

Abrahamic Covenant

But some most worthless persons are in the habit of carrying about the name (of Jesus Christ) in wicked guile, while yet they practice things unworthy of God, and hold opinions contrary to the doctrine of Christ, to their own destruction, and that of those who give credit to them, whom you must avoid as ye would wild beasts.

Ignatius
110 A.D.

War of Seeds

A war of seeds began in Genesis. This was a war of words, a war of DNA, and ultimately, a war of Torahs. In Genesis 3:15, God tells Satan, the serpent that beguiled Eve, as follows:

> **And I will put *enmity* between you and the woman, and between your *seed* and her *Seed*; he shall bruise your head, and you shall bruise his heel (Genesis 3:15).**

God discloses the imminent war between the Seed of Adam and the seed of the enemy. Adam's Seed would crush the enemy's seed in the head, depicting dominion. The word *dominion* in Hebrew means *to tread down, or put under one's feet*, as further depicted in Psalms:

> **You have made him to have *dominion* over the works of Your hands; You have put all things *under his feet* (Psalms 8:6).**

One seed would have dominion over the other. The word *seed* is the Hebrew word *zera*, which means *seed, fruit, plant, sowing, offspring, semen virile, descendants, posterity, children, seed of righteousness or carnality, conceive, fruitful.* The seed is the Word (Luke 8:11), which is also the DNA of God. It is during consummation that the marriage covenant is fulfilled – when the seed enters the womb. In Hebrew thought, the womb is also considered the mind, so consummation and officiation of a marriage occur when the Word of God enters the mind. God told Abraham that he would be fruitful:

> **I will make you exceedingly *fruitful*; and I will make nations of you, and *kings* shall come from you (Genesis 17:6).**

Not only does God tell Abraham that he will be fruitful, but that nations and kings will come from him. In verse 6, the word *fruitful* is the word *parah*, meaning *to bear fruit, grow, increase.* In ancient Hebrew, *parah* is written הרפ, and the root of the word is רפ, meaning *tread, bull, fruitful.* The two letters *pey* (פ) and *resh* (ר) together can be read as "open the head." In these times, heads of grain were scattered on the threshing floor. The ox was then led around the floor, opening the heads of grain through crushing them, thereby revealing the seed inside each head.

Bearing fruit is directly tied to oxen, symbolic of apostles, whose job is to open and reveal the inside of the seeds from their shells. In both 1 Corinthians 9:9 and 1 Timothy 5:18, Paul refers to the original commandment to not muzzle the ox while it treads out the grain (Deuteronomy 25:4). Paul refers to himself as the ox preparing the ground for seeds – he was the apostle preparing the people with revelatory teaching to produce the fruit of God. The spiritual meaning of this commandment is to not silence or stop the apostles from bringing forth the secret teachings of the kingdom.

It is for God to hide a matter and for <u>kings</u> to search out a matter. Solomon writes in his Proverbs:

> **It is the glory of *God* to *conceal* a matter, but the glory of *kings* is to *search out* a matter (Proverbs 25:2).**

As such, the descendants of Abraham are not only oxen (apostles) that reveal the hidden *rhema* word of God, but they are also kings who search out the hidden *rhema*. God's people are called to be *kings* and *priests* (Revelation 1:6, 5:10). This royal priesthood extends beyond the physical high priesthood. The royal priesthood is of the order of Melchizedek, the priesthood of Yeshua (see **Royal Priesthood**).

God further declares an everlasting covenant between Him and Abraham and his descendants:

> **And I will establish My *covenant* between Me and you and your *descendants* (seed) after you in their generations, for an *everlasting covenant*, to be God to you and your descendants after you. Also I give to you and your *descendants* after you the land in which you are a stranger, all the land of Canaan, as an *everlasting possession*; and I will be their God (Genesis 17:7-8).**

Everlasting is the word *owlam*, meaning *vanishing point, time out of mind*, indicating *timelessness.* Before the foundations of the world, the supernatural light of Day One is an everlasting, timeless, eternal light (see **The Light**). The word *owlam* is written in ancient Hebrew, ʍJ⊙, meaning *hide: to be hidden or obscured from sight, covered or unknown*, as well as *ancient: distant time in the past or future, a time hidden from the present.* God has given us access to timelessness in the access of the Holy of Holies. As we step into the role of royal high priests, enter timelessness, and bring the glory back out to the Earth, the dimension of time as understood by human logic disappears into *timelessness*, or the *everlasting covenant* established between God and Abraham. The impregnation of the seed of God results in *eternal* beings.

As eternal beings, we should seek things above – things in the heavens:

> **If then you were *raised* with Christ, seek those things which are *above*, where Christ is, sitting at the right hand of God. Set your mind on *things above*, not on things on the earth. For you died, and your life is *hidden* with Christ in God. When Christ who is our life appears, then you also will appear with Him in glory (Colossians 3:1-4).**

Paul states that we have already died, and our life is *hidden*. The word *hidden* is the word *krupto*, meaning *to hide, conceal, veil*. This death is to our earthly and natural ways of thought and doctrine. Being raised with Christ illustrates the ascension associated with learning the deeper teachings of God, which puts to death carnal teachings and natural interpretations of the Torah. The holy apostles and prophets release the secret life through the hidden mysteries of God into the Earth.

> **. . . and have put on the new man who is *renewed* in *knowledge* according to the image of Him who created him, where there is neither Greek nor Jew, circumcised nor uncircumcised, barbarian, Scythian, slave nor free, but Christ is all and in all (Colossians 3:10-11).**

When we are renewed in knowledge (mindsets) there will be unity with God. When we reach the glory, there will no longer be a distinction between types of people. All will have the same mindset – that of Christ.

A spiritual law exists that every seed must produce according to its kind (Genesis 1:11). Carnal teachings (and natural interpretations of the Torah) produce carnal people. The Early Church pursued the return to the glory of the garden through the secret teachings of Yeshua. They planted the hidden *rhema*, which produced the fruit of the Spirit when revealed.

The covenant that God made with Abraham is a blessing of *multiplication*. The true seed of God will multiply, indicating that the deeper teachings of God are meant to be multiplied by spreading His seed – His Word, the Torah:

> **That in blessing I will bless thee, and in *multiplying* I will *multiply* thy *seed* as the stars of the heaven, and as the sand which is upon the sea shore; and thy *seed* shall possess the gate of his enemies (KJV, Genesis 22:17).**
>
> **For when God made a promise to Abraham, because He could swear by no one greater, He swore by Himself, saying, "*SURELY BLESSING I WILL BLESS YOU, AND MULTIPLYING I WILL MULTIPLY YOU*" (Hebrews 6:13-14).**
>
> **Therefore from one man, and him as good as dead, were born as many as the stars of the sky in multitude—innumerable as the sand which is by the seashore (Hebrews 11:12).**

The true seed of God will possess Satan's gate. They are the descendants of Abraham and will possess the gates of the enemies. The seed extends all the way to the man-child in Revelation 12, at which point a war breaks out in heaven (Revelation 12:7). Michael and his angels fight against Lucifer and his angels, who are *cast down* to the Earth. This occurs after the man-child is *caught up* in the heavens. After the man-child is in his place in the heavens, Satan is displaced. The man-child illustrates a people who die to their own way of thinking, thus becoming living sacrifices. This company of people will ascend to displace Satan, who comes *down* to pursue the inhabitants of the Earth. This remnant of God's elect stand in stark contrast to the majority of people who will remain earthly (those with natural and carnal reasoning). Only the remnant will ascend into the heavenly realms. They will go through the preparation process to become God's elect:

> **You have escaped from great tribulation on account of your faith, and because you did not doubt in the presence of such a beast. Go, therefore, and tell the elect of the Lord His mighty deeds, and say to them that this beast is a type of the great tribulation that is coming. If then ye prepare yourselves, and repent with all your heart, and turn to the Lord, it will be possible for you to escape it, if your heart be pure and spotless, and ye spend the rest of your days of your life serving the Lord blamelessly (Hermas, *The Shepherd*).**

Satan comes down from heaven in the Book of Revelation, just as he fell from heaven as lightning (Luke 10:18). Likewise, Yeshua is likened to lightning flashing from east to west (Matthew 24:27). The word *lightning* is the Greek word *astrape*, whose Hebrew equivalent is the word *baraq*, meaning *lightning, gleam, flashing sword*. The two cherubim guarding the way back into the garden carry swords, indicative of the Word of God and the secrets and parables of the kingdom (see **The Garden**). Lightning falling down to the Earth signifies the revelation of the Word and seed of God entering into our carnal mindsets, the battleground for the war of words, or a war of Torahs. Two seeds exist: one from God and one from Satan. The seed one receives will determine the mark they receive – it will determine their destiny.

Circumcision & The Mark

When God created His covenant with Abraham, He also gave Abraham distinct instructions about circumcision:

> **And God said to Abraham: "As for you, you shall keep My *covenant*, you and your descendants after you**

> **throughout their generations. This is My covenant which you shall keep, between Me and you and your descendants after you: Every *male child* among you shall be *circumcised*; and you shall be *circumcised* in the *flesh* of your *foreskins*, and it shall be a *sign* of the covenant between Me and you" (Genesis 17:9-11).**

Circumcision is the word *mul*, meaning *to cut, be cut off.* In ancient Hebrew, it is written ᒍYʍʍ, and means *front: the front of a long series of the same*; also *the removal of the front part of a male.* We know that in Hebrew thought the past is seen as "in front" and the future is seen as "behind." God's instructions to His people to be circumcised are instructions for them to remove the front (the known past) so that there is only that which is left behind (the unseen future). Pursuing the unseen is pursuing the prophetic realm behind the veil.

God never wanted a circumcision of the flesh but rather of the heart. God tells the people to circumcise the foreskins of their hearts, and Paul reiterates that circumcision is not of the natural flesh but of the heart:

> **Therefore circumcise the *foreskin* of your *heart*, and be stiff-necked no longer (Deuteronomy 10:16).**

> **Circumcise yourselves to the LORD, and take away the *foreskins* of your *hearts*, you men of Judah and inhabitants of Jerusalem, lest My fury come forth like fire, and burn so that no one can quench it, because of the evil of your doings (Jeremiah 4:4).**

> **For he is not a Jew who is one outwardly, nor is circumcision that which is outward in the flesh; but he is a Jew who is one inwardly; and *circumcision* is that of the *heart*, in the Spirit, not in the letter; whose praise is not from men but from God (Romans 2:28-29).**

The natural foreskin, *orlah*, which was physically removed, was considered unclean and deficient. In Hebrew thought, the *heart* is viewed as the *mind*. The Fausset's Bible Dictionary describes the *heart* as including the intellect as well as the affections and will. The *mind* often includes the feelings, will, and intellect. Further, in man's unbelief it is the will that perverts the intellectual perceptions. Paul further portrays the connection between the heart and mind:

> **Because, although they knew God, they did not glorify Him as God, nor were thankful, but became futile in their *thoughts*, and their foolish *hearts* were *darkened* (Romans 1:21).**

Removing the foreskin from the heart and mind is an act of removing all deficiencies in one's thoughts, feelings, and will. God said He would write the Torah on the hearts of the people:

> **But this is the covenant that I will make with the house of Israel after those days, says the LORD: I will put My *law* [Torah] in their *minds*, and write it on their *hearts*; and I will be their God, and they shall be My people (Jeremiah 31:33).**

Covenant is linked to circumcision; the writing of Torah on the people's hearts is a picture of circumcision of the foreskin of the heart and mind (deficient and incorrect understanding). The word *circumcise*, the Hebrew word *mul* (מול), contains the root word מל, meaning *speak, word, continue (a continuation of segments which fill the whole)*. So even the root of *circumcision* is linked to a *word* – the Word of God, which is Torah.

When God created this covenant with Abraham, He established the circumcision as a *sign* of the covenant:

> **And you shall be circumcised in the flesh of your fore-skins, and it shall be a *sign* of the covenant between Me and you (Genesis 17:11).**

The word *sign*, or *token*, is the word *owth*, meaning *mark, miracle*. In ancient Hebrew, it is written †𐤀, which are the first letter (*aleph*, 𐤀) and last letter (*tav*, †) of the Hebrew Aleph-Bet. The word *owth* also means *plow*, and *to arrive (as in traveling toward a mark, destination or a person)*. When an ox plowed the field, the farmer would place a cross at the other end of the field to ensure the ox would walk in a straight line.

God declares multiple times that He is the first and last (Isaiah 44:6, 48:12, Revelation 1:8, 17-18, 21:6-7, 22:13):

> **Listen to Me, O Jacob, and Israel, My called: I am He, I am the *First*, I am also the *Last* (Isaiah 48:12).**

> **I am the *Alpha* and the *Omega*, the *Beginning* and the *End*, the *First* and the *Last* (Revelation 22:13).**

God's original language is Hebrew (see Hebrew Foundations) so when He states, "I am the Alpha and the Omega" what should actually be read is, "I am the *Aleph* and *Tav*" - the ox that takes you to the cross. These are the first and last letters of the Hebrew Aleph-Bet, which spell the very word *owth*, the same word used when God tells Abraham that circumcision will be a *sign* of the covenant. So, this sign is God Himself. Recall that *owth* also means *to travel toward a mark, destination or a person*. The mark, destination, and person are God. Understanding the Word from Hebrew foundations powerfully depicts the heart and true passion of the words of Yeshua.

The sign or mark of God is Yeshua, as Yeshua is God. In the Early Church, the rabbis and priests marked people with the sign of the cross (†, *tav*) on the forehead, signifying the covenant between God and His people. This covenant originates from the covenant God cut with Abraham, the father of many nations.

There are two marks: those who are circumcised receive the mark of God and those who are uncircumcised are given the mark of the enemy (the mark of the beast). As circumcision is of the heart and mind, the two types of markings are also in the mind. Those with correct understanding are circumcised, and those with incorrect understanding are uncircumcised, the latter of which shall be *cut off*:

> **And the *uncircumcised* male child, who is *not circumcised* in the *flesh* of his *foreskin*, that person shall be *cut off* from his people; he has broken My covenant (Genesis 17:14).**

The word *foreskin*, the Hebrew word *orlah*, in addition to meaning *uncircumcised* also means *unlawful, forbidden as food, taboo, obstinacy, opposition to God's law*. The phrase *cut off* is the word *karath*, meaning *to cut down, cut out, eliminate, kill, behead*. A word related to *karath* is the word *keriythuth*, meaning *divorce*. Those who are uncircumcised (go against Torah by wrong interpretation) will be divorced from God and will be cut out of the marriage covenant. There is an imminent dual sacrifice: those who remove their flesh keep their marriage covenant with God, but those who continue to have carnal understanding are removed from the covenant.

Without circumcision, one cannot see and hear spiritually or have right understanding. In Matthew 13, Yeshua speaks about people whose hearts have grown dull, with ears that do not hear and eyes and that do not see.

> **And in them the prophecy of Isaiah is fulfilled, which says: 'HEARING YOU WILL HEAR AND SHALL NOT UNDERSTAND, AND SEEING YOU WILL SEE AND NOT PERCEIVE; FOR THE *HEARTS* OF THIS PEOPLE HAVE *GROWN DULL*. THEIR**

> **EARS ARE HARD OF HEARING, AND THEIR EYES THEY HAVE CLOSED, LEST THEY SHOULD SEE WITH THEIR EYES AND HEAR WITH THEIR EARS, LEST THEY SHOULD UNDERSTAND WITH THEIR HEARTS AND TURN, SO THAT I SHOULD HEAL THEM' (Matthew 13:14-15).**

The hearts of the people have *grown dull.* The phrase *grown dull* is the word *pachuno*, which means *thickened, callous, fatten, stupid.* The people have flesh, or fat, on their hearts, making them dull and stupid – they have no wisdom or right understanding. A circumcision of the heart is required, which is achieved by learning the mysteries of God.

Stubble

God told His children to circumcise their hearts and to cease being stiff necked:

> **Therefore circumcise the foreskin of your heart, and be *stiff-necked* no longer (Deuteronomy 10:16).**

The word *stiff* is the word *qashah,* meaning *hard, as in the stiffness of the stubble or branch.* The word *qashah* (𐤒𐤔𐤄) contains the root word *qash* (𐤒𐤔), meaning *stubble.* God repeatedly warns His children that those who reject His Torah will be as *stubble* and burned in the fire.

> **Therefore, as the fire devours the *stubble*, and the flame consumes the chaff, so their root will be as rottenness, and their blossom will ascend like dust; because they have *rejected the law* of the LORD of hosts, and despised the word of the Holy One of Israel (Isaiah 5:24).**

> **"For behold, the day is coming, burning like an oven, and all the proud, yes, all who do *wickedly* will be *stubble.* And the day which is coming shall burn them up," says the**

> **LORD of hosts, "That will leave them neither root nor branch" (Malachi 4:1).**
>
> Paul mentions *stubble* (translated as *straw*) as one of the materials with which one builds upon the foundation of Christ:
>
> > **Now if anyone builds on this foundation with gold, silver, precious stones, wood, hay, straw [stubble], each one's work will become clear; for the Day will declare it, because it will be revealed by fire; and the fire will test each one's work, of what sort it is (1 Corinthians 3:12-13).**
>
> The wood, hay and stubble point to carnal and natural interpretation of God's Word; whoever builds upon the foundation of Yehoshua – the same foundation of the Early Church Fathers – with wood, hay, or stubble will be destroyed. Thus, God's mandate to circumcise one's heart and to stop being stiff-necked – to no longer be *stubble* – clearly indicates the requirement to remove carnal and natural understanding in order to come into the kingdom.
>
> One's works are driven by one's understanding of His Word. If one only has *p'shat* level understanding, which is a natural understanding of Torah, the corresponding works will only be carnal with no access behind the veil. On the other hand, if one has a *sod*, prophetic understanding of Torah, one's corresponding works will be prophetic, priestly, and spiritual, yielding access through the veil.

God marks those who are circumcised. In the Book of Ezekiel, God tells the angel with the inkhorn to spare those with His *mark*:

> **"Utterly slay old and young men, maidens and little children and women; but do not come near anyone on whom is the *mark*; and begin at My sanctuary." So they began with the elders who were before the temple (Ezekiel 9:6).**

God's judgment is based on understanding His Word. Those who rightly understand His Torah will receive His covenantal mark (Jeremiah 31:33). God instructs the angel to start at His sanctuary, the Church, because judgment will begin first in the house of the Lord (1 Peter 4:17). Circumcision removes the natural interpretation of the Torah, or the soulish nature, represented by the woman or the wife.

Spirit & Soul: Man & Woman

Throughout the Bible are various mitzvahs and instructions depicting rules regarding men and women. The *p'shat,* Outer Court interpretation of these Scriptures would lead one to put restrictions on men and women in the natural. However, God speaks in parables and symbolisms. The man is indicative of the spirit nature, and the woman the soulish nature. Paul writes:

> **Let a woman learn in silence with all submission. And I do not permit a woman to teach or to have authority over a man, but to be in silence (1 Timothy 2:11-12).**

The instruction is to bring the soulish nature (carnal interpretation) in submission to the spiritual nature (the prophetic, *sod*-level interpretation) of Scripture. The soulish nature should not speak over the spiritual nature. It is the soulish nature that is deceived. Adam fell because of the deception of Eve:

> **For Adam was formed first, then Eve. And Adam was not deceived, but the woman being deceived, fell into transgression. Nevertheless, she will be saved in childbearing if they continue in faith, love, and holiness, with self-control (1 Timothy 2:13-15).**

The childbearing points to the offspring – seed or word – that is produced. There are two types of seed, and every tree will produce according to its fruit and seed. The faith, love and self-control of which Paul speaks are the fruit of the Tree of Life (see **The Tree**). Holiness is sanctification and being set apart, which inherently comes with producing the correct fruit.

Natural circumcision of the foreskin requires the use of a knife or dagger. However, the Word of God is sharper than any double-edged sword (Hebrews 4:12), and so the Word is the instrument for spiritual circumcision. When God's Word – His Torah – is written in one's heart, then the heart has been circumcised. Circumcision is a removal of flesh, which is the veil (Hebrews 10:20), and thus entails going through the veil into the Holy of Holies to learn the deeper mysteries of God. Upon enlightenment of the kingdom secrets, one then becomes circumcised – unblemished, perfect, and mature. Ultimately, we are to become a perfect sacrifice just as Yeshua was the perfect sacrifice (see **The Sacrificial Lamb & Temple**).

Becoming a sacrifice entails a death, but a resurrection is promised to follow. In the Book of Colossians, Paul writes that there has already been death with Christ:

> **Therefore, if you *died* with Christ from the basic principles of the world, why, as though living in the world, do you subject yourselves to regulations (Colossians 2:20).**
>
> **If then you were *raised* with Christ, seek those things which are above, where Christ is, sitting at the right hand of God (Colossians 3:1).**

If we are already raised with Christ, then there was already a first resurrection – one from a spiritual death. The Early Church taught that resurrection includes both the spirit and the flesh. So, if a first resurrection has already occurred, it is the spiritual resurrection – whereby the old man (the old, carnal interpretation of God's Word) has died, and the spirit man (the spiritual, prophetic interpretation of His Word) comes alive.

When one steps through the grave of the darkness of Genesis 1, a resurrection occurs through the light (see **The Light**). A transition from the *logos* (carnal, fleshly body) into the *rhema* (glorified body) occurs. The revelation is hidden in His people, just as God hid Himself since the beginning of creation, and the accumulating manifestation of the revelation results in the glory.

On the Mount of Transfiguration, Yeshua went up in a fleshly body and became *illuminated* with glory on the top of the mountain. Peter, James, and John witnessed an *enlightenment* and *ascension* of Yeshua, which is the picture of ascension that comes from learning the secret teachings of God. This same ascension occurs when the royal high priesthood enters behind the veil into the Holy of Holies and begins to see the hidden things visible only to the royal high priesthood but hidden from everyone else.

The Christ Generation

Matthew 1 portrays the 42 generations from David to Christ in three groups of 14 generations. These three groups are the generations from 1) Abraham to David, 2) David to captivity in Babylon, 3) captivity in Babylon to Christ.

Matthew 1:1-6 lists the first set of 14 generations from Abraham to David:

1. Abraham
2. Isaac
3. Jacob
4. Judah
5. Perez
6. Hezron

7. Ram
8. Amminadab
9. Nahshon
10. Salmon
11. Boaz
12. Obed
13. Jesse
14. David the King

Matthew 1:6-11 lists the second set of generations from David to captivity in Babylon:

1. Solomon
2. Rehoboam
3. Abijah
4. Asa
5. Jehoshaphat
6. Joram
7. Uzziah
8. Jotham
9. Ahaz
10. Hezekiah
11. Manasseh
12. Amon
13. Josiah
14. Jeconiah

Matthew 1:12-16 lists the third set of generations from captivity in Babylon to the Christ:

1. Shealtiel
2. Zerubbabel
3. Abiud
4. Eliakim
5. Azor
6. Zadok
7. Achim
8. Eliud
9. Eleazar
10. Matthan
11. Jacob
12. Joseph (Mary's husband)
13. **Yeshua**
14. The CHRIST

Yeshua Himself is the 41st generation. After *Yeshua* comes the *Christ generation*:

> **So all the generations from Abraham to David are fourteen generations, from David until the captivity in Babylon are fourteen generations, and from the captivity in Babylon until the *Christ* are *fourteen generations* (Matthew 1:17).**

The third set of 14 generations ends at the CHRIST. In the Book of Galatians, Paul writes:

> **Now to Abraham and his Seed were the promises made. He does not say, "And to seeds," as of many, but as of one, "AND TO YOUR SEED," who is Christ (Galatians 3:16).**

Yeshua begets the Christ, meaning that the Christ is a *people filled with the Holy Spirit.* These people are the sons of the kingdom, the anointed generation, who are anointed to bring the kingdom back into the Earth. This 42nd generation is part of the holy seed from the garden, who will return back to, and become, the garden. Before the foundations of the world, God purposed for this holy generation to rule the nations as kings and priests (1 Peter 2:9).

Christ is the Greek word *Christos,* and the Hebrew word *mashiach,* meaning *anointed.* Anointing is indicative of the divine wisdom established before the foundations of the world, personified by the Tree of Life. In fact, the anointing oil was considered to be the byproduct of the Tree of Life – the perfume and fragrance of Wisdom (see **Wisdom**).

This Christ generation is a people who clearly understand God's divine purpose and work to bring His kingdom to Earth. While many profess to be Christians, they operate in the anointing of false spirits. Yeshua and many of the Early Church Fathers gave warnings about those who claim to be Yeshua's followers but have no truth in them:

> **But the spirit of deceit preaches himself, and speaks his own things, for he seeks to please himself, for he is full**

> **of arrogance. He is lying, fraudulent, soothing, flattering, treacherous, rhapsodical, trifling, inharmonious, verbose, sordid and timorous (Ignatius, *Epistle to Ephesians*).**

Included in this group are those who may see some truth but choose to take no action for fear of judgment from others – they choose not to defend the truth and Word of God. Though their hearts are to serve Yeshua, they are not fully equipped with His Spirit. There is yet another group that operates with the Spirit of God but has the spirit of compromise. These individuals have no conviction for the truth and are more concerned about self-advancement. The Christ generation is a holy (*set apart*) generation – a people who separate the carnal, soulish desires from the spiritual, prophetic duties to fulfill God's divine plan.

Birthright & Inheritance

The Christ generation is the generation of the many saviors who will come out of Zion:

> **Then *saviors* shall come to Mount Zion to judge the *mountains* of *Esau*, and the kingdom shall be the LORD's (Obadiah 1:21).**

The word *savior* is the word *yasha*, meaning *salvation*, which is part of the name of our Lord: *Yehoshua*. Thus, a multitude of people will bring salvation to the nations through the anointing of our Lord and Savior. Yehoshua will come out of Zion, the New Jerusalem. This will occur by His appearing through His Holy Spirit in the midst of His people, who are of the royal bloodline and of the Abrahamic covenant. Forty-two generations are listed to the Christ. This parallels the Hebrews, who made forty-two stops on the way to the Promised Land. The last stop in the Promised Land correlates to the Christ generation. This is a generation of living tabernacles – the garden of Eden, the New Jerusalem – a people who are the habitation of God.

Obadiah writes that the *mountains of Esau* will be judged. The word for *mountain* is the word *har*, which also means *mindset*. *Har* is written in ancient Hebrew as 𐤓𐤄, the letter *resh* (𐤓) depicting the *mind*, and *hey* (𐤄) depicting *revelation* or *learning*. Mountains thus represent mindsets. Yeshua says, "**I say to you, if you have faith as a mustard *seed*, you will say to this *mountain*, 'Move from here to there,' and it will move; and nothing will be impossible for you,**" (Matthew 17:20). He is saying that a seed – the Word of Yah – can move an entire mindset or way of thinking. The Word of God will change mindsets and break strongholds that are otherwise impossible to overcome by any other means.

Esau, although the firstborn of Isaac, is not listed as one of the forty-two generations from Abraham because he gave up his birthright:

> **And Esau said to Jacob, "Please feed me with that same *red* stew, for I am weary." Therefore his name was called Edom. But Jacob said, "Sell me your *birthright* as of this day." And Esau said, "Look, I am about to die; so what is this birthright to me?" Then Jacob said, "Swear to me as of this day." So he swore to him, and sold his birthright to Jacob (Genesis 25:30-33).**

The word *red* is the Hebrew word *adam*, meaning *Earth*. Esau gave up his high priestly office and royal inheritance as the firstborn son for carnality and the fallen nature of Adam. By giving up his birthright, he removed himself from the lineage of Abraham and the children of God. In the Book of Romans, Paul clearly distinguishes between children of the flesh and children of the promise, who are the seed of Abraham:

> **That is, those who are the children of the *flesh*, these are not the children of God; but the children of the *promise* are counted as the *seed* (Romans 9:8).**

Esau – a picture of the Church full of carnal teachings – is considered to be born of the flesh. Those who do not perceive the deeper revelation of God's kingdom are born of the flesh, not from above (John 3:3). Paul further writes:

> **...for the children not yet being born, nor having done any good or evil, that the *purpose of God* according to *election* might stand, not of works but of Him who calls, it was said to her, "THE OLDER SHALL SERVE THE YOUNGER." As it is written, "JACOB I HAVE LOVED, BUT ESAU I HAVE HATED" (Romans 9:11-13).**

The word *purpose* is the Greek word *prothesis*, coming from the word *protithemai*, meaning *showbread.* The table of showbread was in the Holy Place; it contained twelve loaves of bread, arranged in two rows of six (Leviticus 24:6). The two rows of six loaves of bread represent the 66 books in the current canon of the Bible – the Torah. Thus, the *purpose of Yah* can be read as the *showbread of Yah*, or the *Torah of Yah.* The word *election* is the word *ekloge*, meaning *divine selection, chosen.* The division of the two types of seed and the war of seeds centers on the fulfillment of Torah. This division of seed separates God's remnant – the seed of the promise. The Holy Place, containing the showbread, correlates with the Feast of Pentecost (see **Table 2,** in Chapter 2). This time is the beginning of the summer harvest, which at the end culminates in a sifting of the wheat from the tares (Matthew 13:30). As God said that "the older shall serve the younger," those who have given up their birthright by rejecting the wisdom and revelation of God are sifted from those who have the eyes to see, believe, obey, and act on His divine plan. Early Church Father Origen taught about those who would be removed at the end of the age:

> **...take the good seed to be the children of the kingdom, because whatsoever good things are sown in the human soul, these are the offspring of the kingdom of**

God and have been sown by God the Word who was in the beginning with God (John 1:2) so that wholesome words about anything are children of the kingdom. But while men are asleep who do not act according to the command of Jesus, "Watch and pray that ye enter not into temptation," (Matthew 26:41) the devil on the watch sows what are called tares – that is, evil opinions – over and among what are called by some natural conceptions, even the good seeds which are from the Word. And according to this the whole world might be called a field, and not the Church of God only, for in the whole world the son of man sowed the good seed, but the wicked one tares – that is, evil words – which springing from wickedness, are children of the evil one. And at the end of things, which is called "the consummation of the ages," there will of necessity be a harvest, in order that the angels of God who have been appointed for this work may gather up the bad opinions that have grown upon the soul, and overturning them may give them over to fire which is said to burn, that they may be consumed (Origen, *Gospel of Matthew*).

Chapter Five

Back to Genesis

So then, when the end has been restored to the beginning, and the termination of things compared with their commencement, that condition of things will be reestablished in which rational nature was placed, when it had no need to eat of the tree of knowledge of good and evil...And when death shall no longer anywhere exist, nor the sting of death, nor any evil at all, then verily God will be "all in all."

Origen
184-235 A.D.

The Beginning

> **In the beginning God created the heavens and the earth (Genesis 1:1).**

In the beginning, God established what would take place in the end. The first words of Genesis, "In the beginning," in Hebrew is *bereshiyth*. In ancient Hebrew, *bereshiyth* is written [illegible]. The first three letters are the *bet* ([illegible] *house*), *resh* ([illegible], *son*), and *aleph* ([illegible], *God*), which together mean *to fill or create*. God *filled* a void with His creation. The letters *bet* ([illegible], *house*), *tav* (†, *covenant, marriage*), and *resh* ([illegible], *son*) form the word [illegible] (*beriyth*), meaning *covenant*. In Hebrew thought, marriage is a covenant. God's very first words illustrate His original intention: **God created a house for the covenant marriage of His Son**. His house is the tabernacle, and the marriage occurs in the Holy of Holies. God's house – His temple – is also His people. His original plan, spoken in the beginning, will finally take place in the Book of Revelation, which brings all of creation back to the beginning in full circle.

Rearranging the letters of *bereshiyth* (בראשית) yields אבתשרי, spelling "aleph b'Tishri." This means "the first of Tishri," which is the Feast of Trumpets, *Rosh Hashanah*, the first day of the new year. The first day of creation was Tishri 1. To the Early Church, when God said, "in the beginning," it was the equivalent of Him saying, "the Feast of Trumpets," which is a declaration of a new beginning.

Trumpets

In the beginning, when God said, "Let there be" on the Feast of Trumpets, He prophetically uttered creation into existence. Throughout Scripture, the trumpets directly correlate to the prophets speaking. God instructed Isaiah to lift up his voice:

> **Cry aloud, spare not; lift up your voice like a *trumpet*; tell My people their transgression, and the house of Jacob their sins (Isaiah 58:1).**

Likewise, God calls Jeremiah His prophet and trumpet. Just as physical trumpets were used to alert people about events ranging from war to marriage celebrations, God uses His prophets as spiritual trumpets to alert the people. As prophets are those who understand the hidden things of God (Amos 3:7), sounding trumpets are prophetic utterances of God's hidden mysteries.

The angels that sound the trumpets in the Book of Revelation are prophets and priests revealing mysteries of the kingdom. The sounding trumpets are prophetic utterances of the hidden secrets from behind the veil. When the last angel sounds the trumpet, the mystery of God would be finished:

> **But in the days of the sounding of the seventh angel, when he is about to sound, the mystery of God would be finished, as He declared to His servants the prophets (Revelation 10:7).**

It is His servants the prophets who are the sounding trumpets. It is those who have received revelation – gone behind the veil into the Holy of Holies – and brought back a message of the secret teachings of God in order to fulfill the divine plan of God.

Emptiness and Chaos

> **The earth was *without form*, and *void*; and *darkness* was on the face of the *deep*. And the Spirit of God was hovering over the face of the waters (Genesis 1:2).**

The phrase *without form* is the word *tohu*, meaning *ignore, waste, confusion, chaos, wilderness.* In ancient Hebrew, *tohu* is written Y𓀠†. If the letter *resh* (ᕋ, *man*) is added and the letters rearranged, the resulting word is *torah*, 𓀠ᕋY†. Without the Man (Yehoshua), the *tav*, †, which is a cross (covenant), is meaningless. Yehoshua is also the Sacrificial Lamb. When a lamb was sacrificed, it was cut down the middle and across the back, and skewers were inserted lengthwise along the body and crosswise along the shoulders. The lamb's feet were secured to the lengthwise skewer. Essentially, every sacrificial lamb was placed on a cross, just like Yehoshua. Without a sacrifice to put on the cross, the cross is without form and meaningless.

The cross is also the Tree of Life. In the Book of Acts, Luke writes that Yeshua hung not on a cross but a *tree*:

The God of our fathers raised up Jesus whom you murdered by hanging on a *tree* (Acts 5:30).

Without a mind (𐤓) in which to impart the revelation of God's divine plan, there is chaos and confusion. When the mind is nailed to the cross (𐤕) – when we become dead to our own way of thinking – we can then obtain the mind of Christ. To be without the mind of Christ is to be in a place of wilderness, a place of no revelation. Yeshua became one with the Tree of Life through His sacrifice, just as we are to likewise be nailed to and become one with the Tree (the Torah) as perfect sacrifices.

In the beginning, the Earth was *without form*; it was in a state of *chaos* and *confusion*. Similarly, the Earth was *void*. The word *void* is the Hebrew word *bohu*, which means *need, box, space needing to be filled, rest, empty*. The Earth was thus empty and needed to be filled. It is symbolic of man, for out of the *dust of the earth* man was formed (Genesis 2:7, 3:19). The Earth is the carnal mindset, and an empty mind without form is a mind in darkness and ignorance. Paul tells the Church that they were once in darkness but now are in the light of the Lord (Ephesians 5:8), where the light of the Lord is indicative of the supernatural light of the first day of creation. This supernatural light is the same light associated with the illumination one receives from learning the deeper teachings - the meat of the Word of God.

The word *void* indicates a *box* needing to be filled. The word *void* (*bohu*, 𐤅𐤄𐤁), shares the same root, 𐤄𐤁, as the word *ark*, (*tebah*, 𐤁𐤄𐤕), which means *an empty space that needs to be filled.* The ark of the covenant that resided in the Holy of Holies is in essence a box that was filled with the glory of God. The ark represents the mind. God desires for us to be the ark within the temple as well as the temple itself.

The Ark

The void that existed in Genesis 1 is the ark to be filled with the glory of God. The ark contained three items:

- The two tablets containing the Ten Commandments (Exodus 25:16)
- A golden pot of manna (Hebrews 9:4)
- Aaron's rod that budded (Numbers 17:7-8)

The three items that are in the ark of the covenant reappear in the Book of Revelation:

> **He who has an ear, let him hear what the Spirit says to the churches. To him who *overcomes* I will give some of the *hidden manna* to eat. And I will give him a *white stone*, and on the stone a *new name* written which no one knows except him who receives it (Revelation 2:17).**
>
> **And he who *overcomes*, and keeps My works until the end, to him I will give power over the nations—'HE SHALL RULE THEM WITH A *ROD OF IRON*; THEY SHALL BE DASHED TO PIECES LIKE THE POTTER'S VESSELS - as I also have received from my Father…' (Revelation 2:26-27).**

The overcomers will be given the hidden manna (the Word of God), white stones with new names (His character and function), and a rod to rule the nations (the authority of a high priest). These items that are in the ark of the covenant are given to him who *overcomes*, which is the Greek word *nikao*. The Hebrew equivalents of the word *nikao* include the words *zakhah* (*translucent, innocent, clean*), *chamad* (*beloved, pleasant, precious*), and *natsach* (*to glitter, to be permanent*).

Overcoming is associated with becoming *translucent* or *glittering*. Yeshua took Peter, James, and John up the Mount of Transfiguration with Him:

> **And He was transfigured before them. His face *shone* like the sun, and His clothes became as white as the *light* (Matthew 17:2).**

The word *shone* is the word *lampo*, meaning *to radiate*, whose counterpart Hebrew words include meanings such as *to glitter, to be dazzling white*. As illumination is associated with learning the higher revelation of God, to overcome is to become illuminated, which comes from learning the secrets of the kingdom.

The ark is the mind, created to hold the glory of God. Everything in the ark is in order; no chaos can exist in the glory. God created His people with a void to be filled, to always be seeking Him to fill that place of disorder and chaos. If the void is not filled by His glory, then there will be no order. The order is established when God brings His people out of darkness and into the light, as His light is order.

The Earth was first without form and empty. The word *empty* is also *perdition*. Hence, the son of perdition illustrates a people who are empty – having minds void of God's glory and revelation. The state of perdition is the state to which Adam and Eve fell after eating of the wrong seed in the garden. God desires *order* in His garden, which are His people, and order is obtained with the presence of the eternal light. God said that His Word would not return *void*:

> **So shall My word be that goes forth from My mouth; it shall not return to Me void, but it shall accomplish what I please, and it shall prosper in the thing for which I sent it (Isaiah 55:11).**

Thus, His Word never causes chaos or emptiness. Instead, it brings order and fills the ark with His glory. God's seed imparted into His people will bring a full harvest because His seed produces the fruit of the Spirit – the fruit of the Tree of Life (see **The Tree**).

> **The earth was without form, and void; and darkness was on the face of the *deep*. And the Spirit of God was *hovering* over the face of the *waters* (Genesis 1:2).**

The word *deep* is the word *tehom*, meaning *abyss, subterranean water supply, depth.* The Greek translation is the word *abussos*, meaning *abyss, bottomless pit.* A bottomless pit illustrates a place without light, illumination, or the teaching of the kingdom secrets. The word *deep* is also associated with the word *grave*, which is a place of death. The deep place – the abyss, devoid of revelation and light – is a grave. Without light there is no life.

The Holy Spirit hovered over the face of the waters. The waters and seas are symbolic of humanity: Yeshua told His disciples, "**Follow Me, and I will make you fishers of men**" (Matthew 4:19). The act of hovering is also seen in a marriage. During a Hebrew wedding, the bridegroom would cover his bride with his *tallit*, the prayer shawl worn during the wedding. The *tallit* had four tzit-tzits at each corner, representing the four letters of the name of Yahweh, YHVH (𐤄𐤅𐤄𐤉), as well as Torah (TWRH, 𐤄𐤓𐤅𐤕). This act of the bridegroom hovering over his bride with his tallit is a picture of Yeshua hovering over and covering His Bride with His Torah. The Holy Spirit hovering over the waters – humanity – is a picture of God seeking marriage with His creation.

A large body of water is also seen as a place of chaos because of its storms, turbulent surface, and commotion of waves. Paul wrote that false teachings cause children to be tossed to and fro:

> **That we should no longer be *children*, tossed to and fro and carried about with every wind of doctrine, by the trickery of men, in the cunning craftiness of deceitful plotting (Ephesians 4:14).**

Children are tossed about because they are still immature and in the Outer Court realm. Being tossed to and fro is to be in a state of chaos among the waves in the sea (the chaotic sea is humanity in disorder). Those who are immature do not have the wisdom of the hidden mystery of God:

> **However, we speak wisdom among those who are *mature*, yet not the wisdom of this age, nor of the rulers of this age, who are coming to nothing. But we speak the wisdom of God in a mystery, the hidden wisdom which God ordained before the ages for our glory (1 Corinthians 2:6-7).**

So those who do not see the hidden mysteries of God will be lost in the chaos and emptiness of humanity. But the mature will not be affected, for at the point of maturity and perfection we will reach the measure of the stature of the fullness of Christ (Ephesians 4:13). In maturity there is order because the light of revelation brings order.

Days of Creation & The Temple

The account of creation in Genesis is a pattern of the restoration of the garden, illustrating the progression through the divine and redemptive plan of God:

> **Concerning, then, the creation of the world, what portion of Scripture can give us more information regarding it, than the account which Moses has transmitted**

> **respecting its origin? And although it comprehends matters of profounder significance than the merely historical narrative appears to indicate, and contains very many things that are to be spiritually understood, and employs the letter, as a kind of veil, in treating of profound and mystical subjects; nevertheless the language of the narrator shows that all visible things were created at a certain time (Origen, *De Principiis*).**

Day One: The Light

God created light and divided it from the darkness (Genesis 1:3-5). Yahweh is the light before the physical sun was created. The sun, which was created on Day Four, is an artificial light compared to the supernatural and eternal light of God. As instructed by God, Moses raised up the tabernacle on the first day of the first month:

> **And it came to pass in the *first month* of the second year, on the *first day of the month*, that the *tabernacle was raised up* (Exodus 40:17).**

The first day of the first month corresponds to Tishri 1, *Rosh Hashanah,* the New Year – the same day as the first day of creation in Genesis (see **The Beginning**). Day one corresponds to the first 1000 years of biblical history.

Day One is the creation of the invisible and incorporeal world, the pattern for the following days of creation of the physical world. Barker writes:

> Philo describes the works of Day One as the invisible and incorporeal world. 'First the maker made an incorporeal heaven and an invisible earth and the essential form of air and void.' That was Day One in Genesis. After a lengthy discussion, Philo describes the second

> day: 'The incorporeal cosmos was finished... and the world apprehended by the senses was ready to be born after the pattern of the incorporeal. And first of its parts the Creator proceeded to make the heaven which...he called the firmament.' In other words, everything made on or after the second day was part of the visible world but the works of Day One were beyond matter, beyond the veil. Elsewhere, Philo confirms this by saying that Moses entered this 'unseen, invisible, incorporeal and archetypal essence of existing things and saw what was hidden from mortal sight when he entered God's presence to be made God and King.' On the third day, says Philo, the creator began 'to put the earth in order' (Barker, 1988).

Day Two: The Firmament

The firmament, Heaven, was created and the waters above were separated from the waters below (Genesis 1:3-6). In the construction of the tabernacle, God then instructed Moses to hang the veil of the Holy of Holies:

> **And he brought the ark into the tabernacle, hung up the *veil* of the covering, and *partitioned off the ark of the Testimony*, as the LORD had commanded Moses (Exodus 40:21).**

The veil, separating the Holy of Holies from the Holy Place, is symbolic of the firmament that separates the waters above from the waters below. The Holy of Holies contains the waters, or revelation, above; the Holy Place contains the waters, or revelation, below. Yeshua told Nicodemus that one must be born again, or *born from above*, in order to see the kingdom of God, and that one must be born of water and the Spirit

(John 3:3-5). More importantly, the place from which one is born indicates one's nature:

> **That which is born of the flesh is flesh, and that which is born of the Spirit is spirit (John 3:6).**

As water is likened to teaching, there are teachings from the Holy of Holies, and there are teachings from the Holy Place. The teachings from the Holy of Holies are the divine secrets of the kingdom contained in the glory realm for the royal priesthood. The teachings of the Holy Place correlate to the anointing realm of the Church Age. Likewise, the second day corresponds to 2000 years of biblical history.

Day Three: The Vegetation

On the third day, the Earth and sea were divided, and grass, herbs, and trees were brought forth (Genesis 1:9-13). God specifically called forth the earth to bring grass, the herb with seed and the fruit tree with fruit:

> **Then God said, "Let the earth bring forth grass, the herb that yields *seed*, and the fruit tree that yields *fruit* according to its kind, whose seed is in itself, on the earth" and it was so (Genesis 1:11).**

The word *seed*, *zera*, is the same word used when God makes the everlasting covenant with Abraham and Abraham's seed (see **War of Seeds**). God established the source of life and the expected produce which are the Word of God and the fruit of the Spirit.

The third set of commands to assemble the tabernacle was for Moses to put the bread on the table in the Holy Place:

> **He put the table in the tabernacle of meeting, on the north side of the tabernacle, outside the veil; and he set**

> **the *bread* in order upon it before the LORD, as the LORD had commanded Moses (Exodus 40:22-23).**

To consecrate the table of showbread, the high priest had to place **wine, incense,** and **bread** on it. Wine comes from fruit, and bread and incense come from plants, and so it was on the third day that God created the substance of the offering to be placed on the table outside of the veil.

Day Four: The Celestial Bodies

On Day Four, the sun, moon, and stars were created (Genesis 1:14-19). These celestial bodies are the *containers* for the light of Day One. At the end of the fourth day, the heavenly lights were placed to divide day from night – to divide truth from lies. The lights are for signs and seasons:

> **Then God said, "Let there be lights in the firmament of the heavens to divide the day from the night; and let them be for *signs* and *seasons*, and for days and years" (Genesis 1:14).**

The word *season* is the word *moed*, meaning *appointment, feast, season, sign, rehearsal.* The celestial lights were placed to mark the Feasts of God (Leviticus 23) (see **Rains, Feasts & His Return**). It is also on the fourth day that the 24-hour day came into existence, meaning there was no measurement of time for the first three days of creation because there was no sun.

The fourth set of commands for assembling the tabernacle was to place the lampstand across from the table of showbread:

> **He put the *lampstand* in the tabernacle of meeting, across from the table, on the south side of the tabernacle; and he lit the lamps before the LORD, as the LORD had commanded Moses (Exodus 40:24-25).**

The word *lampstand* is the word *menorah*, which was filled with anointing oil. The menorah is symbolic of the Church filled with anointed teaching (Revelation 1:20). The celestial bodies were created on Day Four as the embodiment of the light of Day One. Likewise, Yeshua came to Earth 4000 years into biblical history as the embodiment of the eternal light of Day One. Scripture tells us that a day is equal to a thousand years (2 Peter 3:8). In Genesis, God foretold that He would send His Son 4000 years into history, which equates to the fourth day since a day is equal to 1000 years. The center shaft of the menorah is called the *shamash* shaft, or the Messiah shaft. Counting from one end of the menorah to the other, the center shaft is the fourth branch. The menorah itself depicts the seven days of creation and the divine plan of God.

Glory to Glory

The celestial bodies created on Day Four each contain different glories. Paul writes to the Corinthian Church:

> **There are also celestial bodies and terrestrial bodies; but the glory of the celestial is one, and the glory of the terrestrial is another. There is one glory of the sun, another glory of the moon, and another glory of the stars; for one star differs from another star in glory (1 Corinthians 15:40-41).**

The moon glory is Satan's glory, as the moon does not have any light on its own but only reflects the light from the sun. The star glory is seen only at night; the light from a star is by far less than the light of the sun. The sun glory is the manifestation of God. These three glories correspond to the three sections of the temple respectively. Just as one travels through each section of the temple, God transforms us from glory to glory:

> **But we all, with unveiled face, beholding as in a mirror the glory of the Lord, are being transformed into the same image from glory to glory, just as by the Spirit of the Lord (2 Corinthians 3:18).**

Each glory realm is increasingly greater than the previous. The Light of the first day is the supernatural light of the incorporeal world, contained in the Holy of Holies while the light of the fourth day is the light of the natural world, contained in the Holy Place. Yehoshua came into the Earth as a manifestation of the light of the first day.

Day Five: The Creatures of Sea and Air

On Day Five, God created the living creatures of the seas and the air (Genesis 1:20-23). He further blessed them to multiply:

> **And God blessed them, saying, "Be fruitful and *multiply*, and *fill the waters in the seas*, and let *birds multiply on the earth*" (Genesis 1:22).**

God created the creatures that would consume the space of the heavens and the waters which were created three days earlier on Day Two. God put the fish in the sea; the fish are symbolic of people and the sea is symbolic of humanity. God also created the birds of the air. There are two types of birds: the prophets (symbolized by eagles) and the enemy (symbolized by fowl).

The creatures of Day Five were representative of the function of the high priest. For example, the high priest was responsible for atoning for the sins (coming from the realm of Satan, or the fowl of the air) of the people (the fish of the sea). The high priest also held a prophetic office as the eagles of the air, and had the responsibility of learning the secrets behind the veil to bring restoration.

The last stop before passing beyond the veil was the golden altar of incense. In the assembly of the tabernacle, the next set of commands given to Moses was to put the golden altar of incense in the tabernacle:

> **He put the *gold altar* in the tabernacle of meeting in front of the veil; and he burned *sweet incense* on it, as the LORD had commanded Moses. He hung up the screen at the door of the tabernacle (Exodus 40:26-28).**

The altar of incense is where the high priest created the cloud of incense in *preparation* to enter through the veil into the Holy of Holies. The high priest entered the Holy of Holies covered in a cloud, where he was caught up in the presence of God. Rabbis teach that the high priest also returned from the Holy of Holies covered in a cloud. God spoke to Moses at Mount Sinai (a representation of the Holy of Holies) in the midst of a cloud (Exodus 19, 34). Yeshua went up in a cloud (Acts 1:9) and He will return the same way:

> **Then the sign of the Son of Man will appear in heaven, and then all the tribes of the earth will mourn, and they will see the Son of Man coming on the *clouds* of heaven with power and great glory (Matthew 24:30).**

> **Then they will see the Son of Man coming in the *clouds* with great power and glory (Mark 13:26).**

> **Behold, He is coming with *clouds*, and every eye will see Him, even they who pierced Him. And all the tribes of the earth will mourn because of Him. Even so, Amen (Revelation 1:7).**

Being covered in the cloud is an indication of a high priestly role and of being in the shadows or under a dark covering, alluding to the *dark sayings* of God, which are the parables and secret teachings:

> **I will open my mouth in a parable; I will utter *dark sayings* of old (Psalm 78:2).**

Yeshua has come, will come, and presently comes in a cloud. As clouds contain rain, and rain is likened to the deeper teachings of God (Deuteronomy 32:2), clouds thereby represent people who are filled with revelation of the deeper teachings of God. As such, Yeshua appears through those have learned the secrets beyond the veil.

Day Six: Man

On Day Six, the creatures on the Earth (the cattle, beasts, creeping things) and man are created (Genesis 1:24-31). God created the living creatures that would consume the substance made on Day Three (the dry land and herbs). On the sixth day, everything is created after its own kind, just as God created man in His image.

> **Then God said, "Let Us make man in Our image, according to Our likeness; let them have *dominion* over the fish of the sea, over the birds of the air, and over the cattle, over all the earth and over every creeping thing that creeps on the earth." So God created man in His own image; in the image of God He created him; male and female He created them (Genesis 1:26-27).**

God created Adam in "our image," indicating that He was speaking to His angelic host. God's nature entails both male and female, as He has the ability to impregnate and to be impregnated. Spiritually speaking, God created mankind with both male and female facets too. The male and female characteristics refer to the soulish and spiritual natures that exist in each one of us (not physical attributes). The purpose of the soulish nature is to be impregnated by the spirit nature, which is the nature of God, to birth out revelatory sons of the kingdom.

Adam was given dominion over the creatures of the Earth. To have *dominion* is *to place under one's feet,* and *to have authority*. Recall that fish are symbolic of humanity, and the birds of the air are symbolic of both prophets and of Satan. Adam therefore had authority over all of humanity and Satan's kingdom, in addition to authority and full understanding of all prophecy and revelation. The return to the garden and the glory realm entails full understanding of all divine knowledge behind the veil.

On Day Three, the grain offerings were created, and on Day Five the poor man's sacrifice was created (dove and pigeon sacrifices). It is on Day Six, however, that the sacrifices for the middle and rich classes (lambs, bulls) were created. Cain brought fruits and vegetables (a grain offering) to God, and Abel brought a meat offering, which was more pleasing to God (Genesis 4:4-5). Even though fruits and vegetables are a type of sacrifice and offering, they are not a complete sacrifice. Grain offerings do not make it into the Holy of Holies and thus do not reach the glory. A full meat sacrifice is required to completely enter into the glory. This illustration follows the pattern of Yeshua as the ultimate sacrifice on the cross. Ultimately it is the sacrifice of our own mindsets to obtain the mind of Christ (1 Corinthians 2:16).

In the construction of the tabernacle, Moses set the altar of sacrifice and brazen laver in the Outer Court, to prepare the priests to enter the tabernacle:

> **And he put the altar of burnt offering before the door of the tabernacle of the tent of meeting, and offered upon it the *burnt offering* and the *grain offering*, as the LORD had commanded Moses. He set the laver between the tabernacle of meeting and the altar, and put water there for washing and Moses, Aaron, and his sons would wash their hands and their feet with water from it. Whenever they went into the tabernacle of meeting, and when they came near the altar, they washed, as the LORD had commanded Moses (Exodus 40:29-32).**

By Day Six, everything was set in place for the priests to enter from the Outer Court into the tabernacle. While the Levitical priests were only allowed in the Holy Place, the high priest alone was allowed to continue from the Holy Place into the Holy of Holies once a year. Entering the Holy of Holies was entering into the seventh day, an eternal rest.

Day Seven: Completion and Rest

After six days of creation, all the heavens and Earth were finished and God rested:

> **Thus the heavens and the earth, and all the *host* of them, were finished. And on the seventh day God ended His work which He had done, and He *rested* on the seventh day from all His work which He had done. Then God blessed the seventh day and sanctified it, because in it He rested from all His work which God had created and made (Genesis 2:1-3).**

The word *host* is the word *tsebaah*, meaning *army, host of angels, host of the sun, stars and moons.* In ancient Hebrew, the word *tsebaah* is written צבא, where the root word, צב means *stand, wall.* The letter *tsaddik* (צ) is a picture of a man on his side, and the *bet* (ב) a picture of a tent; together, these mean "side of the tent," or a wall. Adding the letter *aleph* (א) to צב can then depict a "wall around God."

After assembling the tabernacle, Moses raised up the court all around it, paralleling the *host*, or the "wall around God."

> **And he raised up the court all around the tabernacle and the altar, and hung up the screen of the court gate. So Moses finished the work. Then the cloud covered the tabernacle of meeting, and the glory of the LORD filled the tabernacle. And Moses was not able to enter**

> **the tabernacle of meeting, because the cloud rested above it, and the glory of the LORD filled the tabernacle (Exodus 40:33-35).**

When God finished creating on the sixth day, He rested in the midst of His glorious creation. Similarly, at the end of 6000 years, His glory will fill the entire Earth in a millennial rest. As God's temple, we will be completely consumed in His glory and in a state of rest with our minds being one with His. This understanding was also believed and taught in the Early Church:

> **And the fact that it was not said of the seventh day equally with the other days, "And there was evening, and there was morning," is a distinct indication of the consummation which is to take place in it before it is finished, as the fathers declare, especially St. Clement, and Irenaeus, and Justin the Martyr..." (Justin Martyr, 100-165 AD).**

Just as the high priest was commissioned to restore the Earth when he emerged out of the Holy of Holies, we are commissioned to enter the glory realm and bring restoration back into the Earth. Yeshua tells His disciples that Elijah will come to restore all things (Matthew 17:11). Even though John the Baptist came in the spirit of Elijah, he did not restore all things. In Matthew 17, Jesus was referring to another company of God's people who will come in the spirit of Elijah to bring a final restoration (see **Elijah**). Those called to restore all things are of the royal high priestly office:

> **It is a matter of course that his forerunners must appear first, as he says by Malachi and the angel, "I will send you Elias the Tishbite before the day of the Lord...And he shall turn the hearts of the fathers to the children, and the disobedient to the wisdom of the just, lest I come and smite the earth utterly (Mal. 4:5-6). These, then, shall come and proclaim the**

> **manifestation of Christ that is to be from heaven; and they shall also perform signs and wonders, in order that men may be put to shame and turned to repentance for their surpassing wickedness and impiety (Hippolytus, *Fragments*).**

In following the pattern of the embodiment coming three days after the substance is created, it is then on Day Seven that Yehoshua dwells in His people. God is returning to His people, who are His tabernacle:

> **"Behold, I send My messenger, and he will prepare the way before Me. And the Lord, whom you seek, will suddenly come to His temple, even the Messenger of the covenant, in whom you delight. Behold, He is coming," Says the LORD of hosts (Malachi 3:1).**

> **Do you not know that you are the temple of God and that the Spirit of God dwells in you? If anyone defiles the temple of God, God will destroy him. For the temple of God is holy, which temple you are (1 Corinthians 3:16-17).**

The light of Day One, embodied in Yehoshua on Day Four (4000 years in history), will again be embodied in His people on Day Seven (the start of the Kingdom Age, beginning after 6000 years of history). After the seventh day is the eighth day, symbolic of a *new beginning*. The end will be the beginning: Genesis again. The prophet Isaiah wrote that we would know the end from the beginning:

> **Remember the former things of old, for I am God, and there is no other; I am God, and there is none like Me, declaring the end from the beginning, and from ancient times things that are not yet done, saying, 'My counsel shall stand, and I will do all My pleasure' (Isaiah 46:9-10).**

The seventh day is a day of perfection and rest because the Lord's people will have returned to the original state of glory that Adam experienced in Genesis. The perfection of Day Seven speaks of the mature and perfect mindset of God's people who fully rest in and comprehend His glory.

New Beginnings

Following the seventh day is the eighth day, which is back to the first day – a new beginning. Barnabas, the disciple of Paul, writes:

> **"And God made in six days the works of His hands, and made an end on the seventh day, and rested on it, and sanctified it." . . . This implieth that the Lord will finish all things in six thousand years, for a day is with Him a thousand years. . . . Therefore, my children, in six days, that is, in six thousand years, all things will be finished. "And He rested on the seventh day." This meaneth: when His Son, coming [again], shall destroy the time of the wicked man, and judge the ungodly, and change the sun, and the moon, and the stars, then shall He truly rest on the seventh day. Moreover, He says, "Thou shalt sanctify it with clean hands and a pure heart" (*Epistle of Barnabas*, Chapter 15).**

Barnabas clearly depicts that the sun, moon, and stars will be changed on the seventh day. God will sanctify the Earth by first sanctifying His people. He will remove all iniquity (twisted teaching) and bring righteousness (right teaching and understanding) for His people to be sanctified, who in turn will sanctify the whole Earth. Barnabas further writes:

> **". . . I shall make a beginning of the eighth day, that is, a beginning of another world. Wherefore, also, we**

> **keep the eighth day with joyfulness, the day also on which Jesus rose again from the dead" (*Epistle of Barnabas*, Chapter 15).**

The eighth day, the day of new beginnings and a new world (or age), is the day that Yeshua ascended. Ascension is directly linked to illumination with learning the revelations of God. Thus, the new beginning comes with going beyond the veil and learning the secrets and mysteries of the kingdom.

The Light

On the first day, God spoke light into existence.

> **Then God said, "Let there be *light;*" and there was light (Genesis 1:3).**

The word *light* is the word *owr,* meaning *lightning, happiness, morning, sun, light of the day, light of heavenly luminaries (moon, sun, stars).* In ancient Hebrew, the word *owr* is written 𐤀𐤅𐤓, whose letters can be read together as "the mind connected to the apostolic teaching," or having the mind of Christ. God desires an ox sacrifice, the sacrifice for the rich class – the kingly sacrifice. *Owr* also means a *lamp*, and it is the root to the word *menorah*. The menorah is the seven churches in the Book of Revelation:

> **The mystery of the seven stars which you saw in My right hand, and the *seven golden lampstands*: the seven stars are the angels of the seven churches, and the *seven lampstands* which you saw are the *seven churches* (Revelation 1:20).**

When God said, "Let there be light," He spoke into existence the churches that would carry the light of creation – the divine light with the ability to bring full life into the Earth. The menorah – His Church – was created to house His presence.

Face to Face

The word *light* also pertains to *prosperity, instruction, one's face (face of God)*. When God takes the light out of darkness, we will be in the face-to-face realm with God – the same realm that Moses experienced and also that which Paul speaks of below:

> **For now we see in a mirror, dimly, but then *face to face.* Now I know in part, but then I shall know just as I also am known (1 Corinthians 13:12).**

Paul writes that we will see as in a mirror, but in the time of his writing to the Corinthian Church, there were no glass mirrors like those used today. The water of the brazen laver in the Outer Court was the means by which people could most clearly see their reflections. The water is the revelation of God. To look into the brazen laver is to look into the Word of God and see the purpose of the revealed Word in us, the hope of glory (Colossians 1:27).

The brazen laver sat on twelve oxen (1 Kings 7:23-25), indicative of an apostolic foundation. Thus, the Word of God sits on apostolic teachings – the teachings of Yeshua and the Early Church. Receiving instruction from the apostles is seeing the Father face to face. Rabbis teach that the face of God shines brighter than 1000 suns. The sun, created on the fourth day, is only a dim reflection of the Light of God, created on the first day.

The face to face realm is that of the glory in the Holy of Holies, from which the eternal light comes. When Moses came down from Mount Sinai – the Holy of Holies – he brought the light with him:

> **So when Aaron and all the children of Israel saw Moses, behold, the skin of his face *shone*, and they were afraid to come near him (Exodus 34:30).**
>
> His face shone such that the people were afraid. The word *shone* is the word *qaran*, and actually means *to grow horns.* Moses' shining face indicates his apostolic nature after his face-to-face encounter with God. The word *qaran* is written in ancient Hebrew, [ancient Hebrew glyphs], whose letters *nun* ([glyph], *sprout*), *resh* ([glyph], *mind*), and *kuf* ([glyph], *light gathered at the horizon*), can be read as "sprouting a mind of light." Moses came out of the Holy of Holies with a mind of light – the mind of Christ. Moses' face-to-face encounter with God induced a complete character change into the nature of God, who is the source of the eternal light.

The word *light* (*owr*) also means *order, box, gather*. Light brings order into the void and chaos. Paul speaks about bringing *order* into the Church when he writes, "**Let all things be done decently and in *order***" (1 Corinthians 14:40). The light – revelation of God's deeper teachings – brings *order* and terminates *confusion*. Hence, Paul speaks of all things being done in the revelation of the kingdom mysteries. Even upon entering the tabernacle, the priests had to cleanse themselves. This priestly cleansing, though in the natural, extends to mindsets and thoughts, which had to be in *order*.

Just as the Holy Spirit hovered over the waters (Genesis 1:2), the Holy Spirit also hovered over Mary (Luke 1:35), and the same voice that spoke "Let there be light" in the beginning of creation spoke the Light into Mary. God released His creative Word into Mary, and she became the matrix of the Light of Genesis 1. The Word of God is also His seed, so the Holy Spirit impregnated Mary with the divine seed and DNA of the Father. The Word then became flesh:

> **And the Word became flesh and dwelt among us, and we beheld His glory, the glory as of the only begotten of the Father, full of grace and truth (John 1:14).**

In Hebrew thought, the mind is also considered the womb. When the Father imparts His Word into our minds, He impregnates us with His seed which is meant to be birthed out and manifested in the flesh.

The Light of the New Jerusalem

Light is hidden in darkness. The light on the first day of creation is a spiritual, supernatural light, which is the same light in the New Jerusalem. In the Book of Revelation, the New Jerusalem has no need for a sun, for the Lord is the source of light.

> **There shall be *no night* there [the New Jerusalem]: They need no lamp nor light of the sun, for the Lord God gives them *light*. And they shall reign forever and ever (Revelation 22:5).**

The New Jerusalem is the Holy of Holies, the garden of Eden. God's people will not just return to the garden - they will actually become it. God's return into His children indicates that they will become the light, thereby resulting in no need for any other source of light. His people are called to become the New Jerusalem.

The Outer Court of the temple, having no covering, is lit by the sun; natural light is representative of natural understanding. The Outer Court is also marked by time. Passing through the temple from the Outer Court to the Holy Place to the Holy of Holies does away with time. The Outer Court must pass away because time has to stop for *eternity*. The glory realm is God, and in Him there is no time. As Barker points out, the Holy of Holies "was also beyond time. To enter was to enter eternity" (Barker, 1988).

The sections of the temple clearly represent different *times*. The progression from the east to west is a progression through the ages and the divine plan of God (see **Temple Theology**). The surface area of the hangings surrounding the **Outer Court** is 1500 cubits squared. The time between Moses receiving Torah to Yeshua's First Coming was 1500 years. The volume of the **Holy Place** is 2000 cubits cubed. The time from Yeshua coming to the Earth to present time is 2000 years (the Church Age). The volume of the **Holy of Holies** is 1000 cubits cubed. The millennial reign is 1000 years (the Kingdom Age). The Holy of Holies is a perfect cube (10 x 10 x 10 cubits cubed). The New Jerusalem is also a perfect cube (12,000 x 12,000 x 12,000 furlongs cubed):

> **The city is laid out as a square; its length is as great as its breadth. And he measured the city with the reed: twelve thousand furlongs. Its length, breadth, and height are equal (Revelation 21:16).**

The Holy of Holies is a pattern and scale model of the New Jerusalem. Not only does the New Jerusalem have no need for a sun, but it has no need for a physical temple, because God, the Lamb, and His people become the temple:

> **But I saw no temple in it, for the Lord God Almighty and the Lamb are its temple (Revelation 21:22).**

God used the tabernacle as a pattern of creation to show the way back into the garden of Eden, the habitation of God's glory. The light of Yah in the glory realm is the light of Genesis 1 which was hidden in the darkness. The high priest had to pass through the Holy Place which was lit by the light of the menorah (symbolic of the anointing in the Church Age). From there the high priest went through the veil and into the Holy of Holies which is symbolic of the New Jerusalem and has the eternal light of glory.

This eternal light of Day One is Yehoshua. Salvation was already established before the foundation of the world, but it takes a *revelation* of salvation, a revelation of Yehoshua himself, for Him to manifest. It was by His going to the cross and becoming the Tree of Life that the *void*, the *tohu*, was filled. In the same manner, we also become the same eternal light of Genesis 1 by returning to and becoming the Tree of Life in the garden.

The Tree of Knowledge is the Word of God; the Tree is Torah. Yeshua is the vine, and we are the branches (John 15:5). The Tree bears leaves and fruit, where the leaves are for the healing of the nations:

> **In the middle of its street, and on either side of the river, was the tree of life, which bore twelve fruits, each tree yielding its fruit every month. The *leaves* of the tree were for the *healing of the nations* (Revelation 22:2).**

If there is no healing in the Church, then there is no connection to the source. Likewise, if we produce no fruit, we are not connected to the source. The tree from which Adam and Eve ate was the Tree of Life, the almighty God Himself. In the garden, God came to Adam and Eve in the cool of the day:

> **And they heard the sound of the LORD God walking in the garden in the *cool* of the day, and Adam and his wife hid themselves from the presence of the LORD God among the trees of the garden (Genesis 3:8).**

The word *cool* in Hebrew is *ruach*, which is the breath of God. The breath also symbolizes the character, which is the very genetic code, or the DNA. Walking in the cool (breath) of the day indicates that God's character makes up all of matter. Adam and Eve were constantly infused with His genetic structure, but when they ate of the wrong tree, their genetic structure changed. When God asked Adam, "Where are you?"

(Genesis 3:9), God was inquiring about Adam's change in character due to a change in genetics by impartation of the wrong seed (see **War of Seeds**). The word *genesis* comes from the word *genea* meaning *generation*, which comes from the word *genos*, meaning *genes*. So, Genesis is about the *genes*. Genesis is the first of the five parts of the *ketubah*, the marriage covenant, which outlines the genetic history of the bride and bridegroom (see **The Marriage Covenant**).

Dividing the Darkness and the Night

> **And God saw the light, that it was good; and God *divided* the light from the *darkness* (Genesis 1:4).**

The word *divided* is the word *badal*, meaning *to separate, distinguish, differ, select*. In ancient Hebrew, *badal* is written . The root to the word *badal* is *bad*, written , meaning *separate*, *alone*, *destruction*, which is also the root to the name *Abaddon* (the death angel). To *divide* means to *know something perfectly*. Division occurs with correct understanding. The division that takes place is that between the spirit and soul – between Adam and Eve. As the male is representative of the spirit and the female the soul, correct understanding – righteousness – separates the spirit from the soul, the latter of which is governed by emotion. Eve was *separated* from the side of Adam.

> **Then the rib which the LORD God had taken from man He made into a woman, and He brought her to the man. And Adam said: "This is now bone of my bones and flesh of my flesh; She shall be called Woman, because she was taken out of Man" (Genesis 2:22-23).**

Eve, a type of the soulish nature, became separated from Adam, the spirit nature. Eve was the rib separated. The menorah is a picture of a spinal column with ribs, as well as a tree with branches. Eve is representative of the Church – a rib that originally extended from the spinal column but later became separated. Like Eve, the Jews are a broken off rib. However, Paul writes that we have been grafted back in:

> **You will say then, "Branches were broken off that I might be grafted in." Well said. Because of unbelief they were broken off, and you stand by faith. Do not be haughty, but fear (Romans 11:19-20).**

Unbelief is the cause of being broken off, or being separated. Standing by faith – believing the Word of God, the Torah – opens the way for an engrafting back into the Tree, which is Torah. Paul cautions the Romans not to be haughty but to *fear*, which is associated with learning the secrets of the Lord (Psalm 25:14, see **Secrets**). Through learning the revelation of God, we will be engrafted back into the Tree of Life.

God divided the light from the darkness (Genesis 1:4). *Darkness* is the word *choshek*, meaning *dark, misery, destruction, death, ignorance, sorrow, wickedness, night, obscurity, a secret place*. Through the definition of *darkness*, ignorance is associated with death. As sin is ignorance of Torah (see **The Mystery of *Torah***), ignorance of Torah then leads to death. Darkness is associated with the night, during which stars are visible. Yehoshua is the Light of the world (John 8:12). When He left, the Earth came into darkness, a state in which it is impossible to sustain life. The Church has been in *darkness* for 2000 years (the Church Age), a time of a star glory – the realm of the Holy Place. The word *chosek* comes from the word *chashak*, which means *withholding light, black, darkness, dim, hide*. Paul writes that we see *dimly* in a mirror for now (1 Corinthians 13:12), further indicating a state of darkness. After God divided the light from the darkness, He called the light *day* and the darkness *night*:

> **God called the light Day, and the darkness He called *Night*. So the evening and the morning were the first day (Genesis 1:5).**

The word *night* is the word *layil*, written in ancient Hebrew, ᒍ>ᒧᒍ, where the root word ᒍᒍ pictorially looks like a *scroll*. The Ancient Hebrew Lexicon Bible defines the word *layil* in the following way: "When the night comes, the night sky is rolled out like a scroll. When daylight comes, the night sky is rolled up like a scroll." Isaiah writes:

> **All the host of heaven shall be dissolved, and the *heavens shall be rolled up* like a *scroll*; all their host shall fall down as the leaf falls from the vine, and as fruit falling from a fig tree (Isaiah 34:4).**

When daylight comes – when we enter the eternal light of the glory realm – the night season is rolled up and done away with. This will mark the end of the Church Age and the beginning of the Millennial Kingdom. The night is the time of sleep; thus, the Church has been asleep, or dead, instead of doing the work.

> **I must work the works of Him who sent Me while it is day; the *night* is coming when no one can work (John 9:4).**

However, the eternal light brings resurrection and eternal life. The word *layil* comes from the word *luwl*, written in ancient Hebrew, ᒍYᒍ, which means *spiral step, winding stair*. A spiraling staircase is a picture of Jacob's ladder, the portal to pierce the veil into the Holy of Holies.

Jacob's Ladder

Jacob laid his head on the rock and saw angels ascending and descending on a *spiraling staircase*:

> **So he came to a certain place and stayed there all night, because the sun had set. And he took one of**

the stones of that place and put it at his head, and he lay down in that place to sleep. Then he dreamed, and behold, a ladder was set up on the earth, and its top reached to heaven; and there the angels of God were ascending and descending on it (Genesis 28:11-12).

The place of revelation is the stairway to heaven. Rabbis teach that the staircase contained 72 rungs on which were inscribed the 72 names of God. The spiraling staircase is also a picture of a DNA strand, and so the staircase that Jacob saw was the very Word of God. It is with God's DNA, His character and function, that ascension into the Holy of Holies is accessible.

The angelic beings, illustrative of those who ascend when the secret teachings are revealed to them, have the ability to roll and unroll the scrolls, or bring revelation and glory back to the Earth. The place where Jacob laid his head is the place of access to the Holy of Holies. The angels ascended and descended, illustrative of the high priest entering the Holy of Holies and coming back out with the glory. God desires for His people to access what He created before the foundations of the world and bring it back down the ladder – back through His Word. God calls for us to bring the hidden heavenly elements that were established before the foundations back down to the Earth to manifest restoration. But it first takes a revelation (an ascension up the ladder) to bring about the manifestation.

The same eternal light created on Day One is the light that guided the Hebrews through the wilderness.

> **And the Angel of God, who went before the camp of Israel, moved and went behind them; and the pillar of cloud went from before them and stood behind them. So it came between the camp of the Egyptians and the camp of Israel. Thus it was a cloud and *darkness* to the**

> **one, and it gave *light* by night to the other, so that the one did not come near the other all that night (Exodus 14:19-20).**

A theophanic Angel led the Hebrews out of Egypt. The darkness of Genesis 1 was the same darkness to the Egyptians but to the Hebrews it was light. This is the same light and darkness in which God hides Himself. When the Angel stepped in to guide the children of Israel, heaven stepped in. This was not an earthly event – the Angel placed heaven between God's children and the Egyptians. Egypt, meaning "to limit God," was ruled by Pharaoh, whose name means "double-minded." So those who are double-minded will always be in darkness, and they will be unstable in all their ways (James 1:8).

Stepping Over the Grave

Prior to God calling forth the light, the darkness is associated with the grave. Job writes:

> **If I wait for the *grave* as my house, if I make my bed in the *darkness*, if I say to corruption, 'You are my father,' and to the worm, 'You are my mother and my sister…' (Job 17:13-14).**

The grave is a place of darkness, where there is no light or illumination. As illumination is directly connected to Early Church baptism of the secret teachings, those in darkness have no revelation of the kingdom. Those living in the darkness live in corruption. The fathers of corruption are false teachers who operate in darkness and put people in the grave through dead teachings.

> **The *thief* does not come except to *steal*, and to *kill*, and to *destroy*. I have come that they may have life, and that they may have it more abundantly (John 10:10).**

The word *thief* is a name given to "false teachers, who do not care to instruct men, but abuse their confidence for their own gain" (Thayer, 1889). There are those in the Church who, through false teachings, steal, kill, and destroy. The word *destroy* is the word *apollumi*, which is directly related to the name *Apollyon*, the angel of destruction. There are teachers who are used by this angel to bring destruction through false teachings. Apollyon comes from the bottomless pit, a place of no revelation or deeper understanding. In the Book of Revelation, the harlot rides the beast into the bottomless pit. The harlot, which is the Church without correct teachings, will spend eternity in a place of no light if she does not turn away from twisted teachings and false understanding.

Paul wrote to Timothy about incorruption coming to *light*:

> **...but has now been revealed by the appearing of our Savior Jesus Christ, who has abolished death and brought *life* and *immortality* to *light* through the gospel (2 Timothy 1:10).**

What Paul writes about is a mystery of resurrection and eternal life.

> **Behold, I tell you a *mystery*: We shall not all *sleep*, but we shall all be changed—in a moment, in the twinkling of an eye, at the last trumpet. For the trumpet will sound, and the dead will be raised *incorruptible*, and we shall be *changed*. For this corruptible must put on *incorruption*, and this mortal must put on *immortality* (1 Corinthians 15:51-53).**

The Early Church taught that the first resurrection occurred when one received the first revelation of the secrets of God. The second resurrection was the coming into the glorified body in the Holy of Holies, the New Jerusalem. *Resurrection* is the *reestablishment of spiritual truth*. God established stages of resurrection and glory, and we are transformed from glory to glory (1 Corinthians 15:41-42). Our ascension from glory to glory is a progressive waning of darkness, as we move away from false understanding and come into perfection, maturity and right understanding.

> **He setteth an *end to darkness*, and searcheth out all *perfection*: the stones of darkness, and the shadow of death (KJV, Job 28:3).**

The end to darkness is perfection. Everything in darkness will come into the light, which brings *order* and *restoration*. God's ultimate purpose is not to destroy but to *restore*. In the first of the Forgotten Books of Eden, God tells Eve:

> **For I am God the Creator, who, when I created My creatures, *did not intend to destroy them*. But after they had sorely roused My anger, I punished them with grievous plagues, until they repent. But, if on the contrary, they still continue hardened in their transgression, they shall be under a curse for ever (First Book of Adam and Eve, 6:9-10).**

Our powerful Yah's ultimate purpose is to restore His Church from the darkness (blindness and wrong understanding) back into the light, which is the true revelation of who He is and His divine plan. The restoration comes by learning His deeper teachings. When the light enters our minds, we come out of darkness, or come out of the grave:

> **When His *lamp* shone upon my head, and when by His *light* I walked through *darkness* (Job 29:3).**

The word *lamp* is the word *nerah*, sharing the same root as the word *menorah*. The head is the place of the mind – the place where the ark of the covenant resides. The word *shone* is the word *halal*, meaning *praise, glory, celebrate.* In ancient Hebrew, *halal* is written 𐤄𐤋𐤋, where the root word 𐤄𐤋 means *toward.* The letter *lamed* (𐤋) is the shepherd's staff representing the notion of going *toward* something, since the staff was used to move sheep toward a direction; it is also representative of *teaching* and *authority.* The letter *hey* (𓀠) is representative of *revelation* or *understanding.* Interestingly, the word ᒍᒍ means *night.* Understanding or having revelation of the *night* – the darkness of incomplete truth and false teaching that leads one to the grave – is a cause for *praise, glory, and celebration.*

When the Church steps out of darkness, it experiences resurrection from the grave. Those who have the revelation of stepping out of darkness and into the divine order of the light of Day One will indeed step over the grave into the eternal, glorified state that Adam once had in the garden. This is the glorious state to which Yah desires to restore His people:

> **But these filthy garments, which have been put by you on all who have become Christians by the name of Jesus, God shows shall be taken away from us, when He shall raise all men from the dead, and appoint some to be incorruptible, immortal, and free from sorrow in the everlasting and imperishable kingdom; but shall send others away to the everlasting punishment of fire (Justin Martyr, *Dialogue with Trypho*).**

The Garden

God established the garden of Eden during the creation process in Genesis. Adam and Eve dwelt in the garden until they ate of the wrong seed from the Tree of Knowledge of Good and Evil. After the fall, God separated them from the garden and placed two cherubim to guard the way back into the garden:

> **So He drove out the man; and He placed cherubim at the *east* of the garden of Eden, and a *flaming sword***

> **which turned every way, to guard the way to the tree of life (Genesis 3:24).**

The Early Church taught that the Holy of Holies was Eden. The cherubim are placed at the *east* of the garden. The temple was entered from the east side, and one proceeded westward from the Outer Court into the Holy Place and finally into the Holy of Holies. A river flows from Eden and waters the garden (Genesis 2:10), and a river of living water flows from the throne of God (Revelation 22:1) as well as from those who believe God's Word (John 7:38). The two cherubim on the curtains of the Holy of Holies are direct images of the cherubim guarding the way back into Eden.

To enter into the glory, one must pass the *flaming sword*. The word *flaming* is the word *lahat*, written in ancient Hebrew, **⊗𓀠ᒍ**. The root word *lat*, **⊗ᒍ**, consists of the letters *tet* (**⊗**), a basket meaning *contained* or *hidden*, and lamed (**ᒍ**), a staff meaning *authority* or *teaching*. **⊗ᒍ** can be read as "authority contained or hidden," and also means *cover, veil, secret, a covering that covers and hides one's face*. The letter *hey* (**𓀠**) is indicative of *revelation*, so the word **⊗𓀠ᒍ** can be read, "teachings of revelation that are hidden," or secrets and mysteries. In fact, the Ancient Hebrew Lexicon Bible's definition of *lahat* is *secret.*

The *flaming sword* is thus *veiled secrets*. Dominion and authority are contained within the secrets and must be uncovered. As Solomon writes in Proverbs:

> **It is the glory of God to *conceal* a matter, but the glory of kings is to *search out* a matter (Proverbs 25:2).**

God calls us to be kings and priests (Exodus 19:6, 1 Peter 2:9, Revelation 1:6, 5:10), meaning that we are to search out the secrets of the kingdom (see **Royal Priesthood**). The secrets are in Eden, the Holy of Holies, so when the high priest entered the Holy of Holies, he entered Eden. What Adam lost as the first high priest, Yeshua redeemed - He made a way for us to step back into the royal priesthood in order to restore the Earth. Upon the reestablishment of the high priesthood, both healing and judgment are then released on the Earth. The next move of God is the reestablishment of the king priests who carry the apostolic and prophetic office and will restore, judge, and teach all who desire a deeper relationship with Yehoshua behind the veil. But it all starts with the revelation of the Word:

> **And then a teacher, to train and guide the soul to all requisite knowledge when it is made able to admit the revelation of the Word. Eagerly desiring, then, to perfect us by a gradation conducive to salvation, suited for efficacious discipline, a beautiful arrangement is observed by the all-benignant Word, who first exhorts, then trains and finally teaches (Clement, *The Instructor*).**

The word *lahat* (𐤋𐤄𐤈) also means *burning, fire*. The way back into the garden is through the <u>fire of God</u>. The secrets are the foundations and level field (see **Secrets**). The Lord will not reveal His glory until the foundations are laid. The apostles, who are also foundations of the Church, build upon the *sod*, or secrets of the kingdom.

Reading the Scripture in the Hebrew reveals imperative elements missed in translations of the Bible into other languages. In reading Genesis 3:24 in the original Hebrew language, one finds a particular word which has no direct translation in other languages and is therefore left out of translated Bibles. This word appears three times: once after the word "Eden," once after the word "cherubim," and once after the word "guard." This word is *et*, written in ancient Hebrew, 𐤀𐤕. The word *et* is composed of the first and last letters of the Hebrew Aleph-Bet, which is God Himself, who is the first and the last (Isaiah 44:6, 48:12, Revelation 1:8, 17-18, 21:6-7, 22:13).

This word has the same spelling for *owth*, meaning *mark, sign, destination* – the same mark that God makes on those who understand His divine plan and have His divine love (see **Circumcision & The Mark**). Understanding His plan entails having the *sod* level understanding of His Word, whereby *sod* means both *secret* and *intimacy* (see **Secrets**). The word *et* can be replaced with *Yehoshua*, who is the mark and the sign. This word is actually found all throughout Scripture just as Yehoshua was interspersed all throughout the Torah long before He physically came to Earth. So, Genesis 3:24 can be read:

> **So He drove out the man; and He placed [Yehoshua] cherubim at the east of the garden of Eden [Yehoshua], and a flaming sword which turned every way, to guard [Yehoshua] the way to the tree of life (Genesis 3:24).**

These cherubim are Yehoshua's cherubim – His messengers of secrets. The garden of Eden is Yehoshua, and the way to the Tree of Life is through Yehoshua. There is power in understanding God's original language (see **Hebrew Foundations**) which reveals secrets of Yehoshua that would never otherwise be revealed in current translations and versions of the Bible. Revelation of Yeshua extends beyond merely seeing things hidden in His Word. These revelations are manifestations of truth, which are alive and have the ability to bring life. The Word of God is living and active (Hebrews 4:12). His Word is the life-containing and life-producing *rhema* Word that holds the power to create just as it did in the beginning. It is God's desire to teach His children how to also operate in creation through the manifestation of revelation.

The Glory

When Adam and Eve dwelt in the garden, they were immersed in the glory and were able to see and interact with the heavens.

> **And Adam said to Eve, "Look at thine *eyes*, and at mine, which afore beheld angels in heaven, praising; and they, too, without ceasing. But now we do not see as we did:**

> **our *eyes have become of flesh*; they *cannot see in like manner as they saw before*." Adam said again to Eve, "*What is our body today*, compared to what it was in *former days*, when we *dwelt in the garden*?" (First Book of Adam and Eve, 4:8-10).**

Before the fall, Adam and Eve had eyes to see into the heavens and had direct access to the Father. After the fall, the ability to see into the heavens ceased because their eyes became fleshly. Adam compared the state of their bodies after the fall to that of before the fall, signifying a change in the physical state of being. After the fall, Adam and Eve lost their glorified, heavenly (angelic) bodies and instead had carnal, earthly bodies:

> **Then Adam wept and said, "O God, when we dwelt in the garden, and our *hearts were lifted up*, we saw the angels that sang praises in heaven, but now *we do not see as we were used to do*; nay, when we entered the cave, all creation became *hidden* from us" (First Book of Adam and Eve, 8:1).**

The phrase "our hearts were lifted up" can also be read as "our *minds* were lifted up," since in Hebrew thought the *mind* is the place of emotion and thereby interchangeable with the *heart*. Their minds were lifted up, or enlightened, when they dwelt in the garden. The enlightened state is the same enlightened state of one who has learned the mysteries and secret teachings of the kingdom. It is the state of living in the Holy of Holies – the garden – where one has continuous intimacy with God, paralleling the Early Church teaching that to enter the Holy of Holies was to enter the garden.

> **Then God the Lord said unto Adam, "When thou wast under subjection to Me, thou hadst a *bright nature within thee*, and for that reason couldst thou see things afar off. But *after thy transgression thy bright nature was withdrawn from thee*; and it was not left to thee to see**

> **things afar off, but only near at hand; after the *ability of the flesh*; for it is brutish" (First Book of Adam and Eve, 8:2).**

The *bright nature* is the glory that Adam and Eve lost after the fall. The fact that this bright nature was *within* Adam and Eve further delineates that the Holy of Holies – the garden and the glory of the kingdom – is *within* God's people. After the glory was removed, Adam and Eve (and the rest of humanity) were no longer able see into the heavenly realm, and creation became hidden from them. What they could see was only "near at hand," or things in the earthly realm. But God desires for us to return to the garden, and by returning to the garden we become the garden. Solomon writes of Yeshua pursuing His Bride the garden:

> **A *garden* enclosed is my sister, my spouse, a spring shut up, a fountain sealed. . . . Awake, O north wind, and come, O south! Blow upon my *garden*, that its spices may flow out. Let my beloved come to his *garden* and eat its pleasant *fruits* (Songs of Solomon 4:12, 16).**

The spices of which Solomon speaks are also in the altar of incense, which sits in front of the veil leading into the Holy of Holies. The altar of incense is the last stop before passing beyond the veil into His glory. However, there must be understanding of God's original intention of restoration in order to obtain access behind the veil. Even understanding the Hebrew hermeneutics of the four levels of interpretation – *p'shat, remez, d'rash,* and *sod* – brings us back to the garden (see **Hebrew Foundations**). When we understand the four dimensions of God's Word, we enter *paradise* – we return back to the garden, where God desires to restore all of humanity.

Chapter Six

Eyes to See & Ears to Hear

So by illumination must darkness disappear. The darkness is ignorance, through which we fall into sins and purblind as to the truth. Knowledge, then, is the illumination we receive, which makes ignorance disappear, and endows us with clear vision.

Clement
153-215 A.D.

The Recurring Message

A recurring theme is found throughout the Old and New Testaments: the people do not have eyes to see or ears to hear. This message is not directed to unbelievers, but to the Church.

In Deuteronomy 29, Moses grieved over the people not having eyes to see or ears to hear:

> **And Moses called unto all Israel, and said unto them, Ye have seen all that the LORD did before your eyes in the land of Egypt unto Pharaoh, and unto all his servants, and unto all his land; The great temptations which thine eyes have seen, the signs, and those great miracles: Yet the LORD hath not given you an *heart to perceive*, and *eyes to see*, and *ears to hear*, unto this day (KJV, Deuteronomy 29:2-4).**

The Hebrews saw great signs and wonders in Egypt, coming out of Egypt, and while traveling in the wilderness. They witnessed the Egyptians being tormented by the ten plagues while they were untouched (Exodus 7:14-11:10). They saw the great and terrible Passover during which their own firstborn children were spared because they marked their doors with the blood of the lamb (Exodus 12:29). They experienced being led by a cloud during the day and fire during the night as they departed Egypt (Exodus 13:21-22, 14:19-20), the great parting of the Red Sea (Exodus 14:21-22), and the supernatural daily provision of manna that fell from heaven (Exodus 16:13-14). They witnessed the great appearance of Yahweh at the foot of Mount Sinai and watched Moses ascend the mountain to converse with Yahweh (Exodus 19:16-20). The Hebrews saw numerous signs and wonders, but they still did not perceive God's true message to them.

> **And I have led you forty years in the wilderness: your clothes are not waxen old upon you, and thy shoe is not waxen old upon thy foot. Ye have not eaten bread, neither have ye drunk wine or strong drink: that ye might know that I am the LORD your God (KJV, Deuteronomy 29:5-6).**

The same message that grieved Moses was also given to Isaiah:

> **In the year that king Uzziah died I saw also the Lord sitting upon a throne, high and lifted up, and his train filled the temple. Above it stood the seraphims: each one had six wings; with twain he covered his face, and with twain he covered his feet, and with twain he did fly. And one cried unto another, and said, Holy, holy, holy, is the LORD of hosts: the whole earth is full of his glory. And the posts of the door moved at the voice of him that cried, and the house was filled with smoke. Then said I, woe is me! For I am undone; because I am a man of *unclean lips*, and I dwell in the midst of a people of *unclean***

> **_lips_: for mine eyes have seen the King, the LORD of hosts (KJV, Isaiah 6:1-5).**

Isaiah realized that he was impure and with unclean lips before God. The word *unclean* is the Hebrew word *tame*, meaning *unclean, defiled, polluted.* Out of one's lips come messages and teachings, so unclean lips signify defiled and twisted teaching and understanding.

Uncleanliness

In the Book of Matthew, Yeshua associates the Pharisees with uncleanliness:

> **Woe to you, scribes and Pharisees, _hypocrites_! For you cleanse the outside of the cup and dish, but inside they are full of extortion and self-indulgence. Blind Pharisee, first _cleanse_ the inside of the cup and dish, that the outside of them may be _clean_ also (Matthew 23:25-26).**

The word *clean* is the Greek word *katharos* (note the similarity to the word *catharsis*), which not only means *physically clean*, but also *free from sin and every mixture of what is false.* As sin is missing the mark (not fully understanding the Torah), being clean speaks of correctly understanding Torah.

> **Then flew one of the seraphims unto me, having a live _coal_ in his hand, which he had taken with the tongs from off the altar: And he laid it upon my mouth, and said, Lo, this hath touched thy lips; and thine _iniquity_ is taken away, and thy _sin_ purged. Also I heard the voice of the Lord, saying, Whom shall I send, and who will go for us? Then said I, Here am I; send me (KJV, Isaiah 6:6-8).**

The coal that touched Isaiah's lips is symbolic of revelatory teaching. The coal came from the altar of incense, the last stop before entering the Holy of Holies. This signifies that before entering the glory we must understand the message. The word *iniquity* in Hebrew is *avon*, coming from the word *avah*, meaning *to twist, distort. Iniquity* is thereby *twisted teaching*. Once the coal – revelation – touches the lips, the twisted teaching begins to come undone.

Iniquity and the Eye

In ancient Hebrew, *avon* is written ᓭYY8. The letter *ghah* (8) is a twisted rope and means *twisted, dark, evil.* The letter *ghah* (8) is actually the negative version of the letter *ayin* (◎), the watchful eye, which means *to know, watch*. If *ayin* is a watchful eye, *ghah* is an *evil eye*. Since *iniquity*, or *avon*, means *twisted teaching*, having twisted teaching or understanding causes one to have an evil eye. In fact, rabbis associate the eye with human inclination. The *yeitzer ha-ra* is known as the 'evil eye,' or the 'evil inclination,' that prompts one to act wickedly. Yeshua told His disciples:

> **And if thine *eye offend* thee, pluck it out: it is better for thee to enter into the kingdom of God with one eye, than having two eyes to be cast into hell fire (KJV, Mark 9:47).**

The word *eye* in Greek is *ophthalmos*, whose equivalent in Hebrew is *ayin*, the watchful eye. The word *offend* in Greek is *skandalizo*, which means *to cause to fall away, to cause a person to distrust and desert one whom he ought to trust and obey.* The Hebrew equivalent of *skandalizo* is the word *kashal*, which means *to totter, waver, topple, ruin.* Yeshua did not mean for the disciples to physically gouge out their eyeballs if an immoral thought or action followed from observing something by sight. As He spoke in parables (Matthew 13:34), He was actually telling His disciples that faulty understanding (an evil eye, or twisted teaching) would eventually ruin them, and that they were to gouge out the false teaching such that their eyes would be good, watchful, and perceiving – so that they would have correct understanding.

Being rid of false teaching makes one *righteous*. The Hebrew word for *righteous* is the word *tsaddiyq*, meaning *just, lawful*, and comes from the word *tsadaq*, which means *to be straight, to bring justice in administering the law.* One who brings justice in the law must be somebody with correct or right understanding. The word for *law* in Hebrew is *Torah*. When one transitions from a faulty understanding of the Torah to the way that God intended for it to be understood (in the spiritual interpretation rather than in the natural), one is considered to be made righteous. *Being righteous is correctly understanding and interpreting God's Word.*

The same message God gave to Moses was given also to Isaiah: Tell the people they do not have eyes to see or ears to hear. Isaiah answered the call...

> **And he said, Go, and tell this people, Hear ye indeed, but understand not; and see ye indeed, but perceive not. Make the heart of this people *fat*, and make their ears *heavy*, and *shut* their eyes; lest they see with their eyes, and hear with their ears, and understand with their heart, and *convert*, and be *healed* (KJV, Isaiah 6:9-10).**

The same message that the people did not have eyes to see or ears to hear continued on to Jeremiah:

> **Hear this now, O foolish people, without understanding, who have eyes and see not, and who have ears and hear not (Jeremiah 5:21).**

Ezekiel was also told that the people neither see nor hear due to rebellion:

> **Son of man, thou dwellest in the midst of a *rebellious* house, which have eyes to see, and *see not*; they have ears to hear, and *hear not*: for they are a *rebellious* house (KJV, Ezekiel 12:2).**

The word *rebellious* is the Hebrew word *meriy*, which also means *bitterness*. The root word *mar* means *bitter, weak, trickle*. The word *mar* is written in ancient Hebrew, 𐤌𐤓, where the *mem* (𐤌, *water*) and *resh* (𐤓, *head*) mean "water head," or headwaters, where there is little to no flow. Those who do not learn the deeper teachings of God have little to no flowing water – revelation – in them. Stagnant water that does not flow out becomes bitter and undrinkable. To remain blind and deaf to the secrets of the kingdom is to be bitter and in rebellion.

Throughout Scripture, every prophet warns the people that they do not have eyes to see or ears to hear. In the Book of Matthew, Yeshua refers to Isaiah's prophecy:

> **He answered and said unto them, Because it is given unto you to know the *mysteries* of the kingdom of heaven, but to them it is not given. For whosoever hath, to him shall be given, and he shall have more abundance: but whosoever hath not, from him shall be taken away even that he hath. Therefore speak I to them in *parables*: because they seeing *see not*; and hearing they *hear not*, neither do they *understand*. And in them is fulfilled the *prophecy of Esaias*, which saith, By hearing ye shall hear, and shall not understand; and seeing ye shall see, and shall not perceive: For this people's heart is *waxed gross*, and their ears are dull of hearing, and their eyes they have closed; lest at any time they should *see* with their *eyes*, and *hear* with their *ears*, and should *understand* with their *heart*, and should be *converted*, and I should *heal* them (KJV, Matthew 13:11-15).**

The heart (or the mind) is the seat of thought and emotion. The phrase *waxed gross* in Greek is *pachuno*, which means *to make fat, thick, gross, dull, callous*. One of the Hebrew equivalent words of *pachuno* is *avah*, which means *twisted, crooked, distorted.* The word *avah* in ancient Hebrew is written ቸY8; the letter 8 is the twisted rope and means *dark,* or *wicked.*

The people's hearts (minds) are calloused – they have wrong and twisted teachings. Their ears are dull (burdensome) and their eyes are closed to truth. Yeshua was calling for the people to be converted. The word *converted* is the Greek word *epistrepho*, which means *to turn to the worship of the true God; to cause to return; to bring back to the love and obedience of God, to the love for the children; to love wisdom and righteousness (right understanding).* When the people perceive truth and turn back to God and love Him and His servants, He will heal them:

> **True repentance means to be no longer bound in the same sins for which He denounced death against Himself. Rather it is to eradicate them completely from the soul. For on their extirpation, God takes up His abode again in you (Clement, *Who is the Rich Man that Shall be Saved?*).**

The word *heal* is the Greek word *iaomai*, which means *to cure, to make whole, to free from errors and sins, to bring about one's salvation.* Sin is *missing the mark* (missing Torah), so having eyes to see and ears to hear sets one free from sin, allowing one to fully understand Torah, bringing about spiritual and physical healing – all the way back to the glorified body that Adam once had.

This same message, preached in the Old Testament by all of God's prophets, continued in the New Testament when Yeshua told the nations of Israel they had the same problem as their forefathers. God consistently calls His children to see and hear the revelation of Him, His truth, and His divine plan. This parabolic message must be addressed to fully understand why the Church today is dying. Even in the Book of Revelation, Yeshua says to all seven churches, "**He who has an ear, let him hear what the Spirit says to the churches. . . .**" (Revelation 2:7, 3:6, 11, 13, 17, 22, 29). Yeshua tells the churches to "**. . . anoint your eyes with eye salve, that you may see**" (Revelation 3:18). At the end of the age, the Church has the same problem as every generation before it: not having eyes to see and ears to hear the secrets of the kingdom.

God will close His own eyes and ears to those who are rebellious and do not follow the prophetic Torah. God showed Ezekiel the idol worship in the temple of God:

> **Therefore I also will act in fury. My *eye* will not spare nor will I have pity; and though they cry in My ears with a loud voice, I will not *hear* them (Ezekiel 8:18).**

Essentially, one's harvest correlates with one's spiritual eyesight and hearing. In the parable of the seed and the sower, the seed that fell on good ground yielded different amounts of crop:

> **But others fell on good ground and yielded a crop: some a hundredfold, some sixty, some thirty (Matthew 13:8).**

The thirtyfold crop corresponds to the **Outer Court**, the sixtyfold to the **Holy Place**, and the hundredfold to the **Holy of Holies**. While the ground, indicative of people, was good, not all the seed produced fully. Simply being in the temple is not good enough; God desires for us to enter into the Holy of Holies as royal high priests to receive the hundredfold reward. The full reward is the same glorified body that Adam had in the garden before he fell.

Spiritual Blindness

Having eyes to see is to gain spiritual clarity of sight. Spiritual blindness is caused by being in darkness, a place of no revelation and misery due to sin – ignorance of God's Word. Deuteronomy 28 lists the curses that befall those who do not obey God's commandments:

> **The LORD will change the rain of your land to powder and dust; from the heaven it shall come down on you until you are destroyed. . . . The LORD will strike you with madness and *blindness* and confusion of heart. . . . And you shall grope at noonday, as a *blind* man gropes in *darkness*; you shall not prosper in your ways; you shall be only oppressed and plundered continually, and no one shall save you (Deuteronomy 28:24, 28-29).**

Madness, blindness, and confusion of the heart are part of the curses of not obeying His Word, or not fully understanding Torah. The word *blindness* in Hebrew is *avvereth*, which comes from the word *ivver* (meaning *blind*). In ancient Hebrew, *ivver* is written ᖇY8, with 8 (*ghah*) being the evil eye. Recall that the word *iniquity* is *avon*, meaning *twisted teaching*, or having an evil eye. So not obeying the Word of God – not fully understanding the Scripture on the deeper *sod* level – causes one to be spiritually blind and grope in darkness – a place of no understanding. And so, the message of the prophets throughout Scripture is for God's people to get eyes to see.

The Lord also states that disobedience to His Torah results in plagues with prolonged sickness:

> **If you do not carefully observe all the words of this law that are written in this book, that you may fear this glorious and awesome name, THE LORD YOUR GOD, then the LORD will bring upon you and your descendants extraordinary plagues—great and**

> **prolonged plagues—and serious and prolonged sicknesses. Moreover He will bring back on you all the diseases of Egypt, of which you were afraid, and they shall cling to you (Deuteronomy 28:58-60).**

The plagues are not meant for the Gentiles but for His people who are not listening. Thus, even sickness is a sign of disobedience. However, for those who have eyes to see, the opposite is true: blessings and great increase in health will come. The release of plagues in the Book of Revelation is purposed to make His children repent – turn back – to the truth.

God declares that His Servant, His Elect One (Yehoshua) will come to give a light to the Gentiles, and to "**open blind eyes, to bring out prisoners from the prison, those who sit in darkness from the prison house**" (Isaiah 42:7). Since the Christ is a *generation* of people (see **The Christ Generation**), there will be many saviors coming out of Zion (Obadiah 1:21) who will open the eyes of the spiritually blind by teaching the deeper mysteries of the kingdom. Those who have eyes to see will bring full restoration back into the Earth – this is the light of Day One, the reestablishment of spiritual truth. Yeshua describes the Pharisees as blind leaders, or false teachers (Matthew 15:14, 23:16-17, 23:24, 23:26).

> **Let them alone. They are *blind* leaders of the *blind*. And if the blind leads the blind, both will fall into a *ditch* (Matthew 15:14).**

The Pharisees are spiritually blind because they do not understand the deeper, prophetic meaning of Scripture, and they lead others by their false teachings into a *ditch (or a pit).* The pit – a place of no revelation and truth – is the residence of Abaddon, the principality of destruction and separation, whose job is to stop the Church from seeing the deeper teachings of God. It is also out of the pit from which the locusts come, and Joel indicates that this army of locusts is actually God's own people that destroyed God's Tree (Joel 2:25). The word for *ditch* is the word *bothunos*, coming from the word *bathuno*, meaning *deep, extreme poverty.* The ditch is a place of extreme poverty, illustrative of having no money or *talents*. Yeshua came for the poor – not in finance but in spirit. The spiritually poor are those without revelation, truth, and deeper understanding.

Words have both positive and negative definitions. *Bathuno*, which means *deep, extreme poverty*, also has the following definition: *deep things of God, hidden things above man's scrutiny, especially divine counsels*. This definition indicates that there is another type of depth: the hidden secrets of God. But those without eyes to see are unable to perceive these divine counsels and hidden mysteries.

Talent

Having eyes to see spiritual truth and the deeper teachings of God is associated with being rich. The parable of the talents in Matthew 25 illustrates the true economy of God is based on the kingdom mysteries.

> **For the kingdom of heaven is like a man traveling to a far country, who called his own servants and delivered his goods to them. And to one he gave five talents, to another two, and to another one, to each according to his own ability; and immediately he went on a journey. Then he who had received the five talents went and traded with them, and made another five talents. And likewise he who had received two gained two more also. But he who had received one went and dug in the ground, and hid his lord's money (Matthew 25:14-18).**

The word *talent* is the Greek word *talanton*, whose Hebrew equivalent is the word *kikar*, meaning *round, coin (as a round piece of gold or silver), round loaf of bread, morsel.* The crust of the bread is the *logos* – the shell of the bread, or the dead letter of the Torah.

However, once the bread is broken open, one can reach in and grab the morsel which is the *rhema* (the living Word). Hence, talents are morsels of bread; they're the *rhema,* the hidden and secret Word of God. God bases His economy on the deeper teachings of His kingdom.

The master was pleased with the servants (the prophets) who traded and multiplied their talents – the deeper teachings of God. To them the master said, "**Well done, good and faithful servant; you were faithful over a few things, I will make you ruler over many things. Enter into the joy of your lord**" (Matthew 25:21, 23).

The servants who multiplied their talents had multiplied their revelation, or understanding, of God's kingdom. The initial talents given to the servants were God's provision – His grace – giving the servants the ability to produce more on their own. The praise of the two servants who multiplied their talents illustrates that those who multiply their revelation and understanding obtain the promise.

On the other hand, the selfish servant did not share his talent but instead hid it in the ground. Burying the talent in the ground is indicative of hiding the secret teachings into the *Earth,* or burying the secret teachings underneath carnal reasoning. The talent of the selfish servant was given to the servant who had multiplied his five talents into ten talents. The lazy servant did nothing with the grace given to him and was thrown out – He was thrown out of the Holy of Holies.

God makes it clear that to those who understand the deeper teachings more will be given, but those who do not will find themselves in poverty and in outer darkness:

> **For to everyone who has, more will be given, and he will have abundance; but from him who does not have, even what he has will be taken away. And cast the *unprofitable* servant into the *outer darkness.* There will be weeping and gnashing of teeth (Matthew 25:29-30).**

The master called the profitless servant "wicked" and "lazy" (Matthew 25:26). Wickedness implies dysfunctionality and a lack of understanding. To be rich in the kingdom of God requires one to understand His Word on the *sod* level and to multiply the deeper teachings for others in order to bring them out of spiritual blindness and poverty.

The economy of God is based on the deeper mysteries of the kingdom, or the inner morsels of bread. In the parable of the rich man and Lazarus (Luke 16:19-31), Lazarus (the poor man) represents those with no revelation – no deeper teachings of the kingdom – who desire to be fed with the crumbs of bread that should come from the rich man, the Church. However, the Church lets these morsels of deeper teachings fall from the table. The word *morsel* is further associated with meat. As the meat of the Word is in the Holy of Holies realm, the Church, still on the milk, remains veiled (or outside the Holy of Holies).

Slumber

Darkness, associated with the night season, is a time of slumber. Paul teaches that a lack of true understanding equates to having the spirit of slumber.

> **What then? Israel hath not obtained that which he seeketh for; but the election hath obtained it, and the rest were blinded (According as it is written, God hath given them the *spirit of slumber*, eyes that they should *not see*, and ears that they should *not hear*;) unto this day. And David saith, Let their *table* be made a snare, and a trap, and a stumbling block, and a recompence unto them: Let their eyes be *darkened*, that they *may not see*, and bow down their back always (KJV, Romans 11:7-10).**

The word *slumber* is the Greek word *katanuxis*, which is defined as *insensibility or torpor of the mind which renders their souls so insensible that they are not affected at all by the offer made them of salvation through the Messiah*. The Hebrew equivalent is the word *tardemah*, which means a *deep sleep or trance*. God causes some people to enter into a trancelike state which makes them completely insensitive to salvation. These are the people who do not receive revelation of the kingdom mysteries.

In Verse 9, a *table* is the place of eating – a place of teaching, which should be the Church. But instead, the Church becomes a stumbling block if it has no revelation of the truth, and the people's eyes will be darkened. The word *darkened* in Greek is *skotizo*, which means *to be deprived of light, to cover with darkness: of the eyes, of the understanding, of the mind*. The equivalent Hebrew word for *skotizo* is the word *chashak*, which means *to hide, conceal, confuse*. The Church that has no revelation of the secrets and mysteries of the kingdom will be in a state of *confusion*.

Slumber is also synonymous with *death*. The parable of the virgins in Matthew 25 is actually a picture of a dead system:

> **Then the kingdom of heaven shall be likened to ten *virgins* who took their lamps and went out to meet the bridegroom. Now five of them were wise, and five were foolish. Those who were foolish took their lamps and took no *oil* with them, but the wise took oil in their vessels with their lamps. But while the bridegroom was delayed, they all *slumbered* and *slept*. And at midnight a *cry was heard*: 'Behold, the bridegroom is coming; go out to meet him!' Then all those virgins arose and trimmed their lamps. And the foolish said to the wise, 'Give us some of your oil, for our lamps are going out.' But the wise answered, saying, 'No, lest there should not be enough for us and you; but go rather to those who sell, and buy for yourselves.' And while they went to buy, the bridegroom came, and**

> **those who were ready *went in with him to the wedding*; and the *door was shut.* Afterward the other virgins came also, saying, 'Lord, Lord, open to us!' But he answered and said, 'Assuredly, I say to you, I do not *know* you' (Matthew 25:1-12).**

A virgin is one who has not had intercourse and is not yet married. In a traditional Hebrew wedding, the bride and bridegroom went through *consummation*, which entailed intercourse in the *chuppah* (the bed chamber) as a part of the wedding ceremony. A bride was not considered married until she consummated and was no longer a virgin (see **The Marriage Covenant**). The seed is the sperm and Word of God and the bridegroom impregnating the bride is a picture of God impregnating His Church. When a bride marries, she receives the bridegroom's name just as God seeks a Bride to take His name. In Hebrew thought, a name depicts *character* and *function.* So, when Yeshua states in Revelation 3:12 that He will write a new name on the overcomers, He speaks about a marriage:

> **He who overcomes, I will make him a pillar in the temple of My God, and he shall go out no more. I will write on him the *name* of My God and the *name* of the city of My God, the *New Jerusalem*, which comes down out of heaven from My God. And I will write on him My new *name* (Revelation 3:12).**

A name change is linked to a destiny change. Many times throughout Scripture, God changes people's names in order to change their character and function, and ultimately, their destinies. As the seed is the Word of God, an impregnation of God's seed – His DNA – is receiving the revelation of His mysteries by going through the veil. The mind is also considered the womb, so learning the deeper teachings of God is a mental impregnation. Through opening the womb, the mind, we can be restored:

> **He declared that the Word would become flesh. He declared that the Son of God would become the Son of man. For the pure one opened purely that pure womb which regenerates men unto God. For He Himself made it pure *(Irenaeus, Against Heresies).***

The virgins – those who do not see or hear the mysteries of God – were sleeping. The word *sleep* is the word *katheudo*, which is a euphemism for being *dead*. If the Church, the Bride of Christ, is a virgin and asleep, it has no revelation and is dead. But there is another person in this parable who is not asleep: the one who cries out at midnight that the bridegroom has arrived. This figure, a watchman who has eyes to see, is already inside the door (inside the bedchamber) and already impregnated with God's seed. The wise virgins who have enough oil, representing anointing and teaching from the Holy Spirit, make it into the bedchamber before the door shuts. The foolish virgins who did not study to show themselves approved (2 Timothy 2:15) lacked adequate teaching. As a result, they did not make it into the bedchamber for the wedding and did not receive the impregnation of the seed. They never had access beyond the veil.

Unveiled

God's recurring message is that the Church does not have eyes to see or ears to hear. Being blind is associated with being *veiled*.

> **Unlike Moses, who put a veil over his face so that the children of Israel could not look steadily at the end of what was passing away. But their minds were blinded. For until this day the same veil remains unlifted in the reading of the Old Testament, because the veil is taken away in Christ. But even to this day, when Moses is read, a veil lies on their heart. Nevertheless when one**

> **turns to the Lord, the veil is taken away (2 Corinthians 3:13-16).**

The veil that remains over mindsets hinders the ability to perceive the deeper, *sod* level of Scripture. But if one turns, the veil is taken away. In Verse 15, Paul writes that a veil lies on the people's hearts. The word *veil* is the word Greek *kaluma* with the Hebrew equivalent word *masak* (*a protective covering of God's power*), the same word found in Hebrews 10:20. The cover is over the heart (the mindset) to protect the unrighteous (those with wrong understanding), but once they turn back to the truth, the covering of protection is no longer needed as one can then fully stand in the presence of God.

> **Nevertheless when one turns to the Lord, the veil is taken away. Now the Lord is the Spirit; and where the Spirit of the Lord is, there is liberty. But we all, with unveiled face, beholding as in a mirror the glory of the Lord, are being transformed into the same image from glory to glory, just as by the Spirit of the Lord (2 Corinthians 3:16-18).**

The word *turn* is the word *epistrepho*, whose Hebrew equivalent is *shuv*, meaning *to repent*. Yeshua urges the Church of Ephesus to return to its first love - the teachings of the Early Church, which reveal the secrets of the kingdom. Upon removal of the veil, God transforms His people into His same image. While the veil is the point of access for many to understand the gospel, it also keeps those who do not understand, or those who are perishing, outside:

> **But even if our gospel is veiled, it is veiled to those who are perishing, whose minds the god of this age has blinded, who do not believe, lest the light of the gospel of the glory of Christ, who is the image of God, should shine on them (2 Corinthians 4:3-4).**

Those who perish suffer not only a spiritual perishing, but also a physical perishing, as they have no access into the Holy of Holies (no access back into the garden). When we begin to see Scripture from the prophetic level, through understanding the symbolisms and parables of the kingdom, we are able to spiritually see. Only then will our eyes truly see and our ears truly hear, giving us access to heaven. Heaven resides between the eyes and ears – the mind. Having right understanding, *righteousness*, yields the mind of Christ and access back into the Holy of Holies.

Chapter Seven

Elijah

And it seems to be indicated by these words, that Elijah was to prepare for the glorious coming of Christ by certain holy words and dispositions in their souls, those who have been made fittest for this, which those upon earth could not have endured, because of the excellency of the glory, unless they had been prepared beforehand by Elijah. And likewise, by Elijah, in this place, I do not understand the soul of that prophet but his spirt and power; for these it is by which all things shall be restored (Matthew 17:11) so that when they have been restored, and, as a result of that restoration, become capable of receiving the glory of Christ, the son of God who shall appear in glory may sojourn with them.

Origen
Gospel on Matthew

God will use a company of people who see His divine plan to restore all things. This company of people is a restorative army, an Elijah com-pany. It is prophesied throughout Scripture that Elijah will bring resto-ration in preparation for the return of the Lord. He ascended and experienced resurrection and transfiguration into a glorified state. Elijah had the power to control the rains – the teachings of the kingdom se-crets. He came again in spirit, and will come again through a people, to make the way straight through correct teaching.

Straight & Level

Isaiah prophesied the restoration of Jerusalem and Elijah's arrival to bring restoration:

> **"Comfort, yes, comfort My people!" Says your God. "Speak comfort to Jerusalem, and *cry out* to her, that her warfare is ended, that her *iniquity* is pardoned; for she has received from the LORD's hand *Double* for all her *sins*." The voice of one crying in the wilderness: "Prepare the way of the LORD; Make straight in the desert a highway for our God…" (Isaiah 40:1-3).**

The name *Jerusalem* is compiled of two words: *yaru* (which is the root to the word *Torah*) meaning *to throw, to rain, to teach*, and *shalom* meaning *peace, restoration*. Jerusalem's name (character and function) is to throw the rains of peace, or *to teach the revelation which brings restoration*.

The terms *cry out* and *crying* are the same word, *qara*, meaning *to preach, to proclaim, to summon, to commission, to be chosen*. In ancient Hebrew, *qara* is written 𐤒𐤓𐤀, with the root word 𐤒𐤓 meaning *meeting or bringing together of people or objects by arrangement, accident or purchase*. The Hebrew letters are *aleph* (𐤀, *apostle, God*), *resh* (𐤓, *mind*) and *kuf* (𐤒, *gathering of light*), which together can be read as "the gathering of apostolic minds." This cry out is a commissioning for those who have the apostolic and revelatory understanding of God's Word. It's also a summoning of the Church to see the revelation of His divine plan.

As the Bride receives revelation of God's divine plan, the war of seeds – the war of words, war of Torahs – will cease (see **War of Seeds**). Once iniquity (twisted teaching) is done away with, the Bride will receive a double portion of the blessing - a double portion of revelation.

The one crying out from the wilderness will come to make a straight highway in the desert. The word *straight* is the word *yasar*, written in ancient Hebrew ישר, meaning *to be right, level, smooth.* The root word is שר, where the *shin* (ש, *pressure, anointing*) and *resh* (ר, *mind*) together can be read as "press the beginning," or "pressure on the mind." Anytime God begins to move, pressure occurs, imminently followed by a stripping process. All the leaders in Scripture were stripped. Those who are part of the last move will imminently go through a stripping process. They will be pressed for a new beginning – a return to Genesis.

The word *yasar* (ישר) also means *a cord (as tight rope is straight), righteous (one who is straight and firmly holds up the truth just as the cord is straight and firmly holds the wall of the tent upright).* The tent is the Hebrew letter *bet* (ב), which is the house of God - straight and correct teachings hold up the house of God. As the secrets (*sod*) are also the foundation of God's government (see **Secrets**), the correct teachings are His secrets.

The Ancient Hebrew Lexicon Bible further explains that the word *straight* (*yasar*) is associated with *ropes* and *cords*, which were usually made of bark strips such as from cedar trees, or from the sinew (tendon) of an animal. A bow string was made from the strongest tendons of an animal, usually the thigh muscle, which could withstand the most tension. When Jacob wrestled the angel at Peniel, he was smote on his hip, the place of the most physical strength. However, the message that the angel brought was more powerful than any natural strength.

The word *straight* is also associated with *imagination: the twisting together of thoughts.* Thoughts are bound together, and just as more twists in a rope produce a stronger rope, the more intertwined the thoughts the stronger they are. But when God seeks for repentance, He asks for an *untwisting* of thoughts – a reversal of twisted teaching, or iniquity.

A related word is *asher*, which means *straight, happy*. This word has an additional letter *aleph* (א) at the beginning (אשר), and can be read as "apostolic pressure on the mind." God puts pressure on our mindsets in order to straighten them (untwist them) so that we can have the mind of Christ:

> **For "WHO HAS KNOWN THE MIND OF THE LORD THAT HE MAY INSTRUCT HIM?" But we have the *mind of Christ* (1 Corinthians 2:16).**

Another related word is שור, meaning *ox (as used for pulling heavy loads)*. The ox is symbolic of the apostle and those who are yoked to him have become apostolic also. An ox pulls with a yoke, which is the Hebrew letter *lamed* (ל, *teaching*). To be yoked to Yeshua requires the carrying of a load, which is the teaching of God.

Another definition of the word *yasar* is *remnant (what is left behind), remainder, rest*. Many are called but few are chosen. Only a few – the remnant – go through the pressure, and these few will have rest in their minds. The word *mystery*, in Greek *musterion*, contains the root word *mustees*, which means "one initiated" into "a revealed secret" (see **Discipline of the Secrets & Mysteries**). Those who understand the mysteries of the kingdom are the remnant.

Out of the Wilderness

Isaiah's prophecy indicates that the one crying out in the wilderness brings a leveling and straightening of the land:

> **Every *valley* shall be *exalted* and every *mountain* and *hill* brought *low*; the *crooked* places shall be made *straight* and the *rough* places *smooth*. The *glory* of the LORD shall be *revealed*, and all flesh shall see it**

> **together; for the mouth of the LORD has spoken (Isaiah 40:4-5).**

Elijah would be the one to straighten the path so that the glory of the Lord could be revealed. However, Elijah did not just come once. Long after Elijah physically came and was caught up into heaven, Yeshua told His disciples that Elijah had already come and was *yet to come*:

> **And His disciples asked Him, saying, "Why then do the scribes say that Elijah must come first?" Jesus answered and said to them, "Indeed, *Elijah is coming* first and will *restore* all things" (Matthew 17:10-11).**

The word *restore* is the word *apokathistemi*, which means *to restore to its former state; restoration; perfection; to make restitution*. The former state is the state of glory prior to Adam's fall. So, Elijah comes to restore Eden. If Elijah comes first before Yeshua, then Yeshua is coming back for a Church that is already restored to the glory realm.

In the Book of Matthew, the disciples were looking for a physical Elijah, but Yeshua clearly states that it was John the Baptist who came in the *spirit of Elijah*:

> **"But I say to you that Elijah has *come already*, and they did not know him but did to him whatever they wished. Likewise the Son of Man is also about to suffer at their hands." Then the disciples understood that He spoke to them of *John the Baptist* (Matthew 17:12-13).**

John the Baptist came in the spirit of Elijah, and the Jews judged and killed the very messenger who was supposed to prepare them for the restoration before Yeshua's return. John the Baptist came in the *spirit of Elijah* to make the way straight and level.

Scripture tells us that the Messiah was to be ushered in by the high priest, who would announce Him and learn the teachings of Torah from Him. Caiaphas was the high priest when Yeshua reached the age of ministry. However, Caiaphas had bought his way into the priestly office, because the priesthood had become corrupt. In essence, he was a counterfeit high priest. On the other hand, John the Baptist came from the bloodline of Aaron and was the true high priest. When John the Baptist saw Yeshua, he announced Him as the "Lamb of God who takes away the sin of the world" (John 1:29). John's recognition of Yeshua as a perfect, unblemished sacrifice discloses John's high priestly office. John was God's high priest who ushered in the First Coming of the Messiah, but because the people did not have eyes to see, they killed him.

Just like Elijah before him, John came preaching out of the wilderness:

> **. . .while Annas and Caiaphas were high priests, the word of God came to *John* the son of Zacharias in the wilderness. And he went into all the region around the Jordan, preaching a *baptism of repentance* for the *remission of sins*, as it is written in the book of the words of Isaiah the prophet, saying: "THE VOICE OF ONE CRYING IN THE *WILDERNESS*: 'PREPARE THE WAY OF THE LORD; MAKE HIS PATHS *STRAIGHT...*'" (Luke 3:2-4).**

John came out of the wilderness, a place of desolation and no rain – no revelation. The gematria value for *wilderness*, 246, is also the value for the words *talent, rebellion, thorn, bitter, hide,* and *covered*. Adam and Eve hid from God because they went from the garden to the wilderness. Lacking revelation is similar to *rebellion*, the state into which Adam and Eve fell when they ate of the fruit of the Tree of Knowledge of Good and Evil. After eating of the wrong fruit, they lost their high priestly covering and felt compelled to *cover* themselves and *hide* from God - without their high priestly covering they were naked. Adam and Eve also became in need of water:

> **And Adam said, after he was raised, "O God, while we were in the garden we did not require, or care for this water; but since we came to this land we cannot do without it." Then God said to Adam, "While thou wast under My command and wast a bright angel, thou knewest not this water. But after that thou hast transgressed My commandment, thou canst not do without water, wherein to wash thy body and make it grow; for it is now like that of beasts, and is in want of water" (First Book of Adam and Eve, 10:4-6).**

Adam, while under the command of God, was a "bright angel," for he was under the covering and teaching of God. After transgressing and losing the covering of God, Adam had a need for water – revelation. Just as the natural body requires water to survive, the spirit and soul likewise require the wisdom of God and His revelation to survive.

The *wilderness* is also representative of a system that has *no revelation.* The famines at the end of the age (Matthew 24:7) are not of natural food. The wilderness experience parallels that of the Hebrews coming out of Egypt and into the Promised Land. The Hebrews left Egypt because of the plagues, and in the Book of Revelation, the plagues occur once again. God sent, and will send, the plagues in order to bring people to repentance and the right understanding of His Word. The purpose of the plagues is to bring restoration to His people.

The Church has been wandering in the wilderness, a place without rain, or revelation, for 2000 years (40 jubilees, where a jubilee is every 50 years) – this is the time of the Church Age. The Jews killed John the Baptist who was sent in the spirit of Elijah to bring restoration. It takes righteousness – correct understanding and agreement with God's divine plan – to leave the wilderness and desert. With the revealing of the hidden teachings behind the veil, the time of drought is at an end.

The wilderness and desert are places of habitation for demons. When demons are cast out, they walk through dry places (Luke 11:24). Demons dwell in the desert, which are places of no rain; hence, *demons find habitation in people with no revelation*. While demons dwell in the desert, principalities dwell in the Promised Land. The Hebrews had to pass through the wilderness in order to reach the Promised Land. This is parabolic of the end time Church overcoming demons (the wilderness) and ultimately defeating principalities (Promised Land).

Devils and foul spirits dwell in Babylon, as described in the Book of Revelation:

> **And he cried mightily with a strong voice, saying, *Babylon* the great is fallen, is fallen, and is become the *habitation of devils*, and the hold of every *foul spirit*, and a cage of every unclean and hateful bird (KJV, Revelation 18:2).**

John describes the harlot with "Babylon" written on her head:

> **And on her forehead a name was written: MYSTERY, BABYLON THE GREAT, THE MOTHER OF HARLOTS AND OF THE ABOMINATIONS OF THE EARTH (Revelation 17:5).**

The harlot is the Church at the end of the age. She is Babylon (meaning *confusion*), full of twisted teaching and falsities. The word *Babylon*, or *babel*, comes from *babal*, meaning *mix, anoint*. So, Babylon is a *mixture in the anointing*. It is in the slumbering Church where the demons and devils dwell because of lack of revelation – just like the slumbering virgins who had a lack of oil, or lack of Yeshua's teaching. John the Baptist was sent in the spirit of Elijah to make the way *straight and level*. *Straight and level* is the definition of *sod*, which is also the *secret counsel which governs God*. John came in the spirit of Elijah to teach the secrets of the kingdom and bring the government of God into the Earth.

Those who overcome are given a rod to rule the nations (Revelation 2:27), just as John was given a rod to measure the temple of God and all who worship – or learn – therein (Revelation 11:1). The rod is used to determine if something is level or straight. God lays His foundations upon apostolic teaching and measures our understanding of His divine plan. Those with false teaching and incorrect understanding will be neither straight nor level, and thereby unstable. Instability is associated with *double-mindedness* (James 1:8), the very meaning of the name *Pharaoh*, who ruled in *Egypt*, meaning *to limit God*. The Elijah ministries come to make the way level.

Isaiah's prophecy speaks of the leveling out of high, low, and crooked places:

> **Every *valley* shall be *exalted* and every *mountain* and *hill* brought *low*; the *crooked* places shall be made *straight* and the *rough* places *smooth*. The *glory* of the LORD shall be *revealed*, and all flesh shall see it together; for the mouth of the LORD has spoken (Isaiah 40:4-5).**
>
> **EVERY *VALLEY* SHALL BE *FILLED* AND EVERY *MOUNTAIN* AND *HILL* BROUGHT *LOW*; THE *CROOKED* PLACES SHALL BE MADE *STRAIGHT* AND THE *ROUGH* WAYS *SMOOTH*; AND ALL FLESH SHALL SEE THE SALVATION OF GOD (Luke 3:5-6).**

Elijah's function is to make the way level and straight. Carnal mindsets (the mountains) will be brought low, and the empty vessels (the valleys) will be filled with teaching. The incorrect teachings (the crooked places) will be rectified and made straight. The straight and level foundation that Elijah brings is comprised of the *sod* secrets of God's kingdom.

The word *crooked* is the word *aqob*, meaning *insidious, deceitful*. It further means *restrain, heel: the restraining of the heel when taking a step forward*. The word *aqob* comes from the word *aqab*, meaning *to grab a hold of the heel*, which is the very function of Satan from the first encounter with Eve in the garden. Satan works through crooked teachings. He does not create - he only defiles by making straight things crooked.

In the prophecy of the coming of Elijah, Isaiah states:

> **The *glory* of the LORD shall be *revealed*, and *all flesh* shall see it together; for the mouth of the LORD has spoken (Isaiah 40:5).**

The word *reveal*, or *discover* is the word *galah*, meaning *to remove, uncover, to reveal Himself, to disclose*. The word *galah* is written in ancient Hebrew, 𐤂𐤋𐤄, whose root word 𐤏𐤋 means *work, yoke*, and whose letters can be read, "experience the staff," or "see the teaching." The *eye* represents *knowledge*, so having a good eye indicates having knowledge of His divine plan and true foresight. A true prophet, one with foresight, has true *knowledge*, or a *good eye*. The *lamed* is a yoke, or a staff lifted over the shoulder and attached to an ox to perform work. In Modern Hebrew, the letter *lamed* actually does look like the yoke of an ox: 𐤋. The *lamed* also represents *teaching*, so the teaching of God is placed on the shoulder – in the head, or mind – and replaces carnal teaching and reasoning.

Glory is the word *kabod*, which means *honor, heavy (as in a weight on the shoulder)*. Apostolic and revelatory teachings rest on the shoulder. The head – the mind – rests on the shoulder. It is in the mind (the place of the ark) where the glory will reside. A related word to *reveal* (*galah*, 𐤂𐤋𐤄) is the word *alah* (𐤏𐤋𐤄), which means *to lift, lifting of yoke unto the shoulder: one taken into exile is placed in the yoke for transport and yoke of bondage*. Those who can *see* His divine teaching are *yoked* to Him. The glory will be revealed, and *all flesh* will see it. There is no flesh in heaven, signifying that the revealing of the glory must occur here on the Earth. His ultimate plan is to bring His glory and His kingdom back *into* the Earth. Isaiah emphasizes that "the mouth of the Lord has spoken." Out of His mouth are parables and dark sayings (Psalms 78:2).

To understand what comes out of the mouth of Yahweh, one must understand the mysteries - the symbolism and parables of God.

John the Baptist brought a baptism of *repentance*, which is *the return to spiritual truth. Remission* means *freedom, pardon, deliverance, liberty, release from bondage, forgiveness or pardon of sins.* The Elijah ministries are coming again to *restore* all things and bring back the state of the garden, the realm of the glory of God. John the Baptist's position as a high priest discloses the high priestly office of Elijah and the Elijah ministries.

Rains, Feasts & His Return

Elijah is the only mentioned prophet who commanded the rain - the Spirit of Elijah brings the rains of revelation. The name *Elijah* is made up of the words *El* (*power, strength*) and *Yah* (*God*, the root to the name *Yahweh*). Elijah's character is the *power of God*; his function is to work in the power of God by releasing and withholding the rains which are the teachings of the kingdom.

> **And Elijah the Tishbite, of the inhabitants of Gilead, said to Ahab, "As the LORD God of Israel lives, before whom I stand, there shall not be *dew* nor *rain* these years, *except at my word*" (1 Kings 17:1).**
>
> **But I will more plainly set forth the manner in which this happens. When the close of the times draws nigh, a great prophet shall be sent from God to turn men to the knowledge of God, and he shall receive the power of doing wonderful things. Wherever men shall not hear him, he will shut up the heaven, and cause it to withhold its rains; he will turn their water into blood, and torment them with thirst and hunger; and if anyone shall endeavor to injure him, fire shall come forth**

> **out of his mouth, and shall burn that man *(Lactantius, Divine Institutes).***

Elijah declared that there would be no rain – no revelation – except at his word, which would be at the death of Jezebel, the wife of Ahab. Jezebel is one of the main principalities in the Church, who is a spirit of false prophecy. Jezebel shows up again at the end of the age in the Book of Revelation:

> **Nevertheless I have a few things against you, because you allow that woman *Jezebel,* who calls herself a prophetess, to *teach and seduce My servants* to commit *sexual immorality* and *eat* things sacrificed to *idols* (Revelation 2:20).**

Jezebel resides in the Church, teaching and seducing God's people to commit sexual immorality, which is impregnation of the wrong sperm, or seed – the wrong word, or teaching. Jezebel is a spirit that removes people from the true prophetic gift that God desires for His children: the gift of interpreting the hidden mysteries and teachings at the *sod* level. There are two Torahs (see **The Tree**, **War of Seeds**), and Jezebel teaches the counterfeit Torah. She also makes God's people eat things sacrificed to idols. Eating represents the receiving of teaching, and idols represent worthless things, for God said:

> **You shall not make *idols* for yourselves; neither a *carved image* nor a *sacred pillar* shall you rear up for yourselves; nor shall you set up an engraved stone in your land, to bow down to it; for I am the LORD your God (Leviticus 26:1).**

The word *idol* is *eliyl*, meaning *worthless, good for nothing.* Jezebel brings teachings of worthlessness and emptiness into the Church. As the high priests bring the secrets out from behind the veil, it is the high priestly office operating in the spirit of Elijah that prepares the Church for the coming of our Savior.

God warns His people of His great and terrible day, but before then Elijah will come to turn the fathers to the children and the children to the fathers:

> **Behold, I will send you *Elijah* the prophet before the coming of the great and dreadful day of the LORD. And he will turn the hearts of the fathers to the children, and the hearts of the children to their fathers, lest I come and strike the earth with a curse (Malachi 4:5-6).**

The fathers are the apostles who teach the mysteries of the kingdom. It is thus the function of the Elijah ministries to bring apostolic and Early Church teachings back to God's people.

On top of Mount Carmel, God's fire fell down on Elijah's sacrifice that was soaked with water – revelation. The name *Carmel* means *fruitful land* or *garden.* The falling of God's fire on Mount Carmel is parallel to Moses receiving the Torah on Mount Sinai, the Holy Spirit falling on the apostles' minds on Pentecost, and the end time baptism of those who step through the veil into the Holy of Holies and the glory. After the encounter and execution of the prophets, Elijah released the rains:

> **Then Elijah said to Ahab, "*Go up, eat and drink*; for there is the sound of abundance of *rain.*" So Ahab went up to eat and drink. And Elijah went up to the top of *Carmel*; then he bowed down on the ground, and *put his face between his knees*, and said to his servant, "Go up now, look toward the sea." So he went up and looked, and said, "There is nothing." And *seven* times he said, "Go again" (1 Kings 18:41-43).**

To *go up* is the word *alah*, which means *to ascend.* Elijah gave instructions to ascend by learning the divine teachings and abundance of revelation. Elijah's position of putting his face between his knees (Verse

42) is a picture of the birthing position, symbolic of the preparation of the birthing of offspring – the seed, or the Word of God.

> **Then it came to pass the seventh time, that he said, "There is a *cloud*, as small as a *man's hand*, rising out of the sea!" So he said, "Go up, say to Ahab, 'Prepare your chariot, and go down before the *rain* stops you.'" Now it happened in the meantime that the sky became black with *clouds* and *wind*, and there was a heavy *rain*. So Ahab rode away and went to Jezreel. Then the hand of the LORD came upon Elijah; and he *girded up his loins* and *ran ahead* of Ahab to the entrance of Jezreel (1 Kings 18:44-46).**

Elijah told the servant to check for a *cloud* the size of a *man's hand*, symbolic of the fivefold ministry; God is calling His people to go out and look for the fivefold ministry. At the word of Elijah, the rain came, as the Elijah ministries have the ability to bring the rains of revelation. Verse 46 says that Elijah *girded up his loins*, which is the area of reproduction – where seed is released. Elijah had prepared himself to release God's Word and divine teaching.

Elijah ran and beat not just the footmen, but the horses. Footmen are symbolic of those who do work for the Lord yet are not in the glory, and the horses represent warriors of God who are in His glory. In Jeremiah 12:5, God says, "**If you have run with the footmen, and they have wearied you, then how can you contend with horses?**" If people are made weary by those who serve God yet do not carry the glory, how will they stand in the presence of those who *do* carry the glory of God?

Elijah also had the ability to call the fire down from heaven, or the secrets of the kingdom. The fire of Yah is the fire of baptism in the next and last move, for our God is an all-consuming fire (Deuteronomy 4:24, Hebrews 12:29). The Elijah ministries are thus called to prepare the way for the release of the fire – the deeper teachings of the Word of God – and usher in the restorative plan of God.

Former and Latter Rains

Elijah calls the rains, classified as the *former* and *latter* rains, which are representative of Yeshua's First and Second Comings:

> **Let us know, let us pursue the knowledge of the LORD. His going forth is established as the morning; He will come to us like the rain, like the *latter and former rain* to the earth (Hosea 6:3).**

The former and latter rains are also respectively the spring and fall feasts of God. Leviticus 23 outlines God's (not the Jews') seven feasts.

> **These are the *feasts of the LORD*, holy convocations which you shall proclaim at their *appointed times* (Leviticus 23:4).**

The *former rains* are the spring feasts (Leviticus 23:5-23):

- *Pesach* (Passover)
- *Chag Hamotzi* (Unleavened Bread)
- *Yom Habikkurim* (First Fruits)
- *Shavuot* (Pentecost)

The *latter rains* are the fall feasts (Leviticus 23:24-43):

- *Rosh Hashanah* (Trumpets)
- *Yom Kippur* (Atonement)
- *Sukkot* (Tabernacles)

God makes it clear in Leviticus 23 that His people are to keep holy – to set apart – His appointed feast days. These are His feasts, not Jewish feasts, and they are eternal. The word *feast* is the word *moed*, meaning *appointment, season, congregation, assembly, sign, rehearsal.* God orchestrated major events on His feasts, and parallel themes are found thousands of years apart on the same feast days. These feast days are rehearsals of His return.

On the night that the Hebrews were instructed to put the blood on the doorposts, they ate their last meal in Egypt. That night, the death angel Abaddon passed over the households and killed the firstborn of the Egyptians. **We know that the Hebrews left Egypt on Passover.**	Yeshua ate Passover dinner with His twelve disciples, and **He was crucified on Passover** (Matthew 20:17-20).
Three days after leaving Egypt, the **Hebrews went through the Red Sea on the Feast of First Fruits**.	Three days after He was crucified, **Yeshua was resurrected on First Fruits** (Luke 24:46, Matthew 28:1-2, Mark 16:1).
Fifty days after the Hebrews passed through the Red Sea, Moses went up Mount Sinai – into the Holy of Holies and the glory of God. **He received the Torah from God on Pentecost**.	Fifty days after Yeshua's resurrection, the Holy Spirit fell on the apostles in the upper room, and the **Church was birthed at Pentecost**. God foretold His people that the Church would be birthed in *fire*.

The fall feasts, or the latter rain feasts, depict Yeshua's Second Coming.

> **Be glad then, you children of Zion, and rejoice in the LORD your God; for He has given you the *former rain* faithfully, and He will cause the rain to come down for you— the former rain, and the *latter rain* in the *first month* (Joel 2:23).**

As written in Joel, the latter rain begins in the first month, which is Tishri. The first of the fall feasts, the Feast of Trumpets, occurs on the first day of the first month (called Tishri 1) which is also the first day of creation (see **The Beginning**).

> **Therefore be patient, brethren, until the coming of the Lord. See how the farmer waits for the precious fruit of the earth, waiting patiently for it until it receives the early and latter rain (James 5:7).**

Not only does James indicate the start of end time events, but he clearly writes that they will be released according to the feast calendar of God. God works according to His feast days, so if we wish to be prepared for the coming of our Lord but do not understand His calendar, we will miss His entire plan.

The **Feast of Trumpets** (*Rosh Hashanah*) represents the consummation of a wedding celebration, during which the Bride and Bridegroom enter the bed chamber. On Rosh Hashanah, the doors to the temple are shut at the evening service, which is seen in the door being shut on the foolish virgins who did not make it into the bed chamber with the Bridegroom (Matthew 25:10). It is in the bed chamber that the Bride becomes impregnated with the DNA of the Bridegroom – Yehoshua. It is also upon consummation that the Bride and Bridegroom are officially married. The impregnation with the Bridegroom's seed entails an official change in DNA and name, or character and function. It is upon being filled with the secret teachings of the kingdom that we take on a new name.

The **Day of Atonement** (*Yom Kippur*) is the one day each year that the high priest entered the Holy of Holies to atone for the sins of the people. The word *atonement* in Hebrew is *kippur*, meaning *a cover or lid, a protective covering, or the covering of a debt or wrong.* Atonement is symbolized in the mercy seat (*kapporeth*) that covers the ark of the covenant. The two cherubim that cover the mercy seat are associated with the cherubim that guard the way back into the garden of Eden and the cherubim on the veil entering into the Holy of Holies. The temple serves as a pattern for the Paradise of God in which Adam and Eve once dwelt. The Early Church taught that Moses was shown the six-day process of creation when he was on Mt. Sinai, and the construction of the tabernacle served as a pattern of creation pointing to the return to paradise.

The **Feast of Tabernacles** (*Sukkot*), starting five days after the Day of Atonement, is a seven-day feast during which the Israelites were instructed to dwell in booths (*sukkots*). This was also the ingathering of the first fruit harvest. During this time, the Lord will gather His people and enter into His temple, which are His people:

> **Do you not know that *you are the temple* of God and that the Spirit of God *dwells* in you? (1 Corinthians 3:16).**
>
> **Or do you not know that *your body is the temple* of the Holy Spirit who is in you, whom you have from God, and you are not your own? (1 Corinthians 6:19).**

It is during the latter rain feasts – Yeshua's Second Coming – when He closes the door for those who bought the oil (the anointing and learned the deeper teachings), writes a new name in them, indicative of their understanding of His Torah, and finally enters into a Sabbath rest with them. This final step is the ultimate return to Paradise. In the Book of Matthew, Yeshua speaks about regeneration:

> **So Jesus said to them, "Assuredly I say to you, that in the *regeneration*, when the Son of Man sits on the throne of His glory, you who have followed Me will also sit on twelve thrones, judging the twelve tribes of Israel" (Matthew 19:28).**

The word *regeneration* is the word *paliggenesia*, made up of the words *pali* (*again*) and *genesis* (*birth*). This term is the *spiritual renovation* and *Messianic restoration* – the return to the garden.

The Feasts and His Temple

The grouping of God's seven feasts also aligns with the three sections of the temple. The **Outer Court** contained the altar of sacrifice and brazen laver and was the area to cleanse oneself. The spring feasts of Passover, Unleavened Bread, and First Fruits are a time of cleansing. During the spring feasts, it is customary for Jewish people to clean out their entire households of leaven, which is symbolic of sin.

The **Holy Place** contained the menorah, altar of incense, and table of showbread. The menorah contained the anointing oil, which represents teaching from the Holy Spirit. The Feast of Pentecost is a time of provision. During Pentecost, Moses received the Torah and the Church was birthed.

The **Holy of Holies** contained the ark of the covenant, where the glory of God dwells. The fall feasts of Trumpets, Atonement, and Tabernacles is a time of indwelling with God. It is at this time that God returns to His people – the temple, the garden, the New Jerusalem – who have become the habitation for His glory. This habitation is made manifest by those who have the eyes to see the deeper meaning of God's Word and His divine plan of restoration which He laid out throughout the Torah.

Rains of Restoration

God's divine plan is centered on restoration. Rain is revelatory teaching (Deuteronomy 32:2) and a revealing of kingdom secrets for the high priestly office and those who move behind the veil. Yeshua, who comes as the former and latter rains (Hosea 6:3), brings restoration at the conclusion of the latter rains. The last of the fall feasts, *Sukkot,* is God's indwelling in His people, who are the New Jerusalem. Recalling that the name *Jerusalem* is composed of the words *yaru* (*to throw the rains, to teach*), and *shalom* (*peace, restoration*), the New Jerusalem is a people who bring the *rains and teachings of restoration*. In the Book of Revelation, those who have victory over the beast sing the Song of Moses (Revelation 15:3). The Song of Moses is Deuteronomy 32:

> **Let my teaching drop as the rain, My speech distill as the dew, as raindrops on the tender herb, and as showers on the grass (Deuteronomy 32:2).**

Those who see the deeper things of God bring forth an appearing of Yehoshua into the Earth. The Early Church believed that the appearing of Christ would come first through revelation, followed by His physical return. Deliverance awaits those who recognize that they have been in a state of darkness, slumber, and deception of false teaching and incomplete understanding:

> **And it shall come to pass that whoever calls on the name of the LORD shall be *saved*. For in Mount Zion and in Jerusalem there shall be deliverance, as the LORD has said, among the remnant whom the LORD calls (Joel 2:32).**

This word *saved* is the word *malat*, meaning *deliver, escape, preserve*, and is written in ancient Hebrew, **⊗ᒍ᨞ᨓ**. It shares the root word, **⊗ᒍ**, with the word *lahat* (**⊗𐀀ᒍ**), meaning *cover, veil, secret.* This is the word used in Genesis 3:24 for the *flaming* swords of the cherubim guarding the way back into the garden (see **The Garden**). Thus, salvation is associated with passing through the fire swords of the cherubim – understanding the secrets of the kingdom to ultimately enter the Holy of Holies.

While the rain brings restoration, it simultaneously destroys those who hinder the divine plan of God – those with false teachings and wrong mindsets. Yeshua told His disciples that the coming of the Son of Man would be as in the days of Noah (Matthew 24:37). In the days of Noah, the *Nephilim*, the *fallen ones*, intermingled with the daughters of men (Genesis 6:1-4), and God sent a flood to destroy the mixed bloodlines.

In the same way, we are at a point where a mixed seed (mixed teaching) resides in the Church, and God will send heavy rain – revelation – to clear out the mixture. Recall that the Early Church fathers taught that those who had left the secret teachings were considered *fallen away*. The *Nephilim* illustrate a system that has fallen away from the pure and true teachings of Yehoshua. Just as Elijah destroyed Jezebel, so shall the Elijah ministries send rain to destroy the false teaching and misunderstanding in the Church to bring God's people back into the garden.

Keys to the Kingdom

We know that Elijah had the ability to command the rain, and thus the Spirit of Elijah has the ability to bring restoration through revelation. Elijah released the rain on a land that was in famine. The dry land is representative of people with no revelation of God's divine plan (the sleeping and dead Church). Those who have the keys to the kingdom have access into the Holy of Holies. Keys and doors are widely mentioned throughout the Scripture. It is God's desire to bring us the understanding we need to obtain and utilize the keys of the kingdom in order to bring restoration.

The word *key* is the Greek word *kleis*, which comes from the word *kleio*, meaning *a key (as shutting a lock), literally or figuratively*. The keeper of the keys has the power to open and shut doors, and metaphorically, in the New Testament, the key denotes power and authority. Further, the word *kleio* means *to cause the heavens to withhold the rain*. We know that rain is likened to God's teaching and revelation (Deuteronomy 32:2).

The word *teaching*, *leqach*, not only means *doctrine, teaching, insight, instruction, power, revealing*, but it also means *take, carry, marry, buy*. These words all describe actions of a bridegroom when he comes to retrieve his bride for the wedding ceremony. The bridegroom must *buy* his bride with a down payment, and once he finishes building a house, he *takes* and *carries* away his bride to the bed chamber where they are officially *married* upon consummation – an impregnation of the seed (see **The Marriage Covenant**). Yeshua will have a Bride through His teachings. A related word to *leqach* is the word *melqach*, meaning *tongs: the tool used for taking coals out of the fire.* Tongs were used to bring the coal from the altar of incense to touch and cleanse Isaiah's lips to deliver the message to the people that they had to get eyes to see and ears to hear (see **The Recurring Message**).

The word *kleio* also means *to shut up compassion so that a thing is inaccessible to one; to be devoid of pity; to obstruct the entrance into the kingdom of heaven.* Hence, the key holds the access to the kingdom of heaven. When the door is locked on those who reject the deeper teachings of God, He is devoid of pity and compassion. The kingdom is accessed through the parables, symbolisms, and secrets, as one must pass through the flaming swords – the secret parables – of the cherubim to enter the garden (Genesis 3:24, see **The Garden**).

Yeshua told the Pharisees that they had obstructed the kingdom of heaven. He told them that not only would they not enter in, but that they were hindering others from entering in by being blind guides (Matthew 15:14). The Pharisees – the false teachers – would be cut off because they could not see the deeper teachings and were leading others into the pit, a place of no revelation (see **Spiritual Blindness**).

Withholding the rain is withholding the revelation of God's kingdom. It is the divine revelation of Scripture that will unlock heavenly things, not just mere words of human wisdom. One must have understanding of the revelation in order for His Word and glory to fully manifest.

Receiving Keys Through Revelation

The ability to receive the keys of the kingdom comes by receiving revelation. When Yeshua asked His disciples, **'But who do you say that I**

am?' Simon Peter answered and said, "You are the Christ, the Son of the living God" (Matthew 16:15-16). Yeshua then answered:

> **Blessed are you, Simon Bar-Jonah, for flesh and blood has not revealed this to you, but My Father who is in heaven (Matthew 16:17).**

Simon was *blessed* because he received revelation of who Yeshua was. The word *blessing* is the Hebrew word *barak*, meaning to *kneel and drink the rain.* However, this also means that those who did not receive the revelation of Yeshua were not blessed, or *cursed.* Yeshua then changed Simon's name to Peter:

> **And I also say to you that you are Peter, and on this rock I will build My church, and the gates of Hades shall not prevail against it. And I will give you the *keys of the kingdom of heaven*, and whatever you bind on earth will be bound in heaven, and whatever you loose on earth will be loosed in heaven (Matthew 16:18-19).**

When Peter received the revelation from the Father, Yeshua changed his name. Essentially, Peter became *married.* For Peter, the moment of revelation was the moment of impregnation from the Father. A marriage had taken place, and Peter became the foundation of the Church (the revelatory teachings) and therefore obtained the keys to the kingdom. When Yeshua told Peter, "I will give you the keys," He was saying, "I will give you the ability to lock and unlock the heavens." Peter was given his new name (meaning "rock") upon receiving the revelation of Yeshua, indicating that Yeshua would build His Church upon the *rock* of *revelation.* The body of Christ cannot be built without revelation.

Those who go through the veil and receive revelation of the deeper kingdom secrets gain further access, bringing them into greater maturity and increased responsibility. The remnant will have the ability to ascend the ladder into the Holy of Holies and bring the glory back down into the Earth. Those with the keys of the kingdom have access through the veil, the portal between heaven and Earth. All revelation begins with the revelation of Yehoshua, which is why the Book of Revelation begins with: **"The Revelation of Jesus Christ [Yehoshua Ha Mashiach], which God gave Him to show His servants—things which must shortly take place. . ."** (Revelation 1:1). The revelation of Yehoshua is for His servants the prophets to distribute to the rest of the Church.

Key of the House of David

The terms binding and loosing refer to revelation. Peter had the authority to release or hold back revelation. He was given the authority to put his foot on the serpent's head and given access to the heavens.

> **The *key* of the *house of David* I will lay on his *shoulder*; so he shall open, and no one shall shut; and he shall shut, and no one shall open. I will fasten him as a peg in a secure place, and he will become a glorious throne to his father's house (Isaiah 22:22-23).**

The house of David is the *tabernacle of David*. David brought the ark from the Philistines into his house, and all the priests came for unceasing day and night worship around the ark. The high priest was only allowed to go into the Holy of Holies once a year, but David was in the Holy of Holies continuously, where he wrote the Psalms. All the mysteries are revealed when one is in the glory. David was a high priest - Yeshua said there would be a temple coming like David's temple:

> **In that day will I raise up the tabernacle of David that is fallen, and close up the breaches thereof; and I will raise up his ruins, and I will build it as in the days of old (Amos 9:11).**

> **After this I will return, and will build again the tabernacle of David, which is fallen down; and I will build**

again the ruins thereof, and I will set it up (Acts 15:16).

David's temple is a dwelling place of God's constant presence, which He seeks in His people, who are the temple (1 Corinthians 3:16, 6:19). The physical tabernacle of David was in Jerusalem; the New Jerusalem is the Bride with the fullness of the tabernacle of David, contained within God's people, who have become Eden. The glory resides in the ark, and the ark resides in the tabernacle of David. The coming tabernacle of David at the end of the age is a people. The name *David* means *beloved* - God will dwell in those whom He loves. As love is the ultimate fullness of the Fruit of the Spirit (see **The Tree**), the fullness of God's love is a love for His truth. The only way for the ark to dwell in us is through our love of the revelation of His truth.

In contrast to David's tabernacle, the tabernacle of Moses did not house the ark, indicative of an empty structure or shell – the *logos*. The day that the ark was taken out of God's house and into Philistine captivity, Ichabod was born and was named for the very situation: "The glory has departed." There was no glory without the presence of the ark.

Temple worship will be reestablished to that of David's temple – the temple of the *beloved*. The reinstatement will occur by using the keys of the kingdom and bringing God's glory out from behind the veil. The temple is a pattern of God's glorious creation and divine plan, and God desires for us to return to true temple worship. As worship implies submitting and learning, true temple worship is learning the deeper and secret teachings that the Early Church taught – the hidden secrets behind the veil. As royal high priests, we are meant for temple worship (see **Royal Priesthood**).

The Early Church taught that when Adam left the garden, he took the temple instruments and items needed to perform sacrificial service with him (including gold, frankincense, and myrrh). The Magi brought these temple elements back to Yeshua. If we are restoring what Adam lost, we are restoring the glory in the Earth through temple worship.

The Shoulder

In Isaiah 22:22, the key of the house of David is laid on his *shoulder*. The word *shoulder* is the word *shekem*, written in ancient Hebrew, [ancient Hebrew glyphs]. The letters that make up the word *shekem* indicate that the shoulder is a place of *anointing* ([glyph]), *submission* ([glyph]), and *power* ([glyph]). The shoulder is a place of *government*, which is a high priestly anointing:

> **For unto us a Child is born, unto us a Son is given; and the government will be upon His *shoulder*. And His name will be called Wonderful, Counselor, Mighty God, Everlasting Father, Prince of Peace. Of the increase of His government and peace there will be no end, upon the throne of David and over His kingdom, to order it and establish it with judgment and justice from that time forward, even forever. The zeal of the Lord of hosts will perform this (Isaiah 9:6-7).**

All the names in Verse 6 illustrate Yeshua's high priestly anointing. Yeshua the *Counselor* depicts Him being a revealer of *secrets* (see **Secrets**).

The shoulder is also the place where the yoke is placed on oxen. The yoke (the Hebrew letter *lamed*, [glyph]) is indicative of teaching and instruction, which implies submission to learn – this is true worship. The keys to the kingdom further entail worshiping and learning the hidden things of God.

As the ark is carried on the shoulders, the *glory* is on the shoulders. Just like the head lays on top of the shoulders, the ark is contained in one's mindset, the place where the understanding and revelation of God's plan unfolds. The word *glory* is the Hebrew word *kabod*, meaning *heavy, honor, something that is heavy*. Armaments are heavy weapons carried for battle. The *glory* is thus also the artillery that we carry to come against the false teachings of the enemy.

The shoulder is also where the high priest wore two onyx stones as memorials for the sons of Israel (Exodus 28:9-12). The word *memorial* is the word *zikron*, which comes from the root word *zakar*, meaning *to mark, to recognize*. Hence, the shoulder is a place of marking and recognition; God marks those who have anointing, submission, power, teaching, and glory.

Opening Doors

Keys are used to open doors. The word *door* or *entrance* is the word *pethach*, which means *to loosen, begin, plough, carve, appear, break forth, draw out, ungird, unstop*. So, revelation brings an appearing. The word *pethach* also means *to loosen, to carve, to engrave (being marked by etching)*. God said He would write His Word in our souls, minds, and hearts (Deuteronomy 11:18). He engraves His Torah in His people through revelation. In the Book of Revelation, there are people with His name in their foreheads (those with His character and function). On the other hand, those without His name are sealed in the mark of the beast, or the mark of carnality (see **Circumcision & The Mark**). The keys to the kingdom are therefore instruments of *marking* and *inscribing*. God is *inscribing* with His Word – the sword – which cuts away all carnality and carnal understanding of the Scripture. Having no revelation is equivalent to having no inscription and no circumcision. The Lord desires for us to be circumcised in the Spirit:

> **These things, then, were given for a sign; but the signs were not unsymbolical, that is neither unmeaning nor to no purpose, inasmuch as they were given by a wise Artist; but the circumcision after the flesh typified that after the Spirit. For "we," says the apostle, "have been circumcised with the circumcision made without hands" (Col. 2:11). And the prophet declares, "Circumcise the hardness of your heart" (Deut. 10:16), (Irenaeus, *Against Heresies*).**

The word *pethach* has a gematria value of 488, which is also the value for *tabernacle, door, inheritance, wisdom, cloud, live,* and *purify.* Thus, the *door* is associated with:

- The tabernacle
- The inheritance into the kingdom
- Wisdom, which is personified by the Tree of Life
- Clouds, which are people releasing rain, or revelation
- Everlasting life (resurrection life)
- A pure, or a perfect and unblemished, sacrifice

A related word to the word *pethach* (*door*) is the word *maphteach* (*key, opening instrument*), as well as *pethichah* (*drawn sword*). Another word for *sword* is *maashal,* meaning *parable.* Releasing a parable, or a secret of the kingdom, is pulling the sword out from the sheath.

Just as keys have the ability to shut and lock doors, the heavens can also be shut up. The word *shut* is the word *sagar*, meaning *to close up, cage.* Related words mean *to surrender, to deliver up, to imprison.* When the heavens are shut, imprisonment occurs - meaning that without revelation, the people are imprisoned. Another related word is *sagriyd*, meaning *heavy rain.* God releases *heavy* rains, or heavy revelation. In the Book of Revelation, hail is released (Revelation 16:21). Hail is frozen rain that has the ability to destroy. Just as we proceed through the different sections of the temple, and through different levels of understanding, God brings different levels of rain, culminating in heavy rain and hail.

Doors and Time

Those with the keys of the kingdom are given authority to open and close doors, with an open door being seen as an *opportunity.* In Greek, there are two distinct words for time: *chronos* and *kairos.* The first, *chronos,* is the measure of time as humans know it, with equally spaced segments of counting units, such as seconds, minutes, hours, years, etc. However, the second word, *kairos*, actually means *opportunity*. *Kairos* is the word Yeshua uses when He speaks of discerning "the signs of the *times*" (Matthew 16:3), and which Paul uses when he says that the earthly temple is only "symbolic for the present time" (Hebrews 9:9). This time is a window, or door, of *opportunity*.

Upon entering Day Seven, where we return to the beginning, time is abolished, since in eternity there is no time. There is a return to the *everlasting, timeless* covenant of Abraham. Entering the Holy of Holies through the veil is stepping through a door of opportunity, or entering a *kairos* moment. The keys to these doors are the revelation of the mysteries of the kingdom. The ability to open and shut doors is the ability to control time – these are *kairos* moments.

The Fathers and Sons

We know that Elijah commanded the rains and had the ability to open and shut the heavens. The Elijah ministries will bring forth a straight and level path, and an untwisting of all crooked and false teaching. Just as Elijah killed Jezebel with the rain, we are stepping into one of the final battles in which God's army, having the spirit of Elijah, will destroy the spirit that perverts God's truth. God seeks for a people who come to battle with the armaments of His glory to restore the Church back to her first love – the deep, secret teachings of God. Elijah is the one who comes to turn the hearts of the children back to the fathers, and the hearts of the fathers back to the children:

> **Behold, I will send you Elijah the prophet before the coming of the great and dreadful day of the LORD. And he will turn the hearts of the *fathers* to the *children*, and the hearts of the *children* to their *fathers*, lest I come and strike the earth with a curse (Malachi 4:5-6).**

The fathers are the apostles teaching the secrets of the kingdom and the sons are the true inheritors of the kingdom. Though God seeks a Bride for His Son, becoming the Bride is not the ultimate promise, as the woman does not receive an inheritance. It is the son who receives the inheritance from the father. Eve is symbolic of the Bride, which is the Church. As the mothers are symbolic of the prophets and the fathers the apostles, the Bride is the prophetic nature: God desires to impregnate the prophetic nature with His seed of revelation to produce sons for the inheritance.

Learning the deeper mysteries of God from His holy servants, who are the apostles and prophets (Ephesians 3:5), makes us sons of the prophets and apostles, the mothers and fathers of the Church. When we receive our own revelation straight from God, we then become the sons of God. The apostles purify the Church so that she can be given over to Yeshua. Paul wrote that he, an apostle, was preparing the Church as a chaste bride (2 Corinthians 11:2).

The sons of God are those who receive the full inheritance of the kingdom, which is obtained through revelation of the deeper teachings of God. To the Early Church, the sons of perdition were those who left the secrets - they became empty and worthless. Sons in the kingdom have power and authority to rule as their Father in heaven does. Yeshua said to those who overcome (those who overcome old and false ways of thinking and interpreting His Word), He would give a rod to rule the nations (Revelation 2:27). The overcomers will hold the authority of the key of David, with the ability to open and shut what others cannot:

> **"And to the angel of the church in Philadelphia write, 'These things says He who is holy, He who is true, HE WHO HAS THE KEY OF DAVID, HE WHO OPENS AND NO ONE SHUTS, AND SHUTS AND NO ONE OPENS...'" (Revelation 3:7).**

The Next Move

The Early Church Fathers were not searching for people who would pray a "sinner's prayer." Instead, they were looking for people who could understand the secret teachings of God to bring in His final restorative plan. Those who have eyes to see will be given the keys to the kingdom – the ability to open and shut doors, the opportune *kairos* moments. God will give His remnant access into the Holy of Holies to help bring the restoration and fulfillment of His divine plan.

The coming Elijah ministries will usher in the high priestly office. This company of people will have full access to the secrets and glory that lie behind the veil. The glory is not for everyone; it is for those who recognize and understand the seasons and times of the Lord and are prepared to awaken the sleeping virgin Church so that she can play her role in the great harvest. The final harvest will be revealed and manifested for this time to those who understand God's plan. Those who have eyes to see are friends of the Bridegroom and servants of His will and truth. They bring messages from behind the veil to the sleeping Church, which must be resurrected in order to see the coming restoration through the King of Righteousness.

It is time for the Church to realize that the fathers are here to bring back the Early Church foundational teachings – the *sod*. What a glorious time to enter into partnership with God in restoring spiritual truth and the ultimate return to Genesis. Let those who have eyes to see and ears to hear awaken to God's restorative plan. God is calling us now to pass beyond the veil to obtain the secrets of the kingdom and partake in the coming glory.

References

A. Blumenthal, H. R. Lerner, Ella Werker, Alexandra Poljakoff-Mayber. Germination Preventing Mechanisms in Iris Seeds. 1986, Annals of Botany.

Barker, Margaret. Fragrance in the Making of Sacred Space: Jewish Temple Paradigms of Christian Worship. Moscow: s.n., 2004.

Barker, Margaret. Revelation of Jesus Christ: Which God Gave to Him to Show toHis Servants What Must Soon Take Place. New York: T&T CLARK LTD, 2000.

Barker, Margaret. Wisdom and the Other Tree: A TempleTheology Reading of the Genesis Eden Story. 2012.

Barker, Margaret. Wisdom and the Stewardship of Knowledge. S.l.: Bishop's Lecture Lincoln, 2004.

Barnes, A. Discipline of the Secret. In The Catholic Encyclopedia. New Advent. [Online] 1909. [Cited: March 28, 2015.] http://www.newadvent.org/cathen/05032a.htm.

Barry, W. Parables. In The Catholic Encyclopedia. New Advent. [Online] 1911. [Cited: April 2, 2015.] http://www.newadvent.org/cathen/11460a.htm.

Benner, Jeff A. Ancient Hebrew Lexicon of the Bible. S.l. : Ancient Hebrew Research Center, 2006. 1589397762.

Bivin, D. and Blizzard, R. Understanding the Difficult Words of Jesus. Shippensburg: Destiny Image Publishers, 1994.

Brown, Francis, Driver, Samuel Rolles and Briggs, Charles Augustus. *A Hebrew and English Lexicon of the Old Testament.* 1906. 1-56563-206-0.

Bruce, F. F. *The New Testament Documents: Are They Reliable?* Downers Grove: Wm B. Erdmans Publishing Company & InterVarsity Press, 1981.

Caius. Ante-Nicene Fathers. Volume 4, page 602.

Callan, C. Orthodoxy. In The Catholic Encyclopedia. *New Advent.* [Online] [Cited: October 3, 2015.] http://www.newadvent.org/cathen/11330a.htm.

Clemente of Alexandria. Second Epistle of Clement: True Confession of Christ. Ch. IV.

Clement of Alexandria. The Instructor. Vol. 1, Bk. 1, Ch. 1.

Clement of Alexandria. The Instructor. Vol. 2, Bk. 1, Ch. VI.

Clement of Alexandria. The Stromata. Vol. 2, Bk. 5, Ch. 1.

Clement of Alexandria. The Stromata. Bk, 5. *New Adventfrom Ante-Nicene Fathers, Vol. 2.* [Online] [Cited: April 25, 2015.] http://www.newadvent.org/fathers/02105.htm.

Clement of Alexandria. The Stromata. Vol. 2, Bk. 6, Ch. XV.

Clement of Alexandria. Who is the Rich ManThat Shall Be Saved? Vol. 2, Ch. V.

Clement of Alexandria. Who is the Rich Man That Shall Be Saved? Vol. 2, Ch. XXXIX.

Constitutions of the Holy Apostles. Vol. 7, Bk. 8., Pt. 1, Ch. XIII.

Cyril. Procatechesis. St. Cyril of Jerusalem. *Nicene and Post-Nicene Fathers, Second Series, Vol. 7.* Buffalo: Christian Literature Publishing Co, 1894.

Edwards, James R. The Hebrew Gospel in Early Christianity. *"Noncanonical" Religious Texts in Early Judaism and Early Christianity.* New York: T&T Clark International, 2012, pp. 116-152.

Fausset, Andrew Robert. *Fausset's Bible Dictionary.* 1878.

Hermas. *The Shepherd of Hermas.* Vol. 2, Bk. 3, Pt. 3, Ch. XVI.

Hippolytus. On Christ and Antichrist.

Hippolytus. The Sacred Writings of Saint Hippolytus. Vol. 5, Pt. 1., Ch. XXXI.

Ignatius. Epistle to the Ephesians. Vol. 1, Bk. 2, Ch. VII.

Ignatius. Epistle to the Ephesians. Vol. 1, Bk. 2, Ch. IX.

Ignatius. Spurious Epistles of Ignatius of Antioch. Vol. 1, Ch. II.

Irenaeus. Against Heresies. Vol. 1, Bk. 4, Ch. XVI.

Irenaeus. Against Heresies. Vol. 1, Bk. 4, Ch XXXIII.

Irenaeus. Demonstration of the Apostolic Preaching (Page 75).

Klein, J., Spears, A., Christopher, M. *Lost in Translation: Rediscoveringthe Hebrew Roots of Our Faith.* 2014.

Lactantius. The Divine Institutes. Vol. 7, Bk. 7, Ch. XXII.

Martyr, Justin. Dialogue With Trypho. Vol. 1, Ch. XXXV.

Martyr, Justin. Dialogue With Trypho. Vol. 1, Ch. XLIX.

Martyr, Justin. Dialogue With Trypho. Vol. 1, Ch. CXVII.

Martyr, Justin. Other Fragments from the Lost Writings of Justin. Vol. 1, Ch. XV.

Mathetes. Epistle to Diognetus, Vol. 1, Ch. XI.

McDonald, Lee M., Charelsworth, James H. Introduction: "Non- canonical" Religious Texts in Early Judaism and Early Chrisianity. *"Non-canonical" Religious Texts in Early Judaism and Early Chrisianity.* New York: T&T Clark International, 2012, pp. 1-8.

McHugh, J. New Advent. *Mystery. In The Catholic Encyclopedia.* [Online] 1911. [Cited: April 28, 2015.] http://www.newadvent.org/cathen/10662a.htm.

Methodius. Ten Virgins. Vol. 6, Pt. 2, Ch. VII.

Oegema, Gerbern S. Early Judaism and Modern Culture: Reflections on the Theological Relevance of Early Jewish Literature. *"Noncanonical"*

Origen. Commentary on the Gospel of Matthew. Vol. 9, Bk. 13, Pt. 1, Sec. 2

Origen. Contra Celsus from Ante-Nicene Fathers, Vol. 4. *New Advent.* [Online] [Cited: April 28, 2015.] http://www.newadvent.org/fathers/04166.htm.

Origen. Contra Celsus from Ante-Nicene Fathers. Vol. 4., Bk. 3, Ch. XLVI.

Origen. Contra Celsus from Ante-Nicene Fathers. Vol. 4, Bk. 2, Ch. L.

Origen. De Princiipis. Vol. 4, Bk. 3, Ch. III.

Origen. De Princiipis. Vol. 4, Bk. 3, Ch. VI.

Origen. De Princiipis. Vol. 4, Bk. 4, Ch. I.

Origen. De Princiipis Preface, Vol. 4.

Origen. Gospel of Matthew. Vol. 9, Bk. 10, Pt. 1.

Religious Texts in Early Judaism and Early Christianity. New York: T&T Clark International, 2012,pp. 9-25.

Scannell, T. Catechumen. In The Catholic Encyclopedia. *New Advent.* [Online] 1908. [Cited: March 28, 2015.] http://www.newadvent.org/cathen/03430b.htm.

Skilton, John H. The Transmission of the Hebrew Text. *The Infallible Word: A Symposium by the Members of the Faculty of Westminster Theological Seminary.* Philadephia: Presbyterian and Reformed, 1967.

Strong, James. *Strong's Hebrew and Greek Dictionaries.* 1890.

Svigel, Michael. A Tradition You Can Trust. *Insight.* [Online] [Cited: June 15, 2015.] http://www.insight.org/resources/articles/church- history/tradition.html?referrer=https:// www.google.com/.

Tertullian. Against Marcion. Vol. 3, Bk. 4.

Thayer, Joseph Henry. *Thayer's Greek-English Lexicon of the New Testament.* 1889.

The Canon of Scripture. *Blue Letter Bible.* [Online] [Cited: June 12,2015.] https://www.blueletterbible.org/faq/canon.cfm.

The Complete Word Study Dictionary. Chattanooga: AMG International, Inc., 1993.

Victorinus. Of the Apocalypse of John. Vol. 7.

Wesley, John. 'Address to the Clergy' in Thomas Jackson, ed. *The Works of Rev. John Wesley,* 14 vols. (Kansas City, Missouri: Beacon Hill Press reprint)